Practical SAP® US Payroll

 **PRESS**

SAP PRESS is a joint initiative of SAP and Galileo Press. The know-how offered by SAP specialists combined with the expertise of the publishing house Galileo Press offers the reader expert books in the field. SAP PRESS features first-hand information and expert advice, and provides useful skills for professional decision-making.

SAP PRESS offers a variety of books on technical and business related topics for the SAP user. For further information, please visit our website: *www.sap-press.com*.

Satish Badgi

Practical SAP® US Payroll

Galileo Press

Bonn • Boston

ISBN   978-1-59229-132-8
1st edition 2007

Editor Chuck Toporek
Copy Editor Jutta VanStean
Cover Design Silke Braun
Layout Design Vera Brauner
Production Vera Brauner
Typesetting SatzPro, Krefeld
Printed and bound in Germany

Contents at a Glance

1   Objectives and Purpose 19

2   US Payroll Infotypes: Master Data and
Transaction Data 29

3   Wage Types 51

4   Schemas and Rules 99

5   Benefits Integration 145

6   Garnishments 171

7   Tax Processing 189

8   Advanced Topics 217

A   US Payroll Schema U000 257

B   Wage Type Template 269

C   Commonly-Used Technical Wage Types 273

D   Commonly-Used Model Wage Types 287

E   Commonly-Used Processing Classes and
Specifications 299

F   List of Useful Payroll Operations 307

G   About the Author 317

Contents

Preface 13

1 Objectives and Purpose 19

1.1	What Makes US Payroll Unique	20
	1.1.1	Functional Uniqueness	20
	1.1.2	Technical Uniqueness	23
1.2	The US Payroll Process	24
1.3	Components of SAP US Payroll	26
1.4	Summary	27

2 US Payroll Infotypes: Master Data and Transaction Data ... 29

2.1	Master Data: Conceptual Clarity	29
2.2	Retroactive Accounting	30
2.3	Employee Master Data for US Payroll	32
	2.3.1	Infotype 0008: Basic Pay	35
	2.3.2	Infotype 0009: Bank Details	36
	2.3.3	Infotype 2010: Employee Remuneration	37
	2.3.4	Infotype 0207: Residence Tax	38
	2.3.5	Infotype 0208: Work Tax	38
	2.3.6	Infotype 0167: Health Plans	39
	2.3.7	Infotype 0057: Membership Fees	39
2.4	Employee Transaction Data: US Payroll	40
	2.4.1	Infotype 0014: Earnings/Deductions Transaction Data	44
	2.4.2	Infotype 0169: Savings Plans	44
	2.4.3	Infotype 0015: Additional Payments and Deductions	45
	2.4.4	Infotype 0267: Bonus and Off Cycle	45
	2.4.5	Infotype 0011: External Bank Transfer	46
	2.4.6	Infotype 0210: Changes to W-4 Data	47
2.5	Pre-Payroll Data Verification	47
2.6	Summary	50

3 Wage Types 51

3.1	Overview of a US Paystub and the Concept of Wage Types	51
3.2	Lifecycle of a Wage Type and US Wage Type Catalog	54
	3.2.1 Wage Type Categories	58
	3.2.2 Three Elements of a Wage Type	59
	3.2.3 Wage Type Catalog	61
3.3	Step-by-Step Configuration of a Wage Type	63
	3.3.1 Earnings	64
	3.3.2 Deductions	72
	3.3.3 Taxes	78
	3.3.4 Net Pay	82
3.4	Testing Wage Types	84
3.5	Advanced Topics on Wage Types	88
	3.5.1 Handling Cumulations	88
	3.5.2 Setting Up Payment Models	90
	3.5.3 Priority and Arrears	91
	3.5.4 Posting of Wage Types	96
3.6	Summary	98

4 Schemas and Rules 99

4.1	Examining the US Payroll Driver (RPCALCU0)	99
4.2	Working with US Schema U000	101
	4.2.1 Schema	104
	4.2.2 Subschemas	104
	4.2.3 US Subschemas	106
4.3	Why, When, and How to Change the US Schema	119
	4.3.1 Copy and Modify U000 using the Schema Editor	120
	4.3.2 Running an Error-Free Schema	121
4.4	Overview of the US Public Sector Schema functionality	126
	4.4.1 NRA: Non-Resident Alien Processing	126
	4.4.2 Savings Bonds Processing	127
	4.4.3 Public Sector Savings Plans: 403(B), 457(B)	127
	4.4.4 Employer Benefits and Tax Allocation Rules	128
4.5	Writing Rules in US Payroll	128
	4.5.1 The Rules Editor	129
	4.5.2 Creating a Simple Rule	131
	4.5.3 Creating Complex Rules	135
	4.5.4 Running Error-Free Rules	140
4.6	Summary	143

5	**Benefits Integration**	**145**
5.1	Integration of US Benefits with US Payroll	145
	5.1.1 Processing	147
	5.1.2 Output	147
5.2	Health Plan Integration	148
	5.2.1 Health Plans	149
5.3	Savings Plan Integration	153
	5.3.1 Savings Plans	153
5.4	Insurance Plan Integration	160
5.5	Flexible Spending Account Integration	164
5.6	Sending Data and Remittance to Benefit Providers	167
	5.6.1 Health Plans	167
	5.6.2 Insurance Plans	167
	5.6.3 Savings Plans	168
	5.6.4 Sending Remittance	168
	5.6.5 Sending Data	169
5.7	Summary	169

6	**Garnishments**	**171**
6.1	Configuring Garnishments	172
	6.1.1 Garnishment Infotypes	172
6.2	Disposable Net Income	176
	6.2.1 Definition of Disposable Net Income	176
	6.2.2 Example	178
6.3	Managing Wage Types for Garnishments	180
	6.3.1 Garnishment Deduction Wage Types	180
	6.3.2 Impact of Other Wage Types	181
6.4	Garnishment Subschema	181
	6.4.1 Rule UGIT	182
	6.4.2 Rule UGDN	184
	6.4.3 Function UGARN	186
6.5	Summary	187

7	**Tax Processing**	**189**
7.1	Introduction to US Tax Processing	189
	7.1.1 Tax Infotypes	190
	7.1.2 Earnings and Deductions	192
	7.1.3 Relevant Processing Classes for Wage Types	193

7.2   Tax Models 194

     7.2.1   Tax Authorities 194

     7.2.2   Tax Areas 195

     7.2.3   Tax Types 196

     7.2.4   Tax Class 197

     7.2.5   Tax Models 197

7.3   Year-End Tax Adjustments and Workbench 202

     7.3.1   Starting the Year-End Workbench 204

     7.3.2   Running Payroll 208

     7.3.3   Verification 210

7.4   Overview of Tax Reporter 211

     7.4.1   Preparation Work 212

     7.4.2   Quarterly Reports 212

     7.4.3   Annual Reports 214

7.5   Summary 215

8   Advanced Topics 217

8.1   Overpayments and Claims Handling 217

     8.1.1   Why Claims Are Generated 218

     8.1.2   Identifying Claims in Payroll 220

     8.1.3   Strategy with Claims 221

     8.1.4   Clearing Claims: Payroll-Forgiven 222

     8.1.5   Clearing Claims: Payroll-Not-Forgiven 223

     8.1.6   Clearing Claims: Accounts Taxes (Employee

            Pays Single Check) 224

     8.1.7   Clearing Claims: Accounts Taxes (Employee

            Pays by Payment Plan) 226

8.2   Accruals 227

     8.2.1   Accruals Configuration 228

     8.2.2   Accruals Process and Posting 231

8.3   Interfacing with Third-Party Payroll Systems—Gross to Net 235

8.4   Third-Party Remittance (Accounts Payable Processing) 240

     8.4.1   Required Configuration 241

     8.4.2   Financial Account Management 242

     8.4.3   Running a Third-Party Process 244

8.5   Implementation Tips for US Payroll 247

     8.5.1   Mid-Year Go-Live 247

     8.5.2   Volumes and Complexity 249

     8.5.3   Resource Planning and Knowledge Transfers 249

8.5.4   How to Run a Parallel Payroll   249

8.5.5   Housekeeping Activities   251

8.5.6   Best Practices to Maintain Wage Types,
Schemas, and Rules   253

8.6   Summary   254

Appendix   255

A   US Payroll Schema U000   257

B   Wage Type Template   269

C   Commonly-Used Technical Wage Types   273

D   Commonly-Used Model Wage Types   287

E   Commonly-Used Processing Classes and Specifications   299

F   List of Useful Payroll Operations   307

G   About the Author   317

Index   319

Preface

The SAP Payroll module has traditionally been a "different" module in the sense that people are often fearful of learning about its more advanced topics such as schemas, rules, and wage types. People's fears also partially stem from the fact that mapping payroll processes as well as payroll calculations to an SAP configuration and functionality has its own challenges. This book addresses the US payroll lifecycle from master data to post-payroll processes, including advanced topics such as month-end accruals and overpayment processing.

Practical SAP US Payroll goes a step beyond the standard documentation and training courses by providing you with practical examples and scenarios. The book also covers important US Payroll topics such as schemas, rules, taxes, and garnishments.

Purpose of this Book

SAP HR professionals in the US market have traditionally stayed away from the Payroll module. People are comfortable talking about Personnel Administration (PA), Organization Management (OM), and Benefits, but they always have some amount of fear when it comes to Payroll. SAP users and administrators commonly complain that unlike PA, OM, or the other HR modules, Payroll always feels more technical because of the schemas, rules, and similar technical topics they have to contend with in this module. In addition, there are lots of *moving parts* in the Payroll module when compared with other HR modules. Common examples and complaints I've heard with regard to the Payroll module include:

▶ The schemas and rules are too technical, and I am not a programmer.

▶ I don't understand the taxes and tax structures, so I will not be able to handle it.

▶ I have never worked with a payroll system before.

▶ SAP Payroll is integrated with all other SAP HR modules as well as SAP Financials, and I simply don't know how to approach it.

▶ Payroll maintenance can have challenges such as correcting or reversing payroll results.

These and similar complaints and questions need practical answers and examples. You will find them in this book, which is targeted specifically to configurators and powerusers responsible for configuring US Payroll. Note that while concepts such as wage types, schemas, and rules could be covered in a generic sense, the discussions in this book focus on SAP's US Payroll-delivered objects.

The book also serves as a quick reference guide to those who intend to implement SAP Payroll as well as those who want to learn more about SAP Payroll than what is possible through standard documentation and training classes.

Who Should Read this Book

This book presents a practical, example-based approach to configuring and using SAP's US Payroll module. It offers a real project-based experience to handling complex areas of US Payroll, such as schemas, rules, and wage types. The book is geared toward anyone who would find the following information helpful:

▶ **A complete overview of US Payroll.**
This promotes a better understanding of the implementation considerations.

▶ **Assistance during the configuration.**

▶ **Detailed information about complex issues.**
This includes, for example, information about wage types, rules, and taxes in US Payroll.

▶ **Information on new topics.**
This includes, for example, information on topics such as garnishments, year-end adjustments, overpayments and benefits integration, in case you have not yet explored them in US Payroll.

This book can also serve project teams, consultants, and users as well as anyone looking for a one-stop guide on SAP US Payroll. Note that this book is not intended to teach basic Payroll concepts and tries to always focus on US-specific Payroll functionality not addressed in standard documentation or training. The typical prerequisites you will need before reading this book are:

► **Knowledge of the SAP PA module.**

► **Overall understanding and clarity about payroll operations.**

► **Knowledge of generic concepts covered in SAP's standard documentation.**

While we will try to focus on SAP US Payroll, we will have to discuss many generic concepts and make references to SAP's standard documentation. For example, we will reference but not discuss in great detail the payroll control record because SAP's documentation already provides plenty of help on this topic. Throughout the book you will also find recommendations to refer to standard SAP documentation.

There is a general feeling that US Payroll is easy for those with a programming background; however, that is not entirely true. While the nature of schemas and rules is more technical than other modules, they are based on logic, arithmetic, and mathematical operations. Although, schemas and rules have a programming "look and feel", they are not like a program. In Chapter 4, when you will see the schemas, you will notice that they combine operations, functions and rules in a very logical fashion to drive the payroll processing logic.

What You Will Gain by Reading this Book

By now, you may be wondering what you will be able to do after reading this book. Table 0.1 lists a series of questions that will give you a good idea of what you can expect to learn from reading this book.

Expectation	Response
Will I be able to configure wage types?	☑
Will I be able to understand tax models for US authorities?	☑
Will the book provide me with enough examples on how to create custom US Payroll rules?	☑
Will the book explain the US Payroll schema in detail?	☑
Will the book tell me how to integrate payroll with US benefits, taxes, and accounting?	☑

Table 0.1 What You Can Expect To Learn From This Book

Expectation	Response
Will the book tell me about advanced topics, such as month-end accruals?	☑
Are there any resources that will be useful for my on-going hands-on practice using SAP Payroll system?	☑

Table 0.1 What You Can Expect To Learn From This Book (cont.)

This book uses many practical examples and scenarios to help you understand the covered topics. These scenarios will help you extend your knowledge so you can further your hands-on practice using your SAP Payroll system. Note that across different versions, SAP's US Payroll has not changed in terms of architecture.

SAP Product Version Compatibility

The contents of this book are applicable to all SAP versions from 4.6 to ERP2005 (ECC). There can, however, be minor discrepancies between versions. Where those are known, I will advise you as to what to watch for. Since US Payroll is different from handling payroll in other countries, it is important to discuss some of the differences. You will also find notes—especially for model wage types, technical wage types, and processing classes—in the Appendices.

Structure of this Book

This book has been structured in such a way that it covers the payroll starting with relevant master data and transaction data and then onto the processing part which covers wage types and schemas. The book then covers key chapters on benefits integration as well as garnishments before getting into advance topics. The Appendix also has many useful resources, such as info and wage type tables. The Appendices are referenced throughout the book, especially those on schemas and wage types. This book contains the following chapters:

▶ **Chapter 1: Introduction**
  This chapter starts the book with concepts regarding the US Payroll Process. It also discusses various components used during different stages of the US Payroll process. This Chapter should help you become familiar with the terminology necessary to understand future chapters.

▶ **Chapter 2: US Payroll Info Types**

Chapter 2 discusses the master data and transaction data that uses info types for the US country code. These info types are referred to in subsequent chapters when used in schemas and rules. Although info types is a topic from the PA module, this discussion provides you with the right background for later chapters. Info types also help you further appreciate the functional uniqueness of US Payroll.

▶ **Chapter 3: Wage Types**

The chapter starts with a discussion of a typical US paystub, before diving into discussions on earnings, deductions, and other tax-related wage types. We will study the US model wage types, as well as characteristics, processing classes, and other wage type configuration attributes. Appendix C and Appendix D provide a quick-reference listing for all commonly used US-specific technical and model wage types, respectively.

▶ **Chapter 4: Schemas and Rules**

Chapter 4 explains US Payroll schema **U000**, along with its functions and operations and also attempts to lift the veil of secrecy I've always felt exists around SAP Payroll schemas and rules. To that end, the chapter uses many examples to assist in your journey of learning US Payroll.

▶ **Chapter 5: Integrating US Payroll with US Benefits**

Due to the unique nature of US benefits, this chapter is divided into sections that cover health plans, insurance plans, 401(k) plans, and other benefits such as flexible spending accounts and savings bonds. Note that while it is not my intention to talk about US Benefits in detail in this book, a discussion of US Payroll is not complete unless you talk about integration between the two sub-modules. Benefits is a very US-specific module, and it coexists with Payroll. It's also worth noting that, because of the exhaustive nature of this topic, the chapters on wage types and schemas also cover benefits to some extent.

▶ **Chapter 6: Garnishments**

Garnishments is a very US-specific topic. This chapter provides detailed information on subschemas, wage types, and disposable net income calculations used to handle garnishments.

▶ **Chapter 7: Tax Processing**

This chapter discusses the configuration of Tax Models and also talk about a tax processing engine that US Payroll uses. US tax processing also involves compliance reporting and annual processing of W-2's, 1099's, and 941's. This chapter presents a short discussion around the usage of Tax Reporter for compliance reporting in US Payroll.

▶ **Chapter 8: Advanced Topics**
Chapter 8 covers many often-ignored, but complex US Payroll topics that
lack good information and documentation. Here, you'll learn how to handle overpayments or learn about making the jump from Gross to Net payroll, among others.

The Appendices include some useful templates and reference tables that list
the essential wage types and rules associated with US Payroll. Appendix A
being one of the biggest and important among all appendices, contains the
entire US Payroll schema, **U000**, with its subschemas and explanations. The
appendices are referred to in chapter discussions as needed. It is recommended that you read the chapters in sequence since some of the later chapters are dependent on the discussions in earlier chapters.

Acknowledgments

This book is dedicated to my late mother, Usha Badgi. The book would not
have been completed without constant support from my wife Nanda and my
daughter Shivani. They both left me alone for a long period of time so I could
complete this big task. Thanks to my father for his aspirations and vision for
me and I appreciate the support and encouragement from my father-in-law
during the writing of this book.

I started my SAP HR and US Payroll journey many years back and my customers and colleagues helped me to learn and mature over the years. Many
thanks and appreciation to all my customers. Also, thanks to Ingrid
Schneider for providing me the motivation and support at the work so I
could complete this book.

My sincere thanks to my Editor, Chuck Toporek, for his patience and support during the entire publishing process. He made it so easy! The detailed
and accurate copyedits by Jutta VanStean require a special mention. And
special thanks to Jawahara Saidullah for the support to initiate the writing of
this first book.

Before we get into the detailed discussion and learn about US Payroll, this first chapter presents the unique aspects of US Payroll. The chapter is dividied into the functional and technical features of US Payroll. The discussion on the components of US Payroll and the associated conceptual figures will help you learn more abuot the terminology and overall architecture of SAP US Payroll.

1 Objectives and Purpose

Whether or not you are working with a Payroll system (SAP Payroll or otherwise), I am sure you are familiar with your paycheck and the overall nature of how important a top-notch payroll system is for a company. When employees talk, or when you interview people for new jobs, the obvious discussions are around payroll and benefits, especially in the US. Employees are interested in finding out about benefits and deductions as much as they are about their annual salary.

In our day-to-day life, we always use the terms *take home pay* or *money in the pocket*. It is natural for us to think about taxes and the net money we will take home at the end of the pay period. Similarly, in SAP implementations, when you talk about Human Resources (HR) or Human Capital Management (HCM), payroll, taxes and benefits often become an integral part of the discussion. SAP's Payroll module is well-integrated with other HR sub-modules as well as SAP Financials. Payroll processing also depends very much on the country, thanks to differing tax structures, employment laws, and various regulations.

Before we start the discussion on US Payroll, I would like to present a simple concept diagram for the payroll process. Figure 1.1 is a simple representation of the US Payroll process and shows that:

▶ Employees get paid by their employer.

▶ Employees pay taxes and deductions.

▶ Through the payroll process, employees receive a paycheck.

Later in this Chapter, we will move the discussion to SAP's US Payroll process and provide you with more detailed information.

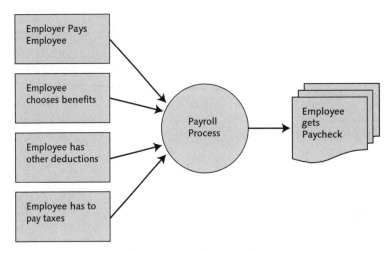

Figure 1.1 The US Payroll Process – Simple Representation

US Payroll is very unique in that you need to understand it from both a functional and a technical perspective. This chapter identifies the unique aspects of US Payroll. It gives you a necessary basic background for pay frequency, payroll control record, and overall payroll processes in the US.

1.1   What Makes US Payroll Unique

I always wondered about the uniqueness of SAP Payroll when I started working with US Payroll and then I realized that US Payroll is different! But why is it so different? The differences can be categorized into two broad areas: functional and technical.

1.1.1   Functional Uniqueness

US Payroll has many unique requirements. SAP's Payroll module addresses these and other functional requirements along with help from other modules, such as PA and US Benefits. These requirements are categorized here for simplicity:

▸ **Unions**
Many US states and industries have unions, and US Payroll creates challenges when handling union agreements (otherwise known as *collective bargaining agreements*), and the calculation complexities involved. Their impact on US Payroll includes:

- Specific infotypes to maintain union dues are provided by SAP.
- You will need to adjust payroll calculations based on union agreements and write custom rules.
- You will need to configure wage types appropriately.

▶ **Taxes**

The US has a multi-tier tax structure: Federal, State, and Local. Also, tax regulations differ from state to state. The impact on US payroll includes:

- Specific infotypes for tax structures relevant in the US.
- Specific tax calculation schemas.
- Specific tax wage types that are generated.
- Configuration of tax models.
- The tax calculation engine that SAP US Payroll uses.
- Compliance reporting and annual reporting.
- Business processes built around a typical tax year of January through December, with a tax return filing date of April 15th.
- Corrections and year-end adjustments for employee tax results.

▶ **Benefits**

US employers offer benefits such as health insurance (medical, dental, vision), life insurance, pension, 401(k), and flexible spending accounts. These benefits and their processing are very tightly coupled with payroll processing. In addition, some employers also allow employees to purchase US Savings Bonds as a standard payroll deduction. The impact of these factors on US Payroll include:

- Deductions for benefits are handled through payroll.
- Wage types are configured for specific benefit plans.
- Pre- and post-tax nature of benefit deductions.
- Remittance to benefit providers is done through payroll.
- Regulations around flexible spending accounts.
- Regulations around 401(k) plans such as annual limits and catch-up contributions.

▶ **Garnishments**

Many countries don't even have the concept of garnishments, and US laws and regulations are very stringent in the way employers handle them. SAP US Payroll provides very comprehensive relevant functionality, which includes:

- Calculations of an employee's disposable net income.
- Built-in models for calculations, including state-based differentiators.
- Reporting and remittance to the authorities.

- **Accruals**
  The financial accruals for payroll expenses are US-specific, and the scenarios include:

  - Specific subschema for accruals.
  - The US public sector has its own requirements around this functionality.
  - Some customers do a once-a-year accrual rather than doing accruals on a monthly basis.
  - Payroll calendars and financial period closings have an impact on accruals, and the scenarios are specific to US customers.

- **Finance Integration**
  SAP US Payroll offers an online real-time integration with the SAP Financials module. US Payroll has a built-in and configurable integration with the following areas of SAP Financials:

  - General Ledger (GL) for expenses and balance sheet accounts postings.
  - Accounts Payable (AP) for vendor postings as well as remittance of money for taxes and benefits deductions.
  - Cost Center Accounting (CCA) for Cost Center postings in the Controlling (CO) module.
  - Funds Management (FM) for Public Sector-specific funds and funds center postings.

- **Pay Frequency**
  Table 1.1 presents the pay frequencies commonly used in US Payroll. Depending on the frequency, the total number of paychecks/pay periods will differ, as shown in the table.

Pay Frequency	Number of Paychecks per Year
Biweekly	26
Semi-monthly	24
Monthly	12

Table 1.1 Typical US Pay Frequencies

Pay Frequency	Number of Paychecks per Year
Weekly	52
Non-standard	22, 20

Table 1.1 Typical US Pay Frequencies (cont.)

The pay frequency discussion directly translates to the concept of payroll areas and payroll control record in US Payroll. The control record has a payroll calendar consisting of payroll period begin and end dates as well as payment dates.

1.1.2 Technical Uniqueness

SAP has built the Payroll module on a central architecture of schemas, rules, and country-specific payroll drivers. However, there are country-specific versions of schemas, rules, drivers, and wage types. Therefore, each country needs to implement its own specific version and, as the title of the book implies, this book focuses on US-specific SAP Payroll only.

The technical uniqueness points for SAP US Payroll are well-known and include the sometimes fear causing topics such as schemas and rules. The uniqueness points include:

▶ **SAP's BSI Tax Product**
The tax calculations and the tax rate tables for various tax authorities are maintained by an embedded product called BSI. Although BSI is a popular acronym in the world of SAP US Payroll, it originated with Business Software Inc. (*http://www.bsi.com*). The BSI Tax Factory, as it is called, works with and is an integral part of US Payroll. It is called Tax Factory because it houses the tax tables and the tax calculation portion of SAP US Payroll. Of course, if you don't need to calculate taxes, and if your net payroll is outsourced, then you don't need a BSI installation. Many US customers run gross payroll in SAP and send that to another provider (e.g., ADP, Ceridian, and so on) for net payroll calculations. However, if the payroll processing is inclusive of taxes and net checks in SAP, you will need to learn SAP's tax processing, inlcuding BSI.

▶ **Schemas**
Schemas tend to scare a lot of people who are new to SAP Payroll. SAP has provided US-specific schemas for payroll calculations. For more information see Chapter 4, which is dedicated to the US-specific schemas.

▶ **Personnel Calculation Rules (PCR)**
SAP has delivered many rules in US schemas. But, in addition, due to the functional uniqueness factors, users normally need to customize rules. An example: Rule **X023** calculates gross amounts while rule **U011** processes infotype **0014** earnings and deductions. SAP US Payroll offers tremendous flexibility through the rules that you can custom create to address your own requirements.

▶ **Model Wage Type Catalog**
Wage types—which translate to earnings, deductions, and tax deductions—are US-specific. SAP delivers a model wage type catalog, which you can use to copy and create custom wage types. BSI Tax Factory also contributes to unique technical wage types (**/301**, **/302**, **/401**, **/402**, etc.), which are generated for US Payroll results.

▶ **Tax Authorities**
The US tax system uses Federal, State, Local (county and city) and school board tax authorities. SAP includes the appropriate Tax Authority tables. These tables are used for the configuration of Tax Models and Tax Combos. Chapter 7 will discuss the configuration of the Tax Models for Tax Authorities. Considering the US tax year of January through December, SAP US Payroll has unique functionality to address end-of-year tax adjustment issues. It is referred to as year-end tax adjustments and we will learn more about it in Chapter 7.

▶ **Retroactivity**
Retroactivity refers to being able to make employee data changes in past payroll periods. SAP US Payroll then automatically recalculates previous periods and adjusts the results. The majority of SAP Payroll users find retroactivity to be one of the most useful functionalities. We will learn more about it in Chapter 2.

The next discussion takes us to the US Payroll process, and dives into topics that will be discussed in later chapters.

1.2 The US Payroll Process

The US Payroll process can be broadly divided into three distinct areas, as follows:

▶ **Pre-payroll Process**
This process involves managing employee data before and during payroll periods.

▶ **Payroll Process**
This process involves running actual calculations along with management of the payroll control record.

▶ **Post-payroll Process**
This process can be broadly divided into sending data and sending money out of the payroll system. For taxes, benefits, and garnishments, the payroll system needs to send data and remittances (deductions) from employees.

Figure 1.2 presents an overall schematic of these three areas. Going from left to right in Figure 1.2, the pre-payroll process starts with the employee data, then moves to the calculation stage and continues on to post-payroll processing. The output of the payroll process is the payroll results tables, which are commonly referred to as *payroll clusters* and is shown in Figure 1.2. The payroll control record serves as a backbone for the entire process. The employee master data and transaction data consist of earnings and deductions, while the payroll results are used to pay employees as well carry out the reporting. The Payroll driver, schema, rules and wage types form the heart of the payroll process.

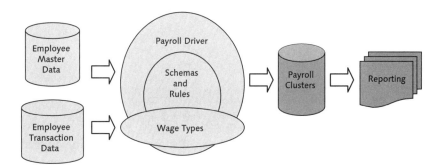

Figure 1.2 The US Payroll Process

This process works with different payroll-related entities such as employees, tax authorities, benefit providers, and the payroll department. Another way to look at the SAP US Payroll system is as an external, entity-based system. For example, employees, vendors, and different authorities receive information from the payroll system.

1.3   Components of SAP US Payroll

Figure 1.3 presents a more detailed view of the SAP US Payroll process and opens up our discussion to many new and different concepts. The contents of Figure 1.3 loosely translate to different submodules and functionality in SAP US Payroll. Before listing these major submodules, it's important to first understand the concepts illustrated in Figure 1.2 and Figure 1.3.

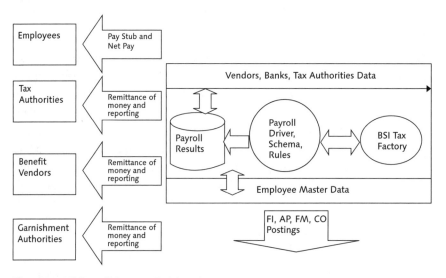

Figure 1.3 US Payroll Process: Entities View

The following list provides simple explanations for various components and terms of SAP US Payroll, as used in both Figure 1.2 and Figure 1.3.

▸ The US Payroll driver **RPCALCU0** (an ABAP program) runs the payroll using a custom schema and is controlled by the payroll control record for its various stages.

▸ The US Payroll schema **U000** uses functions and rules to control the flow as well as actual calculations during the payroll process.

▸ The US Wage Types Catalog comes with delivered model wage types, which are used to create your own custom wage types.

▸ BSI Tax Factory does tax calculations and generates tax wage types along with Tax Authorities and Tax Models maintained in the SAP Payroll module.

▶ Infotypes in the employee master data for benefits, garnishments, bonds, taxes, and other US-specific functions provide the required input to the payroll process. For example, this could include benefits deductions, and the residence tax authority.

▶ Tax reporter, which is used for US tax authority reporting and annual processing.

▶ Third-party remittance, which is used to send money and data to external entities, including tax authorities, garnishment authorities, and benefits providers.

▶ Payroll results (referred to as *payroll clusters*) are the output of a payroll process and are generated by the schema using wage types. They contain many tables for payroll period-related results, year-to-date cumulations as well as taxes.

▶ Financials Accounting (FI), Accounts Payable (AP), Funds Management (FM), and Controlling (CO) are generic references to SAP's Financial modules and are integrated with the SAP Payroll module.

You will typically find people talking about SAP US Payroll functionality in terms of the following major categories or distinct functionalities:

▶ Wage Types Catalog

▶ Payroll Rules and Schemas

▶ Finance Integration

▶ Tax Processing and Year-End Workbench

▶ Garnishments

▶ Integration with other applicable modules

The chapters in this book generally follow this approach so you can easily apply the examples to your own projects.

1.4   Summary

This chapter has given you an overview of SAP US Payroll, and touched on some of the more unique aspects of this module. You have now started to become familiar with the terminology such as schemas, drivers, and rules that SAP Payroll uses. Based on my earlier suggestion, please continue to refer to the standard SAP documentation for more information on conceptual details and basic understanding. In the interest of time, I have stayed away from generic topics in the hope that in this book you will receive more practical and example-based knowledge that you just won't find in any other documentation or training.

In Chapter 2, you will start your journey with a discussion on employee data—both master data and transaction data—as applicable to US Payroll.

The logical point to start the deeper discussion on SAP US Payroll is with relevant employee data. This chapter presents both the employee master data and transaction data used to process payroll. The topic of retroactivity is inevitable when discussing employee data and the payroll process. As such, the chapter also discusses the retroactive accounting concept in SAP.

2   US Payroll Infotypes: Master Data and Transaction Data

In Chapter 1, you learned that employee data is input through US Payroll. Depending upon the payroll calendar, the employee master data as well as the transaction data are managed by the HR and Payroll departments in alignment with payroll calendars and cycles. This chapter focuses on US-specific employee master data infotypes and related topics that govern the payroll process, as well as the output from a payroll process. With a focus on US Payroll-related data, the chapter won't get into the fine details of each infotype or teach you about each of the fields in the infotypes. If you need to know more about any of the infotypes or related topics, please refer to the standard SAP documentation.

2.1   Master Data: Conceptual Clarity

Figure 2.1 presents a simple payroll equation that is applicable to US Payroll calculations, which leads us to the discussion on the topic of input data. The payroll equation is:

Earnings – Deductions = Net Pay

There are two types of deductions: voluntary and involuntary. You will learn more about them throughout this chapter, as well as in Chapter 3 which is related to wage types.

In each organization, the Human Resources (HR) and payroll departments maintain the employee data, which in effect controls the payroll equation. If a data change affects earnings or deductions, the equation will be affected. For example, if an employee receives a salary increase, the change is in infotype **0008**, which changes the equation so it has an impact on the employee's earnings, taxes, and net pay.

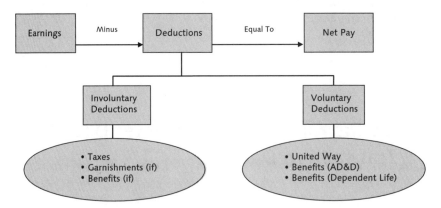

Figure 2.1 The US Payroll Equation

However, it's not enough just to know that the employee data affects the payroll equation; you also need to know about the *timing* of the changes. In Chapter 1, you learned a bit about the payroll control record and calendar. Later in this chapter, you will use the payroll control record status for managing the payroll lifecycle. Although there is plenty of documentation and material available on the topic of retroactive accounting, let's briefly touch on that subject before we go any further.

2.2 Retroactive Accounting

Retroactive (or *retro*) accounting is the bane of many SAP Payroll consultants. Retro accounting is a double-edged sword because it makes the payroll user's life a whole lot better, but at the same time payroll users need to know the why, how, and when of retro accounting. The simple definition of retro states:

> *Master data changes earlier than the current pay period dates trigger a retro payroll for an employee in the next payroll run. SAP recalculates all payroll periods starting with the earliest payroll period that is affected by this change.*

Due to the interesting nature of retro accounting, it's tempting to discuss it in greater detail; however, it's probably best for you refer to standard SAP resources. Figure 2.2 shows the payroll status infotype **0003**, which controls how retro accounting affects an employee record. In addition, the payroll control record also has the *earliest retroactive date*, which controls retroactive calculations.

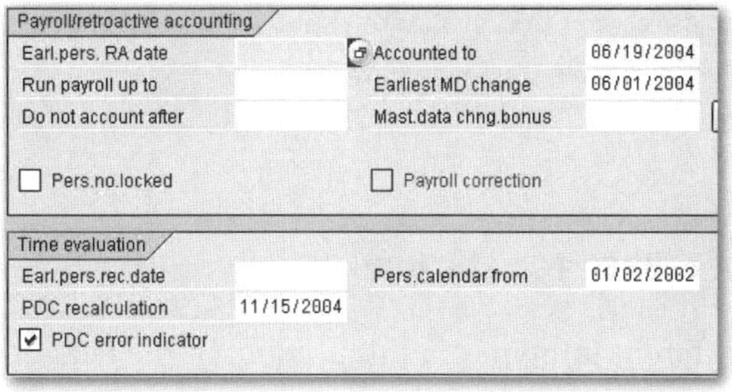

Figure 2.2 Infotype 0003: Payroll Status

Users can go as far back as the earliest MD (Master Data) change date, as highlighted in Figure 2.2 (which in Figure 2.2 is as far as back as 06/01/2004). If the current payroll period is from 07/15/2004 to 07/30/2004, users can change employee data on 6/25/2004 with an effective date of 06/05/2004. SAP Payroll goes back and retroactively calculates the payroll periods starting with 6/05/2004 through the current period of 7/15/2004.

The retroactivity can take place by three different means:

▶ Through the date maintained in the payroll control record.

▶ Through the date maintained in infotype **0003**, as seen earlier.

▶ Forced retroactive payroll if you enter a retroactive date through the payroll driver screen.

In real life, it is often a challenge where HR departments or employees using Employee Self Service (ESS) change the master data, and the payroll department is then faced with conducting a retroactive payroll. It is a good business practice to have established pre-payroll procedures that HR and payroll departments can follow to make sure that everyone is aware of how a retroactive data change affects payroll. Doing so helps reduce the frequency of retroactive payroll runs you need to run so this doesn't become a standard (or substandard) practice. Later in the chapter, you will learn about the pre-payroll verification tools and reports, and how they can be used to reduce the frequency of retroactive payroll runs.

Let's start our discussion around employee master data infotypes and then move on to transaction data.

2.3 Employee Master Data for US Payroll

You will learn about many different infotypes in this section. In the Personnel Administration module, for example, you will see different tabs (infotype menus) when you use transactions such as **PA20** and **PA30** for managing employee data. For the purpose of US Payroll processing, the typical infotype categories are:

▶ Normal employee data, consisting of name, address, and other personal details.

▶ Benefits data, covering benefit plans and deductions.

▶ Garnishment data, which includes garnishment order details, types, and deductions.

▶ Tax data, including information from the employee's W-4, their residence tax area, work tax area, and unemployment worksite details.

▶ Payroll data, which includes basic pay, earnings, and deductions.

Subsequent sections will review the infotypes for these categories. Not all data is mandatory to run the payroll, so let's review the mandatory and additional data for US Payroll.

The employee master data for US Payroll can be split into two categories: what is mandatory for a successful payroll, and what is optional. For example, payroll cannot run without a Basic Pay infotype (mandatory), while payroll can run without the Garnishments infotypes (optional). Table 2.1 lists these infotypes with their applicable master data.

In addition to the list of mandatory infotypes in Table 2.1, there are a number of additional master data infotypes for use with US Payroll. For example, if your implementation uses SAP's Time Management and Benefits functionality, then they include additional infotypes you can use. Another example are voluntary, or employee-dependent, deductions for things such as garnishments.

Infotype	Applicable Master Data in US Payroll
0001: Organization Assignment	▶ Payroll Area ▶ Start date/hire date ▶ Enterprise structure ▶ Cost center for posting
0002: Personal Details	▶ Name ▶ Social Security Number (SSN) ▶ Birth date
0003: Payroll Status (created in the background by SAP during PA actions)	▶ Earliest MD (Master Data) change ▶ Do not run after date ▶ Run payroll up to date
0006: Address	▶ Address with Zip Code (which drives the Residence Tax area infotype 0207)
0007: Work Schedule	▶ Work hours ▶ Capacity utilization %
0008: Basic Pay (earnings)	▶ Basic pay: Hourly rate or pay period rate (earnings)
0009: Bank details	▶ Check or bank transfer ▶ Bank routing, bank account number
0207: Residence Tax (tax deductions)	▶ Residence tax area and applicable tax authorities
0208: Work Tax (tax deductions)	▶ Work tax area and applicable tax authorities
0209: Unemployment (tax deductions)	▶ Unemployment work site and thus get the applicable %
0210: W-4 data (tax deductions)	▶ W-4 status, additional amount

Table 2.1 Mandatory Master Data Infotypes for US Payroll

Table 2.2 lists additional infotypes, which are dependent on additional functionality or employee data details. The table also shows which infotypes are related to maintenance of earnings and deductions.

Infotype	Applicable Master Data in US Payroll
0014: Recurring payments and deductions (earnings and deductions)	Earnings and/or deductions applicable to every pay period
0015: One-time payments and deductions (earnings and deductions)	Earnings and/or deductions applicable for the current pay period
0048: Visa status	Visa status: applicable for Non-Resident Alien (NRA) payroll processing in US Public Sector Payroll
0057: Membership fees (deductions)	Union deduction, a percentage (%) or a specific dollar ($) amount; it is also possible to use infotype 0014 for this deduction
0094: Residence status	Residence status: applicable for Non-Resident Alien (NRA) payroll processing specifically in US Public Sector Payroll
0167: Health plans (benefits deductions)	Master data for health plan enrollment with applicable costs
0168: Insurance plans (benefits deductions)	Master data for insurance plan enrollment with applicable costs, if any
0169: Savings plans (benefits deductions)	Master data for 401(k) and other savings plan enrollment with an applicable percentage (%) of pre- or post-tax contributions
0170: Flexible spending accounts (benefits deductions)	Master data for flexible spending accounts with applicable goal amount
0194: Garnishment (post-tax deductions)	Garnishment document
0195: Garnishment order	Garnishment order
0103: Savings bonds (post-tax deductions)	Savings bond purchase (applicable for US Public Sector Payroll)
0104: Savings bond denomination	Savings bond denomination (applicable for US Public Sector Payroll)
0234: Additional withholding (tax deduction)	Additional US tax withholding information
0235: Other taxes	Used for tax exemptions as well as for NRA processing

Table 2.2 Additional Master Data Infotypes for US Payroll

Infotype	Applicable Master Data in US Payroll
0554: Hourly Rate Movements	Used in US Public Sector Payroll for cost center and position assignments
2010: Employee Remuneration Information (Earnings)	Optionally used by customers to load time data with wage types and rates

Table 2.2 Additional Master Data Infotypes for US Payroll (cont.)

Not all infotypes are applicable to all employees. They will be different for each employee and some of the infotypes may not be even used in some implementations. For example, infotype **2010** is popular for US Payroll implementations without Time Evaluations. However, US Payroll implementations using Time Evaluations will most probably not use this infotype. The Time Evaluation sub-module from SAP's Time Management functionality is used especially for hourly employees. Similar to Payroll schemas and rules, time evaluation also has schemas and rules to manage the generation of time-related wage types.

Now that we learned about the applicable US Payroll master data, the basic question becomes: *How does this impact payroll?* Let's discuss some sample infotypes and focus on the impact of these infotypes on US Payroll. I have chosen the examples in such a way that they will provide you with the necessary background information for subsequent chapters in this book on wage types, schemas, taxes and benefits. It is not my intention to discuss these infotypes from their maintenance perspectives. Instead, I will explain the payroll-related aspects of the infotypes.

2.3.1 Infotype 0008: Basic Pay

Figure 2.3 shows the wage type **M003** with an amount of $1200, which the employee will be paid per-pay period (weekly). This forms the basic pay, or *base pay*, of the employee. If the employee is hourly, you will see an hourly wage type with an hourly rate instead of a per-pay period amount. You can also have more than one wage type to form the basic pay. In US Payroll, there could be situations where you may have multiple wage types in this infotype; however, you will mostly just have one wage type in infotype **0008**.

In Chapter 3 on wage types, you will learn about earnings wage types and how to configure them. In US Payroll, it is not uncommon to change this infotype in the middle of a pay period or to make a change with a past date.

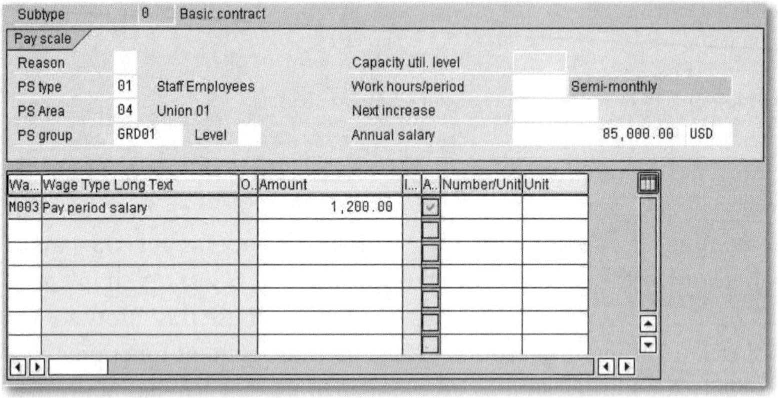

Figure 2.3 Infotype 0008, Basic Pay

2.3.2 Infotype 0009: Bank Details

After the payroll process is completed, the employee's net pay is paid through check or by direct deposit to their bank account. This data is maintained in infotype **0009**. Figure 2.4 shows infotype **0009** with the **Check** option selected for the field **Payment method**. It is good practice to work with your Finance team to configure this infotype. For example, the Payment Method field controls whether the employee gets paid by check or by direct deposit to their bank account. In turn, this field is associated with the Finance configuration. In US Payroll, you will often face situations where an employee would like to send the net pay amounts to more than one bank account or even a combination of check and bank transfer. This infotype allows you to break up the net pay amount by percentage (%) or by dollar ($) amounts. For example, an employee instructs you to send 50% of their net pay to a particular bank account, to send $500 to a second bank account, and the remaining balance to yet another bank account. Of course, the flexibility to do this depends on agreements between employees and their employer, but it is possible.

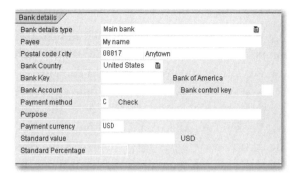

Figure 2.4 Infotype 0009, Bank Details

2.3.3 Infotype 2010: Employee Remuneration

Infotype **2010** is a versatile US Payroll infotype that can be used in many different situations. Some of its possible uses include:

▶ In implementations that don't use time evaluations, this infotype can be used to load data.

▶ Exception basis payments, which are dependent on hours and cost centers.

▶ Exception basis overtime payments, which can capture hours, cost centers, positions, as well as rates.

Figure 2.5 shows a screen for infotype **2010**. This infotype is used by many US implementations to load hourly employees'-related data, for example, if you have school bus drivers that need to be paid a rate based on the number of trips they have made in the day.

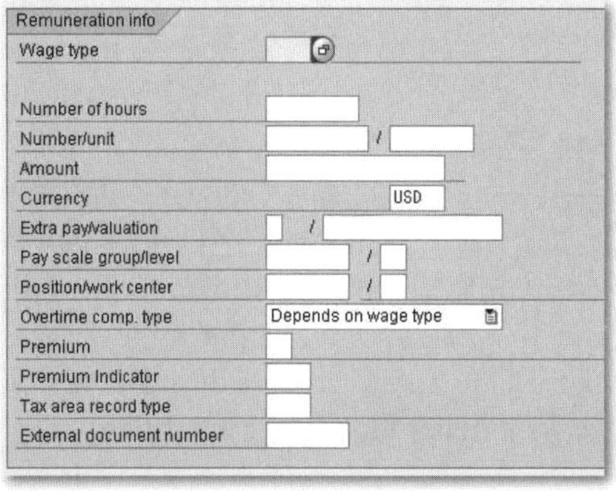

Figure 2.5 Infotype 2010, Useful for Time-Based Payments

2.3.4 Infotype 0207: Residence Tax

You will learn more about tax processing in Chapter 7. However, this chapter (as well as the next few chapters) refers to tax deductions, tax wage types, and tax schemas since they are relevant for the discussion. It's a good idea to briefly discuss infotype **0207** to show how it is used to handle residence taxes. Figure 2.6 shows an example where an employee has federal and state of New Jersey tax deductions. When this master data is used by the payroll schema, the appropriate tax deduction wage types are generated in the payroll run. In Chapter 3, you will see these infotypes used and learn about the tax deduction wage types that are generated.

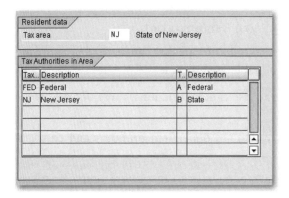

Figure 2.6 Infotype 0207, Residence Tax

Because infotype **0006** holds an employee's address (which includes their zip code), infotype **0207** depends on infotype **0006** to calculate the residency taxes. Tax authority tables are maintained by zip code, so if you make a change to infotype **0006**, SAP's standard dynamic action will pop-up infotype **0207** for any tax authority changes as well.

2.3.5 Infotype 0208: Work Tax

These days, it isn't uncommon for an employee to live in one state and work in another. For example, many employees in metro New York City live in neighboring states, such as Connecticut or New Jersey. In situations like this, the employee's residence tax area will be *CT* or *NJ*, while the work tax area will be *NY01*. Please remember that in situations such as this, the payroll results will use the data to generate wage types for all tax authorities.

2.3.6 Infotype 0167: Health Plans

Figure 2.7 shows the benefit health plan infotype screen. There are many tabs for this infotype, but Figure 2.7 focuses on the relevant *Costs* tab. Based on the plans selected by an employee, the appropriate costs and wage types are processed in payroll. In Chapter 4 on schemas you will learn about the benefits schema and how this and other benefits infotypes get processed by the schema. In addition, Chapter 5 goes into greater depth on this infotype and discusses its impact on payroll.

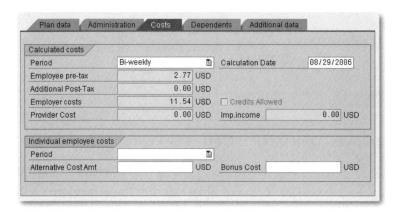

Figure 2.7 Infotype 0167 Benefits, Health Plan

By now, you have probably deduced that master data infotypes have an impact on wage types (earnings, deductions, and taxes) and payroll schemas. You will learn more about both wage types and schemas later in this book.

2.3.7 Infotype 0057: Membership Fees

In US Payroll, many implementations use infotype **0014** to handle union membership deductions. However, I find that infotype **0057, shown in Figure 2.8,** has more functionality to handle union dues. Unlike infotype **0014,** this infotype allows you to use specific dollar ($) amounts or a percentage (%) of an employee's salary. For example, you could apply a 1 % membership fee to all unionized employees, or base it on a certain base pay.

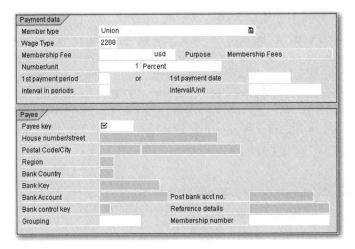

Figure 2.8 Infotype 0057, Membership Fees

2.4 Employee Transaction Data: US Payroll

Transaction data is data related to changes to master data and based on many events that take place in HR and in an employee's life. Transaction data will differ from one payroll period to another. Before picking up an example to help you understand the concept of transaction data, let's look at a typical US Payroll calendar. Table 2.3 presents a sample payroll calendar for different payroll frequencies.

Frequency	Pay Period and Year	Sample Pay Period Start Date	Sample Pay Period End Date
Semi-Monthly (24 payrolls per year)	04/2007	02/16/2007	02/28/2007
Bi-Weekly (26 payrolls per year)	04/2007	02/03/2007	02/16/2007
Monthly (12 payrolls per year)	04/2007	04/01/2007	04/30/2007

Table 2.3 Sample US Payroll Calendar

Changes to employee data need to fit into the payroll calendar, and can potentially force a retroactive payroll depending on when the data change was made. To understand more about these dates, the following list examines the dependent actions/processes based on the calendars:

▶ Managing payroll control record status (Start, Release, Correction, and Exit).

▶ Checking an employee's payroll status infotype **0003** with respect to these calendar dates. (How does the earliest MD change date compare against the calendars?).

▶ From and To dates for infotypes. (How do these dates compare to date ranges in the payroll calendar?)

Let's review a typical data change example using sample dates. Figure 2.9 uses an example of an employee's W-4 change to present the concept of transaction data. The three streams in the figure refer to the business process, the SAP transaction, and the dates. Figure 2.9 shows how the transaction data has a dependency of dates due to the process flow as well as the payroll calendars. If the change takes place with a date earlier than the current payroll period, this will force a retroactive payroll as discussed earlier in Section 2.2.

> **Note**
>
> You can visit the Internal Revenue Service's web site at *http://www.irs.gov* or similar resources to learn more about the US W-4 form.

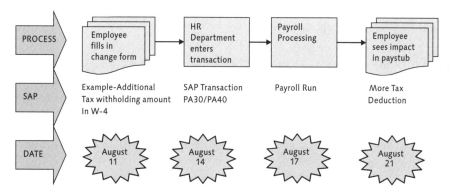

Figure 2.9 Concept of Transaction Data in US Payroll

Table 2.4 and Table 2.5 provide a list of transaction data infotypes. The transaction data tables are divided into two categories: one for the most commonly-used infotypes (Table 2.4), and other used for infotypes related to benefits and time modules, which may not be used in all implementations (Table 2.5).

Infotype	Applicable Transaction Data/Data Changes
0001: Org. Assignment	Changes to enterprise structures and payroll area
0003: Payroll Status	Earliest MD change
0006: Address change	Changes to an employee's place of residence, which also changes the residence tax area (infotype **0207**)
0007: Work Schedule	Changes to work schedules
0008: Basic Pay	Changes to basic pay
0009: Bank details	Changes to bank or check details
0011: External Bank Transfer	Used to directly control the wage type based on payments to a particular bank account
0014: Recurring Payments and Deductions	Changes to earnings and/or deductions
0015: One-time payments and deductions	Changes to earnings and/or deduction
0207: Residence Tax	Changes due to transfers/relocations
0208: Work Tax	Changes due to transfers/relocations
0209: Unemployment	Changes due to transfers/relocations
0210: W-4 data	Changes as requested by employee

Table 2.4 Transaction Data for US Payroll

The majority of the transactions presented in Table 2.4 are changes to infotypes resulting from life events or at the specific request of an employee to change certain data. The following is a list of some sample scenarios for US Payroll transaction data changes:

▶ Employee is promoted and has moved to a new position with additional benefits and pay.

▶ Employee is transferred from one geographical location to another.

▶ Employee has moved from one union to another, and is subject to new union rules.

▶ Employee gets married or divorced.

▶ Employee has child birth, and a new dependent.

▶ Employee moves residence and requests a change of address.

▶ Employee decides to contribute additional funds to their 401(k) or other retirement plan.

▶ Employee's grown up child has moved out of house and is no longer a dependent.

▶ New employee joins the organization.

▶ Employee resigns or is terminated.

▶ A reorganization takes place.

▶ A Merger takes place.

Similar to Table 2.4, Table 2.5 presents additional transaction data depending upon whether benefits or time management is applicable for the implementation Between Tables 2.4 and 2.5, you will be able to relate to the employee life event in the previous list.

Infotype	Applicable Transaction Data in US Payroll
0057: Membership Fees	Additions or changes to union dues
0167: Health Plans	Changes to health plans
0168: Insurance Plans	Changes to insurance plans
0169: Savings Plans	Changes to 401(k) percentage, changes due to age (such as catch-up contribution)
0172: Flexible Spending Accounts	Claims against flex spending account
2001: Absence	Absence details
2002: Attendance	Attendance details; depends upon whether you are using Time Evaluation functionality in SAP
2005: Substitution	Substitution of work schedules and people
2010: Employee Remuneration	When implementations choose to enter hours, wage type and rate through this infotype
0416: Leave Compensation	Employee getting paid for their leave balances

Table 2.5 Additional Employee Transaction Data for US Payroll

Now let's discuss the transaction-related infotypes to see what impact they have on US Payroll.

2.4.1 Infotype 0014: Earnings/Deductions Transaction Data

Figure 2.10 shows infotype **0014**, which is used for transactions related to earnings as well as deductions. Later in Chapter 3, you will learn about infotype groupings and how wage types are applicable to each infotype. If the date of a change is in the past, it triggers a retroactive accounting in payroll.

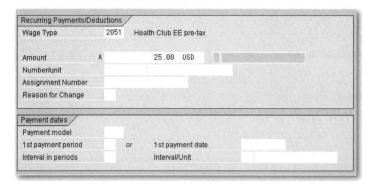

Figure 2.10 Infotype 0014, Transaction Data for Earnings/Deductions

2.4.2 Infotype 0169: Savings Plans

Earlier in the discussion about master data, you saw that benefits infotypes form part of master data. However, depending upon employee life events or in situations where an employee wants to change their 401(k) contribution percentage, there will be transaction data for benefits infotypes. Figure 2.11 presents infotype **0169**, where a contribution percentage is changed.

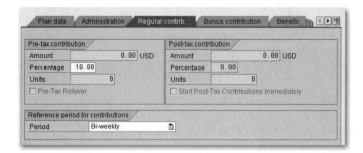

Figure 2.11 Benefits Infotype 0169, Change of Savings Plan Contribution Percentage

When the payroll is processed, the transaction data will be processed by the benefits schema with the appropriate start date for the data change.

2.4.3 Infotype 0015: Additional Payments and Deductions

Infotype **0015** is perhaps the most popular transaction infotype for adjusting earnings and deductions in US Payroll. This infotype can be used to do one-time payments, deductions, and can be used to correct payroll errors. Unlike most other SAP HR infotypes, this infotype does not have a date range and has only one single date. As shown in Figure 2.12, payroll processes this infotype in the payroll period in which the date falls. This applies, for example, when an employee is paid a referral bonus (which is typically not a recurring event but rather a one-time-only payment), as shown in Figure 2.12.

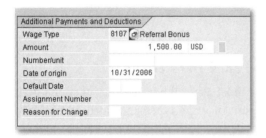

Figure 2.12 Info Type 0015, Adjusting Payments and Deductions

2.4.4 Infotype 0267: Bonus and Off Cycle

Payroll could have a situation where employees need to be paid a bonus or a performance reward based on certain annual events. Some US organizations use infotype **0015** to generate these payments through the regular payroll. Others, however, choose to run a special payroll, for which they can use infotype **0267**.

> **Note**
>
> You should also read SAP's standard documentation on off-cycle payrolls to learn more about this topic.

Figure 2.13 shows infotype **0267** (which is similar to infotype **0015**) with a particular payment date. For example, you might want to pay annual bonuses to all employees on the same date, so you'll need to create infotype **0267** for all eligible employees. In Chapter 8, you will learn about overpayments and claims processing, where infotype **0267** is used again. Off-cycle payrolls are of different types and, as seen in Figure 2.13, the bonus off-cycle run is of type **A**.

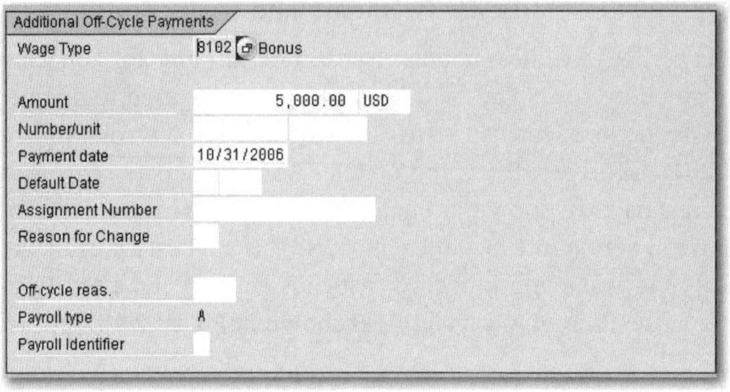

Figure 2.13 Infotype 0267, Off-Cycle Runs

2.4.5   Infotype 0011: External Bank Transfer

This is not a very popular infotype in US Payroll because the functionality is also available through a combination of wage types and third-party remittances. However, you will occasionally run into a situation where a payment needs to be processed through payroll to an external entity that has tax implications. For example, a company leases a car for an employee, which makes the car a taxable perk. In this case, the company pays the bank directly for the lease payment.

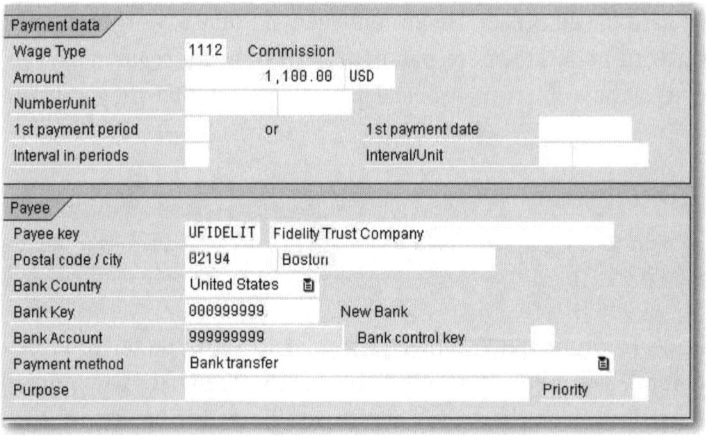

Figure 2.14 Info Type 0011, External Bank Transfer

Figure 2.14 shows infotype **0011** where a particular payment is going out by bank transfer to a payee. Please notice that this infotype is almost a combination of infotypes **0009** and **0014/0015**.

2.4.6   Infotype 0210: Changes to W-4 Data

To wrap up this section, let's look at Figure 2.15, which shows infotype **0210**. Employees typically change W-4 data for allowances as well as for an additional withholding amount. In Figure 2.15, the HR department uses this infotype to change an employee's W-4 data because the employee wants to pay an additional $50 of federal tax withholding every pay period.

Status					
Tax authority	FED	Federal		Tax level	A Federal
Filing Status	02	Married			

Exemptions				
Allowances	3			
Tax Exempt Indicator			☐ IRS mandates	

Withholding adjustments			
Add.withholding		50.00 USD	
Default formula	1 PERCENTAGE M...	Alternative formula	

W-5 filing status	
EIC status	

Figure 2.15 Infotype 0210, W-4 Data Change

To conclude this chapter, we'll discuss data verification prior to the payroll process. You'll also learn about the SAP functionality you can use to verify pre-payroll checks.

2.5   Pre-Payroll Data Verification

Why is pre-payroll data verification a better business practice? To understand this concept, take a look at Figure 2.16, which shows the payroll cycle as controlled by the payroll control record. Notice that the payroll departments only have a limited amount of time to verify entries and make corrections. To minimize data errors and to avoid a last-minute rush, it is normally a good idea to do a pre-payroll verification.

Let's look at some typical data errors you may see when running a payroll, as shown in Table 2.6.

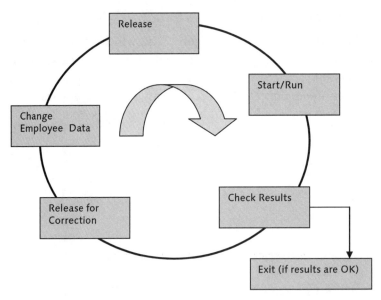

Figure 2.16 Payroll Cycle and Change of Data

Error Condition	Description
1. The amount paid to an employee is enormously large by mistake	Infotypes **0008**, **0014**, or **0015**, which are used to enter amounts do not have controls
2. The date of an earnings or deduction change was mistakenly entered as having occured in the past	Changes to infotypes were made with a retroactive date
3. A wrong wage type was used to enter a deduction	Wrong wage type was entered in infotype **0014** or **0015**, although the amount was correct.
4. Employee got paid even after termination or leaving from company	Termination action along with infotype **0003** maintenance had problems
5. Employee complaint about tax calculations being not correct	An employee requested a W-4 data change and the change was not entered for infotype **0210** in time for payroll

Table 2.6 Sample Data Errors in Payroll

You will be able to identify many such error scenarios and although some of them, such as number 4 from Table 2.6 for example, might sound unrealistic, they do occur.

While it is very difficult to build a completely error-free system, SAP provides many reports and has good configuration controls to help you avoid making such errors. Table 2.7 lists some of those reports and controls:

SAP Feature / Functionality	Description
1. Using Min/Max configuration	Wage types have configuration facility so you can control the inputs within a range of amount.
2. Pre-payroll report	Using SAP's ad-hoc query, you can run a pre-payroll report and look for wage types within a date range and within a certain amount range.
3. Permissibility of wage types	In Chapter 3, we will learn about the permissibility of wage types, which makes it possible to restrict wage types by employee groupings.
4. Running standard SAP reports	SAP has provided standard master data reports such as Employees Joined/Left.
5. Ad-Hoc Query	Develop easy ad-hoc queries to run reports around infotypes within a date range.
6. Transaction SE16 Reporting	Normally, it is not a good idea to give access to users to the SE16 transaction. However, many implementations use the transaction for power users to download data from infotypes.
7. HIS Reporting	Delivered HIS Report in SAP allows you to combine OM structures with PA reporting (i.e., you can select an organization unit and run PA reports for it).

Table 2.7 Sample Tools to Avoid Errors

Whether you use transaction **SE16, HIS** (use the menu path, **Human Resources • Information Systems • Reporting Tools • HIS**) or an ad-hoc query, the types of reporting needs to be around the data that is going to impact payroll processing. Here is a sample list of areas that I normally look for:

▸ New employees have joined during the payroll period and the possible impact of this on gross payroll figures.

▸ During annual performance reviews and promotions season, look for employees who have are part of the promotion as well as salary raise list. Example: Infotype **0008** for all such employees will have change due to salary change.

▸ During bonus or annual commissions season, look for infotype **0015** or **0267** with amounts.

▸ Run reports for any changes to infotypes **0008**, **0014**, and **0015**, which impact the payroll process most.

▶ Run reports if any new wage types were configured and introduced during the current payroll period and are dialogue wage types (user input through infotypes).

▶ Any infotypes that are not normally used in regular payroll (e. g., **0267**, or **0221**).

This concludes the short discussion on employee payroll data. By now, you should be prepared to move into payroll configuration topics.

2.6   Summary

You have learned that the Personnel Administration (PA) infotypes control the master data and transaction data (data changes) to the employee's payroll. Infotypes have country dependence and only US infotypes will be processed later in the US Payroll schema. Payroll-related infotypes fall into multiple categories such as those controlling earnings and deductions, those controlling benefit deductions and others that control tax deductions. Infotypes control the basic philosophy of computer systems: *If the input is good, the output will be good too!*

Infotypes use wage types for inputting hours, numbers, or amounts to the employee payroll process. They are logically linked together, and now that you have a basic understanding of payroll infotypes, it is time to move the discussion on to wage types, covered in Chapter 3.

The payroll equation consisting of earnings and deductions is governed by wage types, which are used to maintain employees' payroll results. This chapter discusses the configuration of wage types along with key concepts such as processing classes and permissibility. The chapter also covers advanced topics such as deduction models, cumulations, and arrears processing.

3 Wage Types

A *wage type* is a messenger that keeps earnings and deductions flowing through the payroll system. In this chapter, we'll examine a sample US paystub to get familiar with earnings, deductions, and taxes. After the discussion on paystubs, we will take a closer look at wage types with the aid of some conceptual diagrams. The chapter shows you how to configure wage types to handle earnings, deductions, and taxes. You'll also see how to test wage types and discover some advanced tips to help you out.

3.1 Overview of a US Paystub and the Concept of Wage Types

One of the best ways to understand what wage types do is to take a look at a typical paystub a US employee takes home, shown in Figure 3.1. Note that the amounts and numbers aren't real, and they don't match with any real tax rates or calculations. The focus here is on wage types, not actual dollar amounts.

When looking at Figure 3.1, you'll notice that the paystub uses many different wage types in US Payroll, including those for:

▶ Earnings

▶ Pre-tax deductions

▶ Post-tax deductions

▶ Taxes, and so on

XYZ Corporation Earning Statement				
My Name			Pay Period Begin: 04/15/2006	
99, Corporate Blvd			Pay Period End: 04/30/2006	
Anytown, NJ 08555			Pay Date: 05/05/2006	
Employee Number: 099999			Location: Plant 1	
Net Pay: $1,882.40			Bank Account # - 999999	
Description	Current Amount	Current Hours	YTD Amount	YTD Hours
Regular Pay	2,500.00	80.00	10,090.34	764.00
Overtime 1.5	554.00	10.00	1,112.00	41.00
TOTAL PAY	**3,054.00**		**11,202.34**	
Imputed Life	6.75		60.75	
TOTAL IMPUTED	**6.75**		**60.75**	
Aetna HMO	42.50		297.50	
Delta Dental	10.00		70.00	
Flex Spending	15.00		105.00	
401K	225.00		1575.00	
TOTAL PRE-TAX DEDUCTIONS	**292.50**		**2047.50**	
FICA-SS	75.50		528.50	
Federal W/H	554.25		3879.50	
FICA-Medicare	75.50		528.50	
NJ W/H	90.00		630.00	
NJ DISAB	25.35		177.45	
TOTAL TAXES	**821.60**		**5567.20**	
AD &D	12.50		87.50	
Group LTD	10.00		70.00	
Savings Bond	25.00		175.00	
TOTAL POST-TAX DEDUCTIONS	**47.50**		**332.50**	

Figure 3.1 A Typical Paystub for a US Employee

In Chapter 2, you saw the following payroll equation:

Earnings – Deductions = Net Pay

Let's expand that equation a little and present it as:

Earnings – Deductions – Taxes = Net Pay

Because taxes are a form of deduction, it's best to pull them out separately in the equation because you will learn more about tax wage types in this chapter. Of course, when taxes are calculated, the pre- or post-tax deductions play an important role, so we'll examine those, too. In addition, some wage types are governed by hours while some (such as 401(k) contributions) are governed by federal regulations. Most wage types also have monthly, quarterly, and annual cumulation. The following discusses various concepts with which we will start our discussion before learning more about wage types. As you read through this list, continue to refer to the paystub shown in Figure 3.1 and use it as a guide to the terms discussed here.

► **Earnings/Pay**

Money earned by an employee as regular pay, overtime pay, sales commission, or bonus is defined as *earnings* (or *pay*). Earnings are subject to taxes from federal, state, and local authorities. Earnings add to the total gross pay of an employee. As seen in Chapter 2, infotypes **0008**, **0014**, and **0015** are used to enter earnings to an employee's payroll data.

► **Pre-Tax Deductions**

This refers to deductions made from the total gross pay before taxes are taken out. For example, if an employee's total pay is $1000 and there is a pre-tax deduction of $200, the remaining $800 is subject to taxes. In Chapter 2 we discussed infotypes **0167** and **0169**, which contribute to pre-tax deductions in US Payroll. In this example, if the tax rate is 25 %, then an employee without the pre-tax deduction will pay $250 in taxes, while an employee with the pre-tax deduction will save $50 on taxes and will only pay $200 because the 25 % is calculated using $800 instead of $1000.

► **Post-Tax Deductions**

Post-tax deductions are taken out of earnings and, unlike pre-tax deductions, have no impact on the taxable base. As noted in Chapter 2, infotypes **0014**, **0015**, **0057**, etc., contribute to post-tax deductions. For example, if the employee in the previous example pays $200 in taxes, the balance will be $600 in pay. Post-tax deductions are then taken out of the $600.

► **Imputed Income**

If an employer extends group life insurance coverage of more than $50,000, then (per the Internal Revenue Service (IRS) rate tables), an imputed income is calculated and is subject to Federal Insurance Contribution Act (FICA) taxes. You will learn more about the tax types later. The example shown in Figure 3.1 adds $6.75 to the FICA taxes. Many web sites, including those of States and Insurance companies, who give details about Imputed income and some aslo give you an age based calculator to calculate the imputed income.

► **Net Pay**

The net pay result of the payroll equation is the amount an employee can take home after all deductions and taxes are taken out of the total pay/earnings. Net pay is either paid by check or by direct deposit to a specified bank account. In Figure 3.1, $1,882.40 is the net pay the employee will take home.

In addition to the different wage type categories, other notable features of the paystub include:

- Some wage types also have hours associated with the amount. For example, note the overtime payment for 10 hours in Figure 3.1.

- All wage types have **YTD** (year-to-date) amounts.

- Paystubs include the name, employee number, pay period, start and end dates, check date, mailing address, bank account number, and similar details for the employee. Some organizations also print the leave/vacation balances on paystubs. Paystubs also include the employee's Social Security number; however, only a portion of the number is typically shown to maintain its privacy. It is very easy to mask the numbers using SAP's HR Forms, which are used to create the paystub.

Let's conclude this section with SAP's definition of wage types:

Monetary amounts or time units that serve different business purposes and that are processed during the payroll run.

Now let's move on to the discussion of wage types using the SAP-delivered wage type catalog.

3.2 Lifecycle of a Wage Type and US Wage Type Catalog

To aid with the discussion on configuring wage types, let's closely examine the next two figures. Figure 3.2 shows a waterfall view of wage types, starting with the creation of a wage type and ending with the employee receiving a paystub. This figure should help you conceptualize the lifecycle of a wage type as the discussion progresses around the steps presented in this figure. For example, a wage type is created and used in infotypes, and then it is manipulated in rules before being posted to Finance.

While the wage type is going through its lifecycle (as shown in Figure 3.2), there are many concepts around the wage type that play an important role. If you use the *Input-Processing-Output*-based approach to study wage types, as shown in Figure 3.3, you'll notice that the boxes on the left represent many different wage type features and characteristics, while those on the right side represent the output or post-processing. Payroll rules and schemas process wage types to get the desired output in the payroll results table.

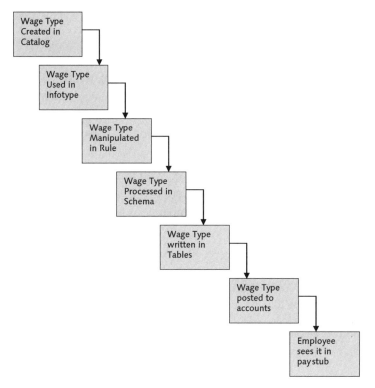

Figure 3.2 Wage Types: Waterfall Diagram

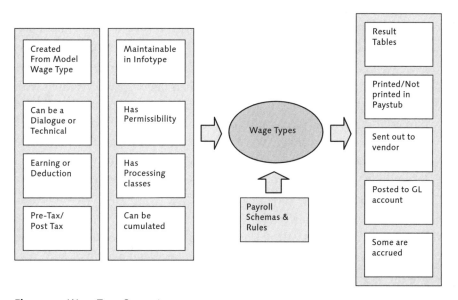

Figure 3.3 Wage Type Concepts

Figure 3.3 introduces many new terms and concepts related to wage types, so let's quickly take a moment to discuss what these terms mean:

▶ **Model Wage Types**

SAP has provided wage types for the US (country code 10), which you can use to copy and create new wage types. Appendix D lists the typical model wage types used to copy and create new wage types in US Payroll. The Appendix is divided into two parts: one for earnings and deductions and another for benefits model wage types.

Model wage types are functioning wage types with preconfigured characteristics. These wage types start with the letter *M* (used for earnings or deductions) or *B* (for benefits), and are numbered as **M001**, **M003**, **BA30**, **BE31**, and so on. The collection of model wage types is referred to as the *model wage type catalog*.

> **Note**
>
> The model wage type catalog differs depending upon the SAP product version you are using. Later, we will examine SAP table **T512W**, which houses the wage types. It is a good idea to know your model wage types from that table along with their characteristics so that you can make the right choices.

▶ **Dialogue vs Technical**

Dialogue wage types, as the name suggests, are typically used by infotypes to enter data. Technical wage types start with a slash (*/*), and are generated during the payroll run. For example, wage type **1000** (Basic Pay) is a dialogue wage type, while **/101** (Total Gross) is a technical wage type.

Dialogue wage types work closely with infotypes, as you have seen earlier in the master data chapter (Chapter 2). When the wage type is input with an infotype, you need to complete a configuration of permissibility and info groups, as noted later in this chapter. Many of the model wage types in Appendix D are dialogue wage types. Appendix C lists technical wage types such as **/101** (Total Gross) or **/559** (Net Pay). Similarly, tax-related technical wage types (some of which will be used later in the chapter) are listed in Appendix C as well.

▶ **Earnings or Deductions**

Earnings is the money earned by an employee, while a *deduction* is the money paid by an employee for things like taxes and benefits.

▶ **Pre-tax vs Post-Tax**

On a paystub, some deductions such as those for health insurance, 401(k) contributions, or flexible spending accounts (FSAs) are taken out before taxes. Deductions such as those for union dues and savings bond purchases are made after taxes are calculated. As such, pre-tax deductions reduce the tax liabilities in your payroll calculations. Whether the wage type is pre-tax and how much of the pre-tax deduction is allowed depends on IRS rules and mandates. Chapter 2 includes a short example on this concept.

> **Note**
>
> To ensure you're up-to-date with the latest US tax rules, be sure to bookmark the IRS's web site: *http://www.irs.gov*.

▶ **Processing Class**

Each wage type has many processing classes and, as the name implies, they control how the wage type is processed in the schema and rules. Chapter 4 studies the usage of the processing classes in rules.

Processing classes are configurable.You will be able to add new and additional specifications for processing classes and then use them in rules. Appendix E lists processing classes with their specifications. It is possible to add new specifications to existing processing classes. For example, if you look at processing class **5** in Appendix E, it has specifications from 0 through 5. You will be able to add a new value 6 and then use it for specific wage types and also in rules for those wage types. Chapter 4 shows you how to use processing class values to drive payroll calculations. Depending on the nature of the wage type, each wage type only has certain processing classes. For example, earning wage types will have processing class **59** related to garnishments. Deduction wage types will have processing class **65** to determine whether a deduction is a pre-tax or post-tax deduction.

▶ **Cumulation**

The Year-To-Date (YTD) amount shown earlier on the paystub (Figure 3.1) is controlled by the cumulation of wage types. SAP automatically maintains the totals for earnings by month and by year. Similarly, you can have Month-To-Date (**MTD**) or Quarter-To-Date (**QTD**) cumulations as well. You can read more about cumulations in the Advanced Topics section of this chapter.

▶ **Permissibility**

You can make a wage type permissible for a certain group or type of employees by using *permissibility*. It is controlled through an employee subgroup grouping and personnel subarea grouping. For example, certain union dues deduction wage types should be permissible only for specific union employees. Or a certain car allowance wage type should be permissible only for specific executive employees. In scenarios like this, the permissibility of wage types ensures that when the wage types are used for data entry in infotypes, they can only be used for specific employee subgroups or personnel subareas. Permissibility also helps to avoid data entry errors in infotypes maintenance. Later in this chapter, you will learn about setting up permissibility.

▶ **Printed or Not Printed**
You can control how wage types are printed on a paystub using *evaluation classes*. Some wage types can be used as intermediate wage types in payroll calculations and don't need to be printed on a paystub. Evaluation classes have a two-digit field associated with the wage type and, depending upon the value of the field, it can be used to control printing.

▶ **Posting Aspects**
Wage types are posted to expense accounts or balance sheet accounts. For example, basic and overtime pay are posted to payroll expenses.

▶ **Third-party Remittance**
Some wage types, such as health plan deductions or 401(k) deductions, need to be sent out to the benefit provider for third-party remittance processing in SAP. Similarly, tax deductions also need to be remitted to respective tax authorities.

3.2.1 Wage Type Categories

Now let's take a slightly different view to examine wage types. This view will help you understand how wage types are processed and treated. Figure 3.4 presents the three categories of wage types you'll come across during the configuration and discussion in the rest of this chapter. The three numbered buckets in the figure are:

▶ Dialogue wage types that are entered through infotypes. These could be both earnings and deductions.

▶ Wage types that are generated during the payroll process due to a configuration. For example, wage types for benefits, savings bond purchases, and garnishments.

▶ Technical wage types generated during the payroll process. Examples include those for tax deductions, total gross pay, and total deductions.

> **Note**
>
> We will refer to Figure 3.4 many times throughout the chapter, as the numbered buckets are referred to along the way.

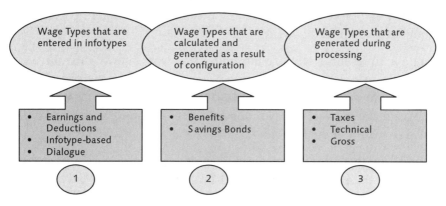

Figure 3.4 Three Wage Type Categories in US Payroll

As important as the three different categories are, each wage type also contains three elements. In the next section we'll look at these three elements to give you a better understanding of how wage types work.

3.2.2 Three Elements of a Wage Type

After the payroll is processed, the wage types end up in the payroll results tables. Payroll results tables are where wage types are written by the payroll process and are subsequently accessed by post-payroll processes. You will learn more about these tables in this and other chapters of the book. The payroll results table contains multiple tables, each with a specific purpose. For example, the **RT** table contains pay period results, while the **CRT** table contains cumulation results.

Each wage type has up to three basic elements which are used in rules as well as in the payroll results table, as follows:

▶ **RTE (Rate)**
   The rate element holds the rates associated with the wage type, such as hourly rate of pay or overtime rates. For example, an hourly employee gets paid a rate of $12 per hour.

▶ **NUM (Number)**
   The number element holds the numbers, such as hours worked. For example, an hourly employee who gets paid a rate of $12 per hour works 40

hours in a particular week. As such, *Number = Hours* is associated with the wage type.

▸ **AMT (Amount)**
The element amount holds the amount for the wage type.For example, an hourly employee was paid $480 in a week at a rate of $12 per hour for working 40 hours that week.

Figure 3.5 presents payroll results with wage types showing the three elements. If you look at the last line of the screen, you will see that the three elements for the wage type **1200** are: **RTE=15.35**, **NUM=40.00**, and **AMT=614.00**. SAP maintains the rate of pay in the field **RTE**, the hours in the field **NUM**, and the amount in the field **AMT**.

You will use these three elements in Chapter 4 to manipulate the wage types in rules. At this stage, however, don't be concerned about the *look and feel* of the payroll results. Instead, try to focus on the conceptual understanding of the elements.

```
1 /001 Valuation b01               15.35
1 /002 Valuation b01               15.35
1 /003 Valuation b01               15.35
1 1000 Hourly rate01               15.35
1 1200 Regular wor01               15.35  40.00              614.00
```

Figure 3.5 Elements of a Wage Type

Not every wage type will have all three elements. Table 3.1 presents sample scenarios around wage type elements and gives you an idea why every wage type may not have all three elements.

Wage Type Scenario	Elements
Basic pay	Has **RTE, NUM**, and **AMT** because employees get paid by the time they worked, based on an agreed rate.
Flexible spending deduction	Has a fixed **AMT** per month, but no **NUM** or **RTE**.
Pension earnings	Base wages for pension earnings has **AMT** and **NUM** because pension plans normally track amounts and hours.
Bonus pay or sales commission	One-time payments with lump-sum amounts only have **AMT** and no **RTE** or **NUM**.

Table 3.1 Different Scenarios for Wage Types

Wage Type Scenario	Elements
Overtime payments	Have **RTE, NUM**, and **AMT**. The **RTE** for overtime payments could be 1.5 times or 2.0 times the normal rate of pay. Therefore, overtime payments need to know the hours as well as the rate at which the hours need to be paid. The **RTE** can be manipulated to any multiplier based on the time management scenarios in SAP. If your implementation is using SAP's Time Evaluation sub-module, then the generation of time wage types will control the RTE and the resulting multiplier.

Table 3.1 Different Scenarios for Wage Types (cont.)

If you refer back to the sample paystub in Figure 3.1, you will notice that both regular pay and overtime pay have three elements. Let's discuss the wage type catalog and then we'll move on to showing you how to use the catalog to create new wage types.

3.2.3 Wage Type Catalog

As noted earlier, SAP has a wage type catalog for each country; however, we will focus on the wage type catalog for country code 10 (US). The wage type catalog is delivered by SAP with model and technical wage types for the US. It isn't good practice to use model wage types directly or to change them for your purpose. This is because during upgrades and installation of support packs, SAP can potentially overwrite your changes. Also, during testing and problem solving, you always need model wage types as a standard for comparison.

Using Model Wage Types

To create new custom wage types, you copy model wage types. For example, to create a deduction wage type, you may choose to use model wage type **M720** (Donation-United Way). Later in this chapter, you will learn the step-by-step process to use a model wage type to create a custom wage type.

Numbering of Wage Types

In a typical US Payroll implementation, you may have a few hundred wage types, depending upon the complexity and requirements. As such, it would be a good idea to follow a numbering scheme that maps to different types, as seen earlier with the paystub (i. e., earnings, pre-tax deductions, etc.). A well-planned numbering scheme will ease your maintenance and reporting. For example, when you only need to run reports on earnings, you will be able to choose a specific range. Many implementations try to follow the same wage type numbering and naming they used in a legacy system. The change and transition could be easier with this approach, but you will most likely face some maintenance issues from the legacy system. A good example is to follow a range for each type, for example, 0100 through 1999 for Earnings, 2000 through 2999 for Post-Tax deductions, and so on. SAP allows you to follow the custom numbering without interfering with upgrades and the installation of support packs.

> **Note**
>
> Remember, all wage types starting with a slash (/) are technical wage types.

Reports that have wage type selection as a criterion can easily use the appropriate range for earnings or deductions. In addition, when you follow a numbering scheme, you will know whether it is an earning or a pre-tax deduction just by looking at the wage type number.

Processing Classes

Processing classes are crucial to wage type configuration, as well as their usage in payroll schemas and rules. Processing classes can be defined as: *Wage type characteristics that control processing steps in payroll.* Each wage type has many processing classes, and each processing class has a different specification. During the payroll run, the schema and rules use the specification values to process wage types. In Chapter 4, you will see more examples that use processing classes. But first, you need to become familiar with the processing classes applicable in US Payroll and which govern the wage type in the payroll schema. Although Appendix E presents a complete list of processing classes, Table 3.2 presents some of the more commonly used processing classes with a short description.

Processing Class	Description
3	Cumulation and storage
6	Previous pay period process
10	Monthly factoring
20	Cumulation and storage at end
24	Transfer control

Table 3.2 Commonly-Used Processing Classes

Processing Class	Description
25	Behaviors after end of payment
30	Cumulation update
41	Splits
59	Disposable net for garnishment
60	Save garnishment wage type
65	Pre- or post-tax
66	Deduction goal/deduction (replaced by processing class 50 in newer versions)
68	Payment type for tax calculation
69	Taxable or non-taxable
71	Tax classification
73	Third-party sign assignment
78	Third-party remittance
72	Employee/Employer tax
76	Regular or bonus runs
82	Set this for infotype 0221 runs (you will learn more about infotype 0221 payroll runs in Chapter 7)

Table 3.2 Commonly-Used Processing Classes (cont.)

The next chapter shows you how to further use wage types with their processing classes for manipulation in payroll rules.

Because you are now familiar with the basic concepts, terms, and processing classes, it's time to see how to configure wage types using examples relevant for US Payroll. Please refer to the wage type template in Appendix B, which you can use to create new wage types. This template captures various characteristics that we will configure for wage types in the sections that follow.

3.3 Step-by-Step Configuration of a Wage Type

This section is divided by the three different wage types for earnings, deductions, and taxes discussed earlier. For both earnings and deductions, the central theme for configuration is the same. However, depending on whether it is an earning or a deduction, the processing class treatment will differ.

Deductions also have additional features and functions that may require additional configuration. This discussion starts by examining earnings wage types.

3.3.1   Earnings

Earnings is the money earned by an employee as regular pay, overtime, bonus, sales commission, and so on. If you refer back to Figure 3.4, earnings fall into the first bucket. The typical qualities of US earnings are:

▶ They are mostly dialogue and entered through infotypes **0008**, **0014**, **0015**, and so on.

▶ They are taxable (either normal rate or supplemental rate).

▶ They are added to gross wages.

▶ Typical examples for different types of US earnings are:

  ▶ Regular pay for both salaried (fixed salary per paycheck) and hourly (variable salary per paycheck, based on the number of hours worked and the hourly rate) employees.

  ▶ Overtime, shift duty allowance, call-in pay, and all such time- (hour-) dependent earnings.

  ▶ Sales commission, awards, merit pay, bonuses, and other one-time payments.

  ▶ Hazard allowance, teaching allowance, higher duty allowance, heavy machinery operator allowance, and pay for job- or duty-based special allowances.

Appendix D shows model wage types such as **M001** (hourly rate), **M003** (salary), **M101** (bonus), etc. Earnings have different types of taxabilities, including normal or regular rate and supplemental rates. One-time earnings, such as a bonus, are taxed at supplemental rates which are lower than the normal tax rates and are decided by tax authorities.

Now let's create a wage type from a US model wage type: We want to create an earning wage type for this example. Therefore, we will use earning model wage type **M101**. The custom wage type we are going to create will be numbered as **0750** and is intended to be used in infotype **0015** to reimburse tuition fees. The custom wage type number can be any number based on the numbering discipline that you may be following. Because wage type **0750** will be an earning wage type, it will potentially have an impact on gross pay as well as taxability.

Step 1: Create the Dialog Wage Type

In the first step of the example, you will create a dialogue wage type for entering a payment. The wage type will be used through infotype **0015**. Follow the configuration path in the IMG menu under **Personnel Administration · Additional Payments · Wage Types · Create wage type catalog**.

1. In the IMG, **Create wage type catalog** is available in many different places, such as Basic Pay configuration, Additional Payments configuration, etc. Use this configuration node with country code **USA** and you will see the screen shown in Figure 3.6.

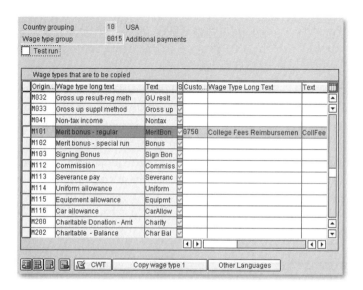

Country grouping	10	USA
Wage type group	0015	Additional payments
☐ Test run		

Wage types that are to be copied

Origin...	Wage type long text	Text	S	Custo...	Wage Type Long Text	Text	
M032	Gross up result-reg meth	GU reslt	✓				▲
M033	Gross up suppl method	Gross up	✓				▼
M041	Non-tax income	Nontax	✓				
M101	Merit bonus - regular	MeritBon	✓	0750	College Fees Reimbursemen	CollFee	
M102	Merit bonus - special run	Bonus	✓				
M103	Signing Bonus	Sign Bon	✓				
M112	Commission	Commiss	✓				
M113	Severance pay	Severanc	✓				
M114	Uniform allowance	Uniform	✓				
M115	Equipment allowance	Equipmt	✓				
M116	Car allowance	CarAllow	✓				
M200	Charitable Donation - Amt	Charity	✓				▲
M202	Charitable - Balance	Char Bal	✓				▼

CWT | Copy wage type 1 | Other Languages

Figure 3.6 Copy and Create a Wage Type using the US Model Wage Type

2. Select a model wage type from the left column. SAP shows all applicable wage types that are permissible for a particular infotype. (Wage types for infotype **0015** are displayed for this example.) Because you want to create an earnings wage type, select **M101** as shown in Figure 3.6.

3. Enter the number and text in the right column. In Figure 3.6, we used **0750** as the number for the wage type and entered a description of *College Fees Reimbursement*. The short text has a limitation of number of characters while the long text can be used to describe the wage type fully. You may want to think through the short text with the limited number of characters because many times, the short text can be used for printing in the pay stub.

Please note the **Wage type group** field (shown at the top of Figure 3.6) refers to infotype **0015** because I used the **COPY** node from the configuration menu in the IMG under Additional Payments configuration. If you use the **COPY** node under the Basic Pay configuration (**Personnel Administration • Basic Pay • Wage Types • Create wage type catalog**), you would have seen **0008** instead of **0015** in the grouping. You will be able to create a custom wage type applicable to the infotype. The advantage here is that SAP includes the list of model wage types that are only appropriate to that group/infotype. This answers the questions we raised earlier about knowing which model wage type to use. Of course, you won't always find a matching description from the model wage types. In those situations, you should select the closest earnings wage type and then modify the processing classes or other characteristics as necessary. Earnings are normally entered in US Payroll through infotypes **0008**, **0014**, **0015**, and **2010**. Therefore, you should use the **COPY** node in the IMG as appropriate under each of the infotypes related to configuration.

4. The *Test Run* button helps you to test what you have done before you actually update the database. It also helps you to know if there are any errors in your work. Figure 3.7 shows the error-free report you will get at the end of the copy. After receiving an error-free report, the remaining steps can be performed in any order. It will depend on your individual comfort level whether you will follow **IMG** nodes to carry out these steps or whether you will maintain them directly through tables. If you are confident about your knowledge, you can go directly to the tables listed in Figure 3.7 to change the wage types.

```
▽ 🗀 Copy wage type(s)  Test run  maintain manually:  012 Errors:  000
   ▷ 📁 Documentation
   ▷ 📁 T511        Wage Types
   ▷ 📁 T512T       Wage Type Texts
   ▷ 📁 T512W       Wage Type Valuation
   ▷ 📁 T512Z       Permissibility of Wage Types per Infotype
   ▷ 📁 T528C       Wage Type Catalog
   ▷ 📁 T52D7       Assign Wage Types to Wage Type Groups
   ▷ 📁 T52DZ       Assignment: Customizing - Model Wage Type
   ▷ 📁 T52EL       Posting of Payroll Wage Types
   ▷ 📁 T52EZ       Time-Dependency of Wage Type Posting
   ▷ 📁 T539J       Base Wage Type Valuation
   ▷ 📁 T54C3       Cumulation of Wage Types
```

Figure 3.7 An Error-Free Copy of a Wage Type

Figure 3.8 shows a menu option in the IMG that runs a simple transaction to check the assignment between wage types and infotype groups. When in doubt, you can always verify things through this menu option.

Step 2: Verify the Wage Type Characteristics

In the next steps, you will verify the wage type's characteristics by following the configuration IMG node of **Additional Payments • Wage Types**, as shown in Figure 3.8.

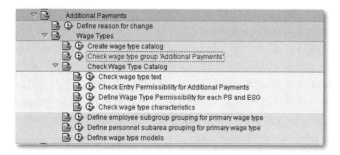

Figure 3.8 Additional Payments Wage Type Configuration in IMG

1. Use the **Check wage type characteristics** node to get to the screen shown in Figure 3.9. Rather than spending time digging into the details of each field, you can use the standard SAP documentation to learn about the characteristics. Earlier in the chapter, you learned about the three elements a wage type can have: **RTE**, **NUM**, and **AMT**. The *Input combination* field in Figure 3.9 controls the use of these elements. Also, if you recall the discussion on errors and controls while entering data, you'll notice the *Minimum amount* and *Maximum amount* fields. In Chapter 2 on Master Data, we discussed that infotypes **0014** or **0015** can control the wage type amount's input with a range of values; that range is controlled by these two fields.

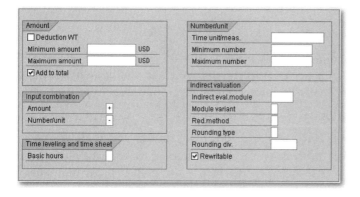

Figure 3.9 Wage Type Characteristics

2. From Figure 3.8, use the **Define Wage Type Permissibility for each PS and ESG** (which stands for *Personnel Sub-Area Grouping* and *Employee Sub-Group Grouping*) node to adjust the permissibility so the wage type can be used only for applicable employee subgroup groupings and personnel sub-area groupings. This configuration helps you control certain wage types for a specific category or type of employee. For example, if there is more than one union your employees belong to, you can make certain wage types permissible only for employees belonging to a particular union. Figure 3.10 shows the *piano boxes* (as many users refer them because they look like piano keys) for making the wage type permissible for certain types of employees or certain locations, depending upon how the groupings are designed. In the example in Figure 3.10, because all the boxes have been assigned a value of 1, the wage type is applicable to all employees—all ESG's and PSG's.

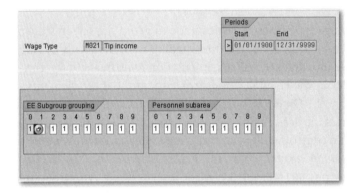

Figure 3.10 Wage Type Permissibility

Step 3: Adjust the Processing Classes of Wage Types

If you refer to the wage type template in Appendix B, you will see the key processing classes you need to use to complete the configuration. At this stage, let's examine a very important guideline around wage type configuration.

In the configuration IMG, you will find many nodes which allow you to maintain appropriate processing classes, cumulation, or the taxability of the earnings wage type. For example, the IMG node under cumulation allows you to maintain a processing class for cumulation, while the IMG node for deductions allows you to maintain deduction-related processing classes. However, most of the experienced configurators follow an approach of table-based maintenance. Many configurators use transaction **SM31** and access table **T512W** (for some tables, SAP gives you access to views; in this case access the table view: V_521W_D), and maintain the wage types for all processing classes and cumulation classes. The advantage of taking this route is that you get to see everything about the particular wage type on one screen. Figure 3.11 shows the T512W screen for maintaining wage types. Processing classes 1 through 6 are visible; use the down arrow on the side to get to processing classes 7 and beyond. (See Appendix E for a list of processing classes and their values.)

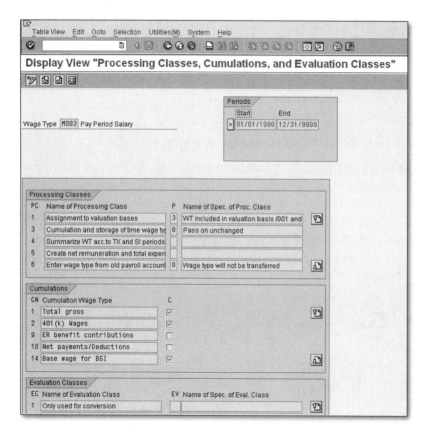

Figure 3.11 Maintaining Processing Classes of Wage Type: Table T512W View

Step 4: Determine the Cumulation Wage Types

Refer to Figure 3.11 where the cumulation is checked for **1**, **2**, and **14**. As such, this wage type is added to **/101** (Total gross), **/102** (401(k) Wages), and **/114** (Base wage for BSI). The other relevant examples here for US Payroll are the pension calculations. For instance, say a pension plan requires 5% of pensionable wages to be placed into a particular account. For that, you will need to determine which earnings wage types are pensionable (such as regular or overtime pay) and which are not.

Step 5: Maintaining Custom Cumulation

For all such wage types, which need to be used for cumulation towards pensionable wages, if you check cumulation 17 (not shown in Figure 3.11), the payroll process generates a technical wage type /117 and places all pensionable wages accumulated into it. Subsequently, in benefits as well as in any applicable payroll rules, you can use wage type /117 to calculate the pension amount. SAP has used many of the cumulations already. If you need to create new cumulations, you can use unused numbers. If we look back to our custom wage type 0750 from earlier steps, it will get added to /101 because earnings are added to gross pay.

Step 6: Determine the Factoring for the Wage Type

Factoring refers to a partial pay period or partial month amount determination. For example, if an employee's monthly pay is $3000 and she joins the company mid-month, you would need to factor the wage type with a processing class. Figure 3.12 shows processing class 10, which controls wage type factoring. Some wage types are factored proportionately to the duration the employee worked during the payroll period, while some wage types cannot be factored.

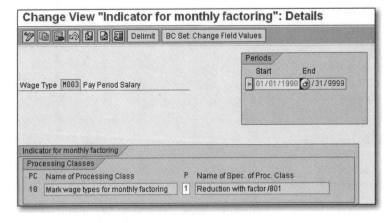

Figure 3.12 Monthly Factoring of Wage Types

Table 3.3 lists some of the more commonly used processing classes used for earnings wage types. However, it is worth your time to review all of the processing classes by reviewing SAP's model wage types. This gives you a better understanding of how SAP sets the processing classes.

Processing Class	Description
1 – Valuation	Valuation of wage type.
10 – Monthly Factoring	For employees joining or leaving in mid-month; used for partial month factoring cases.
20 – Storage and cumulation	For storage in Results Tables (RT).
30 – Cumulation	For YTD cumulation.
59 – Garnishment disposable net income	For transferring to disposable net income.
68 – Regular Payment	Regular or supplemental; for example, bonus payments are supplemental.
69 – Taxable earning	Most earnings are taxable.
71 – Tax classification	Earnings will mostly have a specification of 1- regular.
79 – Accruals	Earnings will mostly have a specification of 1.

Table 3.3 Earning Wage Type Processing Classes

Earlier, you learned that technical wage types are generated during the payroll process. Let's take a closer look at which technical wage types are normally impacted by earning wage types.

Technical Wage Types Associated with Earnings

Table 3.4 lists the technical wage types associated with earnings.

Technical Wage Type	Relationship to Earnings
/101	Gross wages: Earnings are cumulated to **/101**; as such, the cumulation class 1 for earnings should be checked ON.
/102	401(k) wages: All normal earnings are cumulated to 401(k) base wages. This wage type is used to calculate a percentage in 401(k) calculations.
/114	Base Wage for BSI calculation: This is sent over to BSI for tax calculations.

Table 3.4 Technical Wage Types Impacted by Earnings

Technical Wage Type	Relationship to Earnings
Custom cumulations	Earnings are typically used for pension or performance bonus calculations. However, overtime and other earnings are often excluded from such base calculations. You may have to create a custom cumulation wage type for such situations.

Table 3.4 Technical Wage Types Impacted by Earnings (cont.)

After completing the discussion on earnings wage types, let's move on to deductions. The overall philosophy of configuration remains the same as far as processing classes and cumulations are concerned. However, for deductions, there are additional features not applicable to earnings that we need to discuss.

3.3.2 Deductions

As noted earlier, a *deduction* is money paid by an employee from their earnings for items such as health insurance, 401(k) contributions, union dues, and so on. (In Figure 3.4, deductions fall into the first and second buckets.) The typical qualities of US deduction wage types include:

- They are dialogue wage types in certain cases and are entered through infotypes such as **0014**, **0015**, **0057**, and so on.
- In other cases, such as benefits and garnishments, deductions are calculated and generated in the payroll process based on configuration as well as input of data in infotypes.
- They can be either pre- or post-tax.
- They are added to technical wage types.
- In some cases, a deduction can have a predefined balance or goal.

Taxes also form part of deductions, but we will study them separately. As with earnings, SAP provides US model wage types for deductions, as listed in Appendix D. First, let's look at pre-tax deductions. Deductions appear with a minus sign (–) in the payroll results. If you refer back to Figure 3.9, the wage type can be turned into a deduction if *Deduction WT* is checked.

Before you learn how to configure a deduction, it's important that you first know more about the pre- and post-tax qualities of deduction wage types. (Both pre- and post-tax deduction wage types fall into buckets 1 and 2 in Figure 3.4.)

Pre-Tax Deductions

The IRS, along with state and local tax authorities, decides which deductions are pre-tax and how much is allowed in a tax year. (The US tax year is from January 1 to December 31.) The most common pre-tax deductions include:

▸ Savings plan (401(k)) deductions. These deductions have annual cumulation limits as prescribed by the IRS from year-to-year.

▸ Health plan deductions.

▸ Dental plan deductions.

▸ Flexible Spending Account (FSA) deductions for qualified health and child care expenses.

▸ Qualified transit programs for commuter expenses.

You will learn more about these and other benefit-related deductions in Chapter 5. US Payroll uses processing class 65 to decide whether a deduction is pre- or post-tax. As shown earlier in the sample paystub (see Figure 3.1), pre- and post-tax deductions are printed under separate headings. You will learn about pre- and post-tax deductions later in the chapter when we discuss the deduction wage type configuration.

Post-Tax Deductions

Post-tax deductions are taken out of an employee's earnings after tax calculations have been performed and taxes have been deducted. Examples of some typical US post-tax deduction include:

▸ Union dues.

▸ Charitable donations (such as to the United Way or some other non-profit organization).

▸ Loans.

▸ Garnishments.

▸ Savings bond purchases.

Deduction configuration involves the same steps used to create earnings wage types. Earnings are grossed (cumulated) in technical wage type **/101**, and deductions are grossed in technical wage type **/110**. Figure 3.13 shows wage type **/110** in the payroll results. If you need to use total earnings or total deductions in any reports or rules, you can use technical wage types such as **/101** or **/110**.

```
Table RT - Results Table (Collapsed Display)
A Wage type      APC1C2C3ABKoReBTAwvTvn One amount/one number    Amount
* /101 Total gross                                               575.63
* /102 401(k) Wage                                               575.63
* /104 NQP Eligibl                                               575.63
* /109 ER benefit                                                184.58
* /110 EE Deductio                                                62.64-
* /114 Base wage f                                               575.63
```

Figure 3.13 Technical Wage Types /101 and /110 from Payroll Results

Steps for Configuring Deduction Wage Types

As noted earlier in Figure 3.4, deduction wage types can fall into one of two buckets, and they can either be input through infotypes or are generated by configuring deductions such as benefits, savings bonds and garnishments.

The steps to configure the wage types that fall into the first bucket are the same as those for earnings. Rather than repeating the same steps listed earlier in Section 3.3.1, Figure 3.14 recaps the steps. If you are planning to create a new wage type for use in infotype **0014**, just follow the steps used to create an earnings wage type. The difference is that the model wage type is a deduction wage type instead of an earnings wage type.

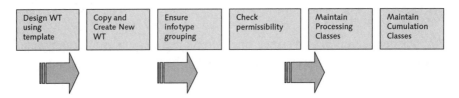

Figure 3.14 Reiterate Steps for Dialogue Wage Types

Depending on the type of deduction, however, creating a deduction wage type could have more steps to follow than an earnings wage type. Figure 3.15 includes boxes to show the extra steps. Note that not all of the steps are mandatory for all deduction wage types.

Figure 3.15 Additional Configuration Steps for Deductions

We will start the additional configuration discussion with balance and deduction wage types. Later in this chapter, we will cover arrears processing, deductions not taken, as well as posting of wage types (including third-party processing).

In US Payroll, you will often have a situation where a regular per-pay deduction has a certain goal amount (also called a *balance*) and stops when the goal amount is reached. The following steps should be used to manage these paid wage types:

1. First, select wage type **2200** (based on model wage type **M720** (deduction)) and **2202** (based on model wage type **M721** (goal and balance)) from the US model wage type catalog. **2200** is used through infotype **0014** for deductions, and **2202** is used through infotype **0015** for calculating the goal. (As mentioned earlier, please confirm the correct model wage type for your SAP version.)

2. In the IMG, follow the path **Payroll-USA • Deductions • Wage Types for Deductions with Balances and Totals** to further configure these wage types. This configuration maintains the processing class **66** (replaced by processing class **50** in newer versions), as well as a link between the three wage types. The third wage type, **2203** (based on model wage type **M722**), is used to display the running balance in the payroll results. (You will see this wage type in the results, shown later in this section.) Figure 3.16 shows the IMG path to configure the wage types with balances and deductions. This path leads to Figure 3.17, which shows how to link three wage types together. The configuration table in Figure 3.17 has an indicator column; please note the entries numbered 10 and 11. These two entries link the wage types **2200** to **2202** and **2202** to **2203**.

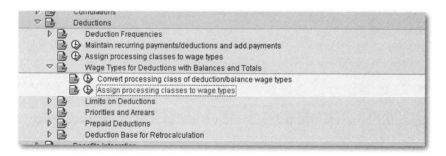

Figure 3.16 Configuring Deduction Wage Types with Balances

Indicator	W. type	Wage Type Long Text	From	To	W. type	Long tex
10	2200	United Way donation amt	01/01/1900	12/31/9999	2202	United V ▲
11	2202	United Way balance	01/01/1900	12/31/9999	2203	United V ▼

Figure 3.17 Linking Balance and Deduction Wage Types

3. Figure 3.18 presents infotype **0014** and Figure 3.19 presents infotype **0015** to show how **2200** and **2202** are linked, respectively. After completing the configuration in the previous step (when you create an infotype with wage type **2200**), SAP automatically pops-up infotype **0015** with **2202**. In this example, it will take the employee 10 payroll runs to pay the $250 goal amount, deducted at a rate of $25 per pay period. Figure 3.18 shows the payroll results where wage type **2202** is reduced from $250 to $225 after first payroll. That is how SAP keeps reducing **2202** in each payroll.

Recurring Payments/Deductions				
Wage Type	2200	United Way donation amt		
Amount	A	25.00 USD		Weekly
Number/unit				
Assignment Number				
Reason for Change				

Payment dates				
Payment model		First Pay Period of Month		
1st payment period	or	1st payment date		
Interval in periods		Interval/Unit		

Figure 3.18 Infotype 0014: Per Pay Deduction Wage Type M720

Additional Payments and Deductions		
Wage Type	2202	United Way balance
Amount	250.00	USD
Number/unit		
Date of origin	06/20/2004	
Default Date		
Reason for Change		

Figure 3.19 Infotype 0015: Goal or Balance Amount against the Deduction in Figure 3.18

Figure 3.20 presents the payroll results table. In addition to wage types **2200** and **2202**, you will notice that wage type **2203** is used to maintain the running totals for deductions.

These wage types are useful for processing cash advances and personal loans with a per-payroll deduction. As with earnings, Table 3.5 lists some commonly-used processing classes for deduction wage types.

```
* 2200 United Way                          25.00-
* 2202 United Way                         225.00
* 2203 United Way                          25.00-
```

Figure 3.20 Balance and Deduction Wage Types in Payroll Result

Processing Class	Description
20 – Storage and cumulation	For storage in the Results Tables (RT).
30 – Cumulation	For YTD cumulation.
65 – Pre-tax or after-tax	For certain benefit deductions such as 401(k); this processing class is pre-tax.
73 – Third-party sign assignment	For sign reversal of negative amounts in payroll results for deductions. For example, an employee benefit contribution has a negative sign in the payroll results, but before sending it out to the benefit provider, you change its sign to a positive.
78 – Third-party remittance	Used when sending money out to third-party vendors; for example, 401(k) deductions.

Table 3.5 Deduction Wage Type Processing Classes

Note
In earlier versions of SAP, the balance/deduction wage types were controlled by processing class **66**. Newer versions use processing class **50**. The upgrade process will take care of the changes to the processing class as well as changes to the appropriate lines in the payroll schema.

Deduction wage types are cumulated into a few technical wage types, as you will see in the next sub-section.

Technical Wage Types Associated with Deductions

Table 3.6 lists the technical wage types associated with deductions.

Technical Wage Type	Relationship to Earnings
/110	Total Deductions: Deductions are cumulated to **/110**; cumulation class **10** for deductions should be enabled in the configuration.
/109	Total benefits; employer contributions.

Table 3.6 Technical Wage Types impacted by Deductions

The next set of wage types handles tax deductions. Compared to earnings and deductions, taxes are not controlled by user inputs. Instead, they are based on tax authorities, who set the rates for taxable income and deductions. To that extent, the earlier discussion on earnings and deductions provides input to tax calculations and generation of tax wage types.

Splits

For earnings, deductions, and tax deductions, you need to know the concept of *splits*. Wage types are stored in the payroll results table (**RT**), which means they can be linked with additional information in other tables using wage type splits. These links are created using a two-character split indicator, as shown in the following examples:

▶ Wage type **/559** (Net Pay) is split with indicator **01** and **02** when infotype **0009** is divided to send employee net pay to two different banks.

▶ Wage type **M003** (Basic Pay) is split with indicator **01** and **02** when an employee is transferred to a different department in the middle of a pay period and belongs to two different cost centers.

▶ Wage type **/401** (withholding tax) is split with indicators **01** and **02** for federal and state taxes.

There are different split types and SAP's standard documentation will give you more information on those types and how to interpret splits.

3.3.3 Taxes

Tax processing will be covered in detail in Chapter 7. However, the wage type discussion won't be complete without discussing tax deduction wage types. In Chapter 1, you learned about **BSI** and tax calculation options. You won't be able to see the tax wage types in your payroll results without the BSI Tax Factory implementation. The good news is, however, that all tax wage types are technical and are generated by the system. As such, you will have to do less work on your configuration.

Tax wage types fall into the third bucket in Figure 3.4. Unlike earnings and deductions, you don't have to copy, create, and modify the tax wage types. They are delivered by SAP and, after you configure the tax models (discussed later in Chapter 7), the tax wage types are generated in the payroll schema.

The earnings and deduction wage types seen earlier, and their applicable tax-related processing classes, decide the tax calculations. Appendix C has a complete list of the technical wage types, ranging from **/300** to **/700**. Processing classes **67** through **71** affect the tax processing. Figure 3.21 shows an earnings wage type **M003** with the associated processing classes that will impact the taxes.

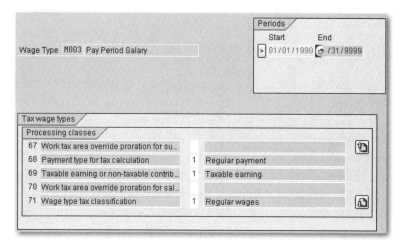

Figure 3.21 Tax Related Processing Classes for Wage Types

Although you haven't learned much about or seen the payroll results tables, let's examine some screenshots showing the tax-related wage types in payroll results. These screens, shown in Figures 3.22 and 3.23, will give you a better idea of the tax wage types to be discussed later in this section.

```
/101 Total gross                          1,750.00
/102 401(k) Wage                          1,750.00
/104 NQP Eligibl                          1,750.00
/109 ER benefit                             453.97
/110 Net payment                            177.37-
/114 Base wage f                          1,750.00
/301 TG Withhold    01                    1,753.15
/301 TG Withhold    02                    1,753.15
/303 TG EE Socia    01                    1,753.15
/304 TG ER Socia    01                    1,753.15
/305 TG EE Medic    01                    1,753.15
/306 TG ER Medic    01                    1,753.15
/310 TG ER Unemp    01                    1,750.00
/310 TG ER Unemp    02                    1,753.15
/401 TX Withhold    01                      120.81
/401 TX Withhold    02                       68.57
/403 TX EE Socia    01                      108.69
/404 TX ER Socia    01                      108.69
/405 TX EE Medic    01                       25.42
/406 TX ER Medic    01                       25.42
```

Figure 3.22 Tax Wage Types in Payroll Results (Part 1)

```
/601 TB Withhold  01                        1,595.65
/601 TB Withhold  02                        1,595.65
/603 TB EE Socia  01                        1,753.15
/604 TB ER Socia  01                        1,753.15
/605 TB EE Medic  01                        1,753.15
/606 TB ER Medic  01                        1,753.15
/610 TB ER Unemp  01                        1,750.00
/610 TB ER Unemp  02                        1,753.15
/700 RE plus ER                             2,203.97
/701 RE Withhold  01                        1,595.65
/701 RE Withhold  02                        1,595.65
/703 RE EE Socia  01                        1,753.15
/704 RE ER Socia  01                        1,753.15
/705 RE EE Medic  01                        1,753.15
/706 RE ER Medic  01                        1,753.15
```

Figure 3.23 Tax Wage Types in Payroll Results (Part 2)

Figure 3.22 shows the first part of tax wage types, covering series **/3xx** through **/4xx**, while Figure 3.23 shows the tax wage types covering series **/6xx** through **/7xx**. Table 3.7 presents the different types of tax wage types from both of the figures, along with a brief description. Remember that tax wage types come in groups, such as **/303**, **/403**, **/603**, and **/703**, which all correspond to employee Social Security taxes. Similarly, **/304**, **/404**, **/604**, and **/704** correspond to employer Social Security taxes. Why does SAP need so may wage types for each tax type? Table 3.7 helps to explain these different wage types.

Wage Type	Description
/3xx – Taxable Gross	These wage types contain taxable gross.
/4xx – Tax Deductions	These are actual tax deductions.
/6xx – Taxable Earnings	These are taxable earnings.
/7xx – Reportable Earnings	These are reportable earnings. Each /6xx wage type has an accompanying /7xx wage type. However, /7xx stops when there is a maximum wage limit, while /6xx continues. For example, Social Security limits will make the /703 wage type appear with an amount of $94,200, while /603 will be $102,000.

Table 3.7 Tax Wage Types from the Payroll Results

Tax wage types generated in tax calculations are impacted by two factors:

▶ Taxable earnings and pre-/post-deductions.

▶ The tax rates provided by **BSI** are based on tax authorities in tax infotypes **0207**, **0208**, **0209**, and **0210**.

If you refer back to the sample paystub (see Figure 3.1), look under the tax sections and you'll see many different tax types. To better understand the tax wage types, you need to know the tax authorities and tax types. (This is discussed in greater detail in Chapter 7.) Table 3.8 lists a broad category of the tax authorities and tax types, along with the tax wage types, as seen earlier in Figure 3.22.

Tax Authority	Tax Types	Wage Types from Figure 3.22
Federal	▶ Federal Withholding ▶ Social Security (FICA) ▶ Medicare (FICA)	▶ /401 Split 01 ▶ /403 and /404 (for employee and employer portions) ▶ /405 and /405 (for employee and employer portions)
State (the following States do not have a state income tax: Alaska, Florida, Nevada, New Hampshire, South Dakota, Tennessee, Texas, Washington, and Wyoming)	▶ State withholding ▶ State unemployment	▶ /401 Split 02
Local	▶ City taxes ▶ School taxes ▶ Occupational taxes	

Table 3.8 Tax Authorities and Tax Types

Depending on an employee's residence and work location, you may see different tax wage types in the payroll results. For example, employees in states such as Ohio or Pennsylvania will have local taxes, while employees in states like New Jersey will have unemployment-related taxes. The three different federal tax types from Table 3.8 are applicable to employees in every state.

> **Note**
>
> For some tax types in US taxes, the employee and employer both pay a portion of the tax. One example are the Social Security and Medicare tax types, shown by wage types **/403**, **/404**, **/405**, and **/406** in Table 3.8.

As noted earlier, wage types **/101** and **/110** are used for gross earnings and deductions, respectively. Similarly, all employee US tax deductions are grossed in wage type **/5U0**, and all employer US tax deductions are grossed in **/5U1** technical wage type. If you are looking for total taxes in a pay period for the employee or employer, you only need to consult these two technical wage types.

After covering earnings, pre-tax deductions, post-tax deductions, and taxes, the last wage type category to discuss is related to net pay.

3.3.4 Net Pay

Net pay brings us to the end of the equation. Earnings, pre- and post-tax deductions, and the tax calculations help the payroll process to arrive at *net pay*. Net pay is the amount an employee takes home at the end of a pay period. In some unique situations, the net pay can be zero (e.g., when an employee has no money left over to take home after deductions); however, the net pay can never be a negative amount (i.e., in arrears). There are situations where an employee might owe money to their employer, and these are defined as *Overpayments and Claims* in SAP. Situations like this are discussed in Chapter 8 *Advanced Topics*.

Net pay calculations have only few wage types:

- **/559 (Net Pay)**
  This wage type can have splits if an employee asks for options in infotype **0009**, which is used in instances where an employee wants some of their pay transferred to a bank account and the remainder as a check. Figure 3.24 shows **/559** with split 01, which means the entire amount in **/559** is paid by one check or one bank transfer, as the case may be with infotype **0009**. If infotype **0009** has part check and part bank transfer in the payroll results, **/559** will have two splits: 01 and 02. Figure 3.25 shows **/559** wage types with two splits, which means the employee has selected two different bank accounts or two different split amounts.

- **/560 (Amount Paid)**
  /559 and **/560** will have the same values in many cases. However, **/560** is further discussed in Chapter 8 *Advanced Topics*.

- **/5PY (Good Money)**
  Normally good money should be a positive amount (taxes aren't calculated unless **/5PY** has a positive amount). Chapter 8 discusses overpayments and claims, so look there to learn more about **/5PY**.

```
* /550 Statutory n                          1,426.51
* /559 Payment              01              1,249.14
* /560 Amount to b                          1,249.14
* /5PY Good Money                           1,750.00
* /5U0 Tot EE tax                             323.49
```

Figure 3.24 Net Pay Wage Types in the Payroll Results

```
* /559 Payment          01                              150.00
* /559 Payment          02                              308.33
* /560 Amount to b                                      458.33
* /5PY Good Money                                     3,333.33
```

Figure 3.25 Net Pay Wage Type with Splits in Payroll Results

Obviously, the employee needs to get paid, and in US Payroll they either get paid by check or by direct deposit to a specified bank account, the details of which are discussed in the next section.

Using Net Pay for Money Transfer

Infotype **0009** (as discussed in Chapter 2), helps decide whether an employee is paid by check or direct deposit to their bank account. SAP has a common process with the Accounts Payable module called **DME** (Data Medium Exchange) to manage checks and bank transfers. In the latest version, SAP provides the DME Workbench to help you manage this process. The payroll process writes the data in Bank Transfer (**BT**) tables in the payroll cluster. Figure 3.26 shows the **BT** table and how wage type **/559** is used to transfer the amount ($1219.14) to the employee's bank account. (**DME** programs access this table to pay the employee).

```
Table BT - Payment Information

TA  WType Max.amount in  ayroll currency          PymtMeth Recipient
Location                Ctry  Bank number      Bank account        Rec.        Purpose
InvType    Date     Time       Transfer ID         Trans.  Post bank          Street
Amt. in Payment Currency      Currenc  Region  POR number    POR ref.

01  /559  Payment                              1,249.14  T
                          US    123445678          887660607526
           08/06/2004  05:53:42                     00
```

Figure 3.26 Bank Transfer (BT) Table

Earlier in this chapter, we mentioned that net pay can be zero in US Payroll processing, and that there is a special functionality used to print *Zero-Net-Checks*. Figure 3.27 shows the IMG path for **DME** management. You can get to this path from the configuration menu in the IMG: **Payroll USA · Electronic Fund Transfer (EFT)**.

After you complete the short configuration steps listed in Figure 3.27, it isn't difficult to print Zero-Net-Checks (if any) after payroll is processed. We won't get into a detailed discussion about checks and bank transfers, because standard SAP documentation covers these topics.

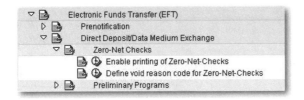

Figure 3.27 Handling Zero-Net-Checks

Now that you've learned how to configure earnings and deductions, in the sections that follow, we will review the steps to test wage types.

3.4   Testing Wage Types

After creating wage types, you need to test them. First off, wage type testing is divided into two areas: configuration completeness checks and the runtime or actual usage test.

- **Configuration Checks**
  Depending on whether a wage type is an earnings or deduction wage type, there can be many configuration steps. SAP has provided good reports to check the configuration and verify processing classes and posting attributes of wage types.

- **Wage Type Utilization Report**
  Figure 3.28 shows how to access the wage type utilization report in the menu under **Tools**. When you run the report, you can accesss all wage types with a particular processing class with the specifications. This report is very useful for examining the processing classes and cumulations of wage types. You can use the wage type template to verify this report and ensure that all processing classes are properly configured. This report allows you to verify:

  - Processing classes

  - Cumulation classes

  - Evaluation classes (used for print controls)

This report allows you to drill down into individual processing classes to discover the wage types associated with a particular processing class. Figure 3.29 shows an example for processing class **65** with pre-tax deductions specifications.

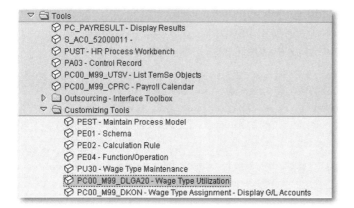

Figure 3.28 Accessing the Wage Type Utilization Report

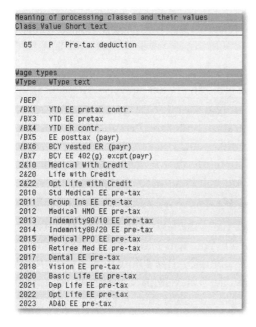

Figure 3.29 Output of the Wage Type Utilization Report

► **Characteristics Checks**

To avoid data entry errors, it's good practice to use the wage type template from Appendix B and verify the configuration for permissibility and input controls.

► **Run-time Checks**

Running wage types have three broad areas: input, processing, and output. Let's start with input first. As discussed earlier, wage types are linked to infotypes. Depending upon whether it is an earning or a deduction, the wage type is entered by specific infotypes. Table 3.9 lists some sample scenarios that you will test with the input of wage types.

Infotype Scenario	Test Conditions
Infotype 0008 and Basic Pay	▶ Defaults of wage types as per features
	▶ Defaults of rates as per configuration
	▶ Permissibility as per type of employee
Infotype 0014 and Payments and Deductions	▶ Permissibility for infotype group
	▶ Permissibility as per type of employee
	▶ Goal and deduction linkage
	▶ Payment model for deductions
	▶ Combination of amount and/or number
Infotype 0015	▶ The test conditions for infotype 0015 are similar to infotype 0014

Table 3.9 Infotype-Based Wage Type Tests

A common problem revolves around grouping between wage types and infotypes. Figure 3.8 shows the IMG configuration for assigning wage types to infotypes. (You will find this configuration under the **Personnel Administration** module in SAP.) When you use this path, you can attach wage types to infotypes as shown in Figure 3.30. The figure shows wage types as applicable to infotype group **0015**. Similarly, you will be able to configure wage types for infotype grouping **0008**, **0014**, **2010**, etc.

After you successfully enter the wage types through their relevant infotypes, you then need to process the payroll. You will learn more about payroll tables in Chapter 4, which also helps you understand how to test wage types during payroll processing and how the rules impact wage types during processing. You can examine the schemas and rules to *see* the wage type while it is processing.

Finally, to check the output, you need to get to the payroll results tables. Payroll results is the best place to check the output of a wage type. As noted earlier, the wage type can have **NUM, AMT**, and **RTE**, depending upon the type and configuration parameters. Figure 3.31 shows the payroll results tables and, among the list of tables, **RT** tables provide you with the output of all wage types with the three elements. You can access the payroll results tables as shown in Figure 3.31 using transaction **PC_PAYRESULT** or through the **Payroll USA • Tools** menu.

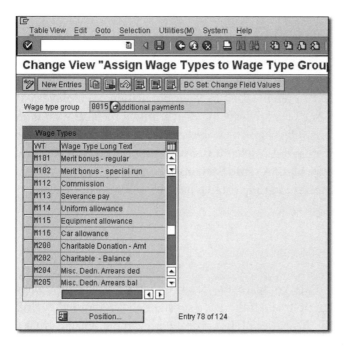

Figure 3.30 Assigning a Wage Type to an Infotype

Name	Name	Nu...
WPBP	Work Center/Basic Pay	1
RT	Results Table	73
RT_	Results Table (Collapsed Display)	73
CRT	Cumulative Results Table	189
BT	Payment Information	1
C0	Cost Distribution	1
V0	Variable Assignment	5
PCALAC	Status info. for subsequent programs	1
VERSION	Information on Creation	1
PCL2	Update information PCL2	1
VERSC	Payroll Status Information	1
TAX	Employee tax details	2
TAXR	Residence and unemployment tax details	4
TAXPR	Tax proration table	1
GRDOC	Garnishment document	1
GRORD	Garnishment order	1
TCRT	Cumulated tax results	501
NAME	Name of Employee	1

Figure 3.31 Payroll Results Tables

The most commonly used payroll report is the wage type reporter, which uses the payroll results tables. The next section discusses this report.

Wage Type Reporter

The wage type reporter is very simple to use, and is one of the best tools for checking the output of payroll results. Payroll results (seen earlier in Figure 3.31) help you to look at one employee at a time, while the wage type reporter allows you to run reports for a broader population of employees. It also helps you to run one or more wage types at a time for a location, for an employee group or for a subgroup. The wage type reporter also gives you the ability to compare two payroll results. It is a very simple report, which you can access from the **Payroll USA • Info Systems** menu. Many SAP customers use the wage type reporter to group wage types by:

▶ Earnings

▶ Benefits deductions

▶ Taxes

Subsequently, these users compare the total amounts for the groupings between two payroll periods and if there is a substantial difference, they drill down further to verify the causes of difference. For example, imagine that a number of employees are promoted, and subsequently receive a pay raise, during the current pay period. In this pay period, the wage type totals for gross pay wage type **/101** will be higher than for the previous pay period.

Although we could continue to discuss wage types forever, in the interest of time, let's address just a few advanced topics about wage types and then wrap up this chapter.

3.5 Advanced Topics on Wage Types

There are few more wage type topics, including cumulations and arrears processing, that have been separated from our main discussion earlier. You will use them for earnings as well as deductions, as explained in the following sections.

3.5.1 Handling Cumulations

In US Payroll, the term *cumulation* can refer to two aspects of wage types:

▶ Cumulating a wage type to another technical wage type. For example, the basic pay wage type **1000** has cumulation class 1 and is added (or *cumulated*) into technical wage type **/101**. This is the easy side of the cumulation. While configuring this cumulation, you can decide whether to base the cumulation on a number and/or an amount.

▶ The other side of cumulation (or rather the *true cumulation*) is to cumulate the wage type by month, quarter, year, or by another calendar period, as needed. Typically, we refer to these as **MTD**, **QTD**, and **YTD** cumulations. In some unique situations, you may encounter a requirement to do a custom cumulation based on a period you specify. Figure 3.32 shows the configuration steps in the IMG for cumulation.

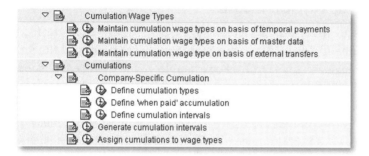

Figure 3.32 Cumulation Configuration

Although the configuration looks and feels difficult, after you understand the fundamental concepts, it isn't that tough. These concepts include:

▶ Decide the wage types and their cumulation approach by using processing class **30**.

▶ Define cumulation types and frequency: yearly, monthly, or another custom period which you define.

▶ Decide cumulation types and their start dates. For example, annually starting on January 1, or monthly starting on the first of each month.

▶ Assign years and from-to dates to the cumulation types.

▶ Tell the system whether you want to do amount and/or number cumulation. With certain wage types it helps to cumulate the numbers. For example, overtime hours in a year or, in case of certain pension wages, you only need to cumulate the number of hours.

Configuration results are visible in the **CRT** (Cumulative Results Table), as shown in Figure 3.33. The rows for the year 2004 are visible in the first column of the figure, with **M** (Month), **Q** (Quarter), and **Y** (Year) cumulations.

2004	07	M	/101	Total gross	0.00	3,500.00
2004	06	M	/101	Total gross	0.00	3,500.00
2004	05	M	/101	Total gross	0.00	3,500.00
2004	04	M	/101	Total gross	0.00	3,500.00
2004	03	M	/101	Total gross	0.00	3,500.00
2004	02	M	/101	Total gross	0.00	3,500.00
2004	01	M	/101	Total gross	0.00	3,500.00
2004	03	Q	/101	Total gross	0.00	3,500.00
2004	02	Q	/101	Total gross	0.00	10,500.00
2004	01	Q	/101	Total gross	0.00	10,500.00
2004	01	Y	/101	Total gross	0.00	24,500.00

Figure 3.33 CRT Table Showing Cumulations

3.5.2 Setting Up Payment Models

Payment models are used with deduction wage types. They give you the flex-ibility to determine if a deduction can be taken at a predetermined time of the year and through certain payrolls. For example, if you input a deduction in infotype **0014** within a date range, the deduction will be made every pay period. However, if you don't want that to happen and only want the deduc-tion to be made at certain times of the year, you can use payment models to control that. Figure 3.34 shows the IMG path in Payroll-USA for configuring deduction models.

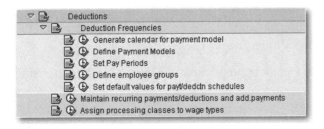

Figure 3.34 Deduction Payment Models

If you follow the IMG path shown in Figure 3.34, you will be able to create your own payment models or use the SAP-delivered payment models. Figure 3.35 shows an example from one of the SAP-delivered payment models. In the example, a biweekly payroll with 26 pay periods per year has deductions taken out only 12 times per year, as noted by the checkmarks. The deduc-tions are selectively taken in the payroll periods with checkmarks. Note that the deduction models are dependent on individual years and need annual maintenance.

If you refer back to infotype **0014** where deductions are stored, you will see the **Payment model** field. In reality, each employee has multiple pre- and post-tax deductions. Therefore, SAP Payroll needs to know which deduction is more important and what treatment to adopt if there is not enough money in an employee's pay to cover their deductions. Let's learn more about this.

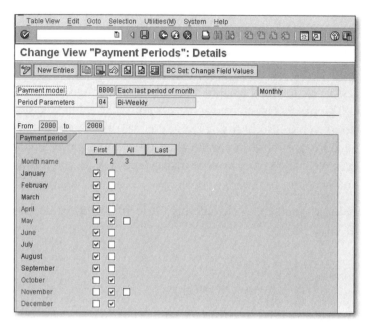

Figure 3.35 Payment Model Deduction Frequency

3.5.3 Priority and Arrears

Normally, deductions are fine when an employee has enough money to pay for them and everything is normal. But life is never normal and perfect! Payroll processes need to know how to handle situations when there is not enough money for all of an employee's deductions. The questions to ask include:

▶ Is there enough money to take the deductions?

▶ If there isn't enough money, is a portion of the money available?

▶ If there isn't enough money, will the deduction be dropped or put in arrears for future payroll periods?

That introduces some new concepts: priority of deductions, arrears processing, and deductions not taken. We will also discuss these concepts when we get to payroll schema discussions in Chapter 4 and learn about the US Payroll schema functions that handle them. The configuration steps discussed in this section will assist you in managing these concepts. In Chapter 4, when we discuss schema **UDD0**, we will talk about arrears processing as well as the deductions not taken table which uses this piece of the configuration for the wage type.

Step 1: Priority and Arrears Processing

When working with deductions, you will often encounter a situation where the payroll process needs to know what to do if there isn't enough money to take a deduction. This process is referred as *arrears processing*. While the system is looking at arrears, it also needs to know the priority of each deduction—some deductions are more important than others. The garnishment deduction, for example, has a higher priority than a deduction for the United Way or for union dues.

1. In the IMG, select **Payroll-USA • Deductions • Priorities and Arrears**, as seen in Figure 3.36.

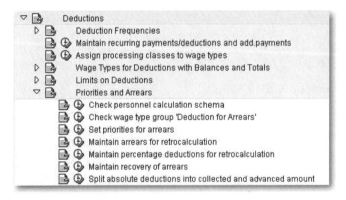

Figure 3.36 Configuration of Priorities and Arrears

2. Figure 3.37 shows the configuration related to priorities processing. As noted in the screen, deductions with Priority A take a higher priority than those with Priority B or C.

3. After the system knows the priority of a deduction, and if there isn't enough money for the deduction, then system needs to make a decision on arrears. When a deduction is sent to arrears processing, subsequent payroll processes will look for money to take the deduction. For example, in payroll period 10, a certain deduction went to arrears for $50, so that amount will be deducted in payroll period 11. Figure 3.38 shows the arrears configuration screen.

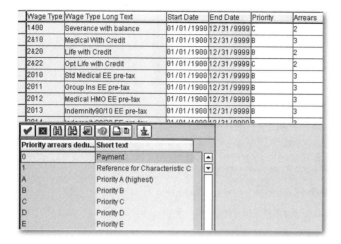

Wage Type	Wage Type Long Text	Start Date	End Date	Priority	Arrears
1400	Severance with balance	01/01/1990	12/31/9999	C	2
2&10	Medical With Credit	01/01/1900	12/31/9999	B	3
2&20	Life with Credit	01/01/1900	12/31/9999	B	2
2&22	Opt Life with Credit	01/01/1900	12/31/9999	C	2
2010	Std Medical EE pre-tax	01/01/1900	12/31/9999	B	3
2011	Group Ins EE pre-tax	01/01/1900	12/31/9999	B	3
2012	Medical HMO EE pre-tax	01/01/1900	12/31/9999	B	3
2013	Indemnity90/10 EE pre-tax	01/01/1900	12/31/9999	B	3
2014	Indemnit90/20 EE pre-tax	01/01/1900	12/31/9999	B	2

Priority arrears dedu...	Short text
0	Payment
1	Reference for Characteristic C
A	Priority A (highest)
B	Priority B
C	Priority C
D	Priority D
E	Priority E

Figure 3.37 Arrears and Priority for Deduction Wage Types

Wage Type	Start Date	End Date	Priority	Arrears
1400	01/01/1990	12/31/9999	C	2
2&10	01/01/1900	12/31/9999	B	3
2&20	01/01/1900	12/31/9999	B	2
2&22	01/01/1900	12/31/9999	C	2
2010	01/01/1900	12/31/9999	B	3
2011	01/01/1900	12/31/9999	B	3
2012	01/01/1900	12/31/9999	B	3
2013	01/01/1900	12/31/9999	B	3

Arrears characteri...	Short text
1	Deduct total amount
2	Deduct what is possible
3	Write remainder to arrears table
4	Garnishment, not a reduction
5	Deduct all or nothing
6	All or nothing, write to arrears table
7	Loan, no reduction

Figure 3.38 Arrears Characteristics Configuration

4. Obviously, arrears processing can have a retroactive impact because the payroll process has to span the periods. Therefore, the retroactive arrears treatment has some additional configuration, as shown in Figure 3.39.

5. When a deduction is not taken in the current payroll period, it is written in a payroll table **DDNTK** and, depending upon the arrears processing configuration, the deduction will either get dropped or go to arrears processing. For example, a deduction is not taken and is written to the **DDNTK** table in the payroll results. However, if there isn't a corresponding arrears processing configuration, the deduction will get dropped and won't be processed in the next or any subsequent payroll periods.

Wage Type	Wage Type Long Text	Start Date	End Date	Retroacct.
1400	Severance with balance	01/01/1900	12/31/9999	1
2810	Medical With Credit	01/01/1900	12/31/9999	1
2820	Life with Credit	01/01/1900	12/31/9999	1
2822	Opt Life with Credit	01/01/1900	12/31/9999	1
2010	Std Medical EE pre-tax	01/01/1900	12/31/9999	1
2011	Group Ins EE pre-tax	01/01/1900	12/31/9999	1
2012	Medical HMO EE pre-tax	01/01/1900	12/31/9999	1

Arrears deducts.in RA...	Short text
1	Take old amount, write difference to arrears table
2	Take old amount, only write positive difference to arrears
3	Take old amount, only write negative difference to arrears
4	Take old amount, forget difference

Figure 3.39 Arrears Processing in Retroactive Payroll

Later in Chapter 4, you will learn about subschemas and where the applicable payroll tables, **ARRRS** and **DDNTK**, are generated. The configuration explained here plays a role in generating these tables in the payroll subschemas. Considering the complexity of this topic, let's look at another example to show the effect of this configuration.

Figure 3.40 shows an infotype **0014** deduction for an employee for $10,000 (I have purposely used a large amount so the deduction will go into arrears and won't be taken).

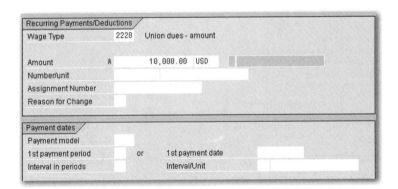

Figure 3.40 Deduction in Infotype 0014

Subsequently, we have run a payroll to demonstrate how the deduction can go to the **ARRRS** and **DDNTK** tables. Figure 3.41 shows the wage type **2220** in the payroll results for an amount of $1,632.38, which is the amount the process could afford to take with the available earnings for this employee.

```
1 /002 Valuation b01                    23.70
1 /BER Benefits ER01                                          114.65
1 /BT1 EE GTLI Tax01                                            2.22
1 1001 Hourly rate01                    23.70
1 1200 Regular wor01              23.70 80.00               1,896.00
1 2220 Union dues 01                                       1,632.38-
1 2320 Basic Life 01        B 01                                0.89
1 2420 Basic Life 01        B 01                                0.89
```

Figure 3.41 Wage Type 2220 Deduction in Payroll

Actually, the payroll should have taken a deduction of $10,000, leaving a short fall of $8,367.62 ($10,000 − $1,632.38 = $8,367.62). Figure 3.42 shows the **DDNTK** table (Chapter 4 discusses how this table is generated) and Figure 3.43 shows the **ARRRS** table. In the current pay period, the balance of $8,367.62 is written to the deductions not taken table. In addition, the same amount is written in the **ARRRS** table so the next pay period can take the possible deduction (either full or in part) for this wage type.

Table DDNTK

Wage typ	Wage type text	Amount	VT	VN	Origin
2220	Union dues - amount	8,367.62		00	A

Figure 3.42 DDNTK Table with Balance Amount

Table ARRRS

WType	Wage type text	Amount
2154	Defer Comp-B EE after-tax	33.12-
2154	Defer Comp-B EE after-tax	22.08-
2154	Defer Comp-B EE after-tax	1.38
2154	Defer Comp-B EE after-tax	9.66-
2154	Defer Comp-B EE after-tax	11.04-
2154	Defer Comp-B EE after-tax	34.50-
2154	Defer Comp-B EE after-tax	11.04
2154	Defer Comp-B EE after-tax	11.04-
2154	Defer Comp-B EE after-tax	11.04-
2154	Defer Comp-B EE after-tax	45.54-
2154	Defer Comp-B EE after-tax	55.20
2154	Defer Comp-B EE after-tax	55.20
2154	Defer Comp-B EE after-tax	59.34
2154	Defer Comp-B EE after-tax	300.00
2220	Union dues - amount	8,367.62

Figure 3.43 ARRRS Table with Balance Amount in Arrears

Table 3.10 presents a list of the configuration nodes for this wage type.

IMG Node (Refer to Figure 3.36)	Configuration Details (Refer to Figures 3.37 through Figure 3.39).
Check wage type group deduction for arrears	Wage type 2220 is part of this group.
Set priorities for arrears	Priority C and Arrears characteristics=3 (write the remainder to the arrears table).
Maintain arrears for retrocalculation	Arrears characteristics for retro=1 (take the previous amount and write the difference to the arrears tables).

Table 3.10 Configuration Steps for Arrears and Retro of the Wage Type

The next section briefly discusses the postings of wage types.

3.5.4 Posting of Wage Types

As you know, SAP's strength is in its integration across modules. SAP Payroll and SAP Financials are well-integrated. When users post documents from payroll, they are instantly posted to General Ledger (GL) and Accounts Payable (AP), and the accounts are updated. The configuration resides in Payroll-USA, but needs to be worked out by the financials team. Integration between Finance and Payroll is beyond the scope of this book, so let's limit the discussion to a simple overview. The posting programs are run after payroll *Exit*.

GL Posting

US Payroll wage types are posted to one of two accounts: expense or financial (balance sheet) accounts. Typically, regular pay, overtime, bonus pay, etc., are expenses and will be appropriately mapped to expense accounts. (Refer to the standard SAP documentation to read about the concept of symbolic accounts and how they are used to map GL accounts.)

It is worth noting a very useful SAP report, **RPCPCC00 (Payroll USA · Info System · Payroll Results)**, which is very helpful for drilling down into the wage type postings. This report wasn't available in pre-4.6 versions of SAP, and it is useful because it provides the GL accounts and the cost center postings for wage types. Figure 3.44 shows the output of this report. You can see that this single report gives you the ability to drill down to cost center postings, payroll results, as well as GL account postings.

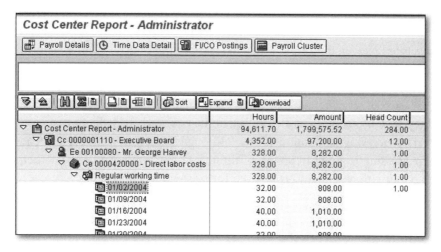

Figure 3.44 Cost Center Report, RPCPCC00

AP Posting (also called Third-Party Remittance Posting)

Before we get to account posting, let's go back to Chapter 1 and Figure 1.2. There, you can see that taxes, benefits, and garnishments are sent out to different vendors or authorities. During payroll processing, various deductions are calculated and then the actual money needs to go out to proper authorities. For example, say you deducted $400 as federal tax from an employee's pay. You then need to send that money to the IRS within a certain timeframe. The same logic holds for benefit providers and garnishment authorities, also. While SAP's standard documentation gives you enough information about this topic, let's quickly recap the list of important steps to follow:

▸ Work with the finance team to configure the appropriate vendor accounts. Additionally, you will need help from the finance team to attach a *Clearing Account* to the wage types that need to go out to vendors.

▸ Revisit processing classes **73** and **78** for the wage types to ensure that third-party processing and sign assignments are correct.

▸ Work with your interface development teams as they will need these wage types and their associated characteristics to send the information to benefit providers or garnishment authorities.

You will learn more about this topic in Chapter 8, *Advanced Topics*.

3.6 Summary

Wage types play an important role when processing US Payroll. They control the inputs, processing, and output from the process. A wage type's life revolves around processing classes, and you need to have a good understanding of each processing class and what it means to the wage type. SAP provides you with many features and functionalities, such as deduction models, arrears processing, and cumulations. Although not every wage type in payroll processing is going to use all of these features, you need to know them well because they will always be used for processing US Payroll.

This Chapter has provided you with insight into earnings, deductions, and tax wage types. So far, you have learned about the configuration and characteristics of certain wage types. However, you have yet to see the wage types used to process payroll. Chapter 4 will lead us to that discussion.

When you combine wage types with schemas and rules, you get a very powerful—but nonetheless very flexible—sub-assembly of US Payroll! Chapter 4 takes you to the discussion of schemas and rules to help you overcome the much-talked-about fear of *rules*.

US Payroll schema U000, with its associated subschemas and rules, forms the core of the US Payroll processing system. In addition, writing rules is one of the challenging areas in SAP Payroll and is a much-required skill to explore the flexibility of US Payroll. This chapter explains the functionality of the US schema and presents examples to assist you with writing your own rules.

4　Schemas and Rules

This chapter forms the heart and soul of the book. While many of you will agree that there is a fear factor associated with writing schemas and rules in US Payroll, this chapter intends to discuss the US Payroll schema U000, followed by the subschema discussion. The chapter discusses modification of schemas and rules, including the run-time environment. It uses many practical examples to support rule writing and provides you with guidance for future rule-writing initiatives. Dealing with schemas and rules requires lot of practice; the chapter helps you overcome initial fears so you can start using the examples to create your own custom rules. The US Payroll schema consists of a series of statements that control the logic for payroll calculations and the payroll process. Rules are an integral part of the schema and they normally contain arithmetical and logical operations such as multiplication and division. You will be able to use these operations to manipulate the rate, number, and amounts in wage types. Let's dive in and examine the US payroll driver.

4.1　Examining the US Payroll Driver (RPCALCU0)

Before jumping into the schema discussion, it's important to understand where and how the schema is used in the payroll process. The payroll driver is used whenever you run the payroll, either in simulation mode or start mode (as per status of the payroll control record). Payroll driver is just another term for an ABAP program, **RPCALCU0** (the *U* in the name of this program refers to the US payroll driver). Figure 4.1 shows the opening screen of the driver as you'll see it on your own system.

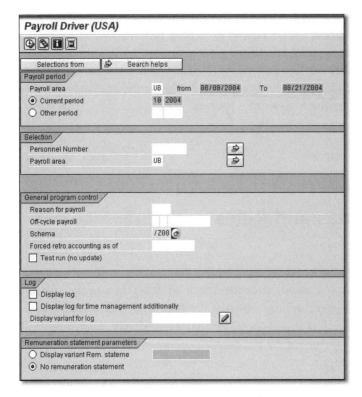

Figure 4.1 RPCALCU0, US Payroll Driver

The payroll driver helps you with multiple tasks, including:

▶ Managing the payroll process based on the status of the payroll control record (Start/Correction/Exit)

▶ Managing off-cycle/bonus runs, in addition to regular payroll runs

▶ Allowing you to perform forced retroactive payroll runs

▶ Allowing you to use a custom schema for payroll calculations based on your own requirements

Since the discussion here is about schemas, let's focus on using custom schemas. Custom schemas give you tremendous flexibility for payroll calculations. You can also use different schemas to run different payroll areas. For example, if you have a weekly payroll for hourly employees and a biweekly payroll for salaried employees, you will have two payroll areas: one for weekly and one for biweekly. You can also create two schemas, one for each area. The payroll areas should be kept simple and straightforward for overall ease of maintenance. For example, if different geographic locations have different payroll rules and scenarios, you'll need to create separate payroll areas for them. Of course, you can also use one schema for both payrolls and create separate rules for salaried and hourly employees. You will learn how to create rules later in Section 4.5. The example in Figure 4.1 relates to the payroll driver, which uses schema **/Z00** to run the payroll. That means the logic and rules coded in schema **/Z00** are used by the payroll run.

During testing, you have the ability to turn logging *ON*, so you can dissect the schema and learn more about any errors and issues that occur. More examples will be discussed later in this chapter. For now, don't set this flag to *ON* for a full payroll run because it can create too large a log and may create a program dump if the output becomes too large (for example, if your payroll contains thousands of employees).

At this stage, it is important for you to read through the standard SAP documentation on payroll control record topics if you are not familiar with the different possible statuses of the payroll control record. It is important for you to have this knowledge before going on to the next section, which dives into the US schema (U000), and walks you through the important subschemas.

> **Tip**
>
> The SAP documentation is available online, at *http://help.sap.com/*.

4.2 Working with US Schema U000

For many, a common question is: *What is a schema?* Perhaps some of you have already heard of database schemas or XML schemas. The US Payroll schema consists of a set of statements which drive the logic of payroll processing. As the word suggests, it is a defined plan to run the payroll.

The payroll schema helps the payroll driver with calculation rules, functions, and the overall flow of processing of employees in a payroll. The schema gives you the ability to "arrange" the processing as you will see in the examples later in this chapter. Imagine that in your legacy payroll system, for example, a single payroll program is used to control the processing, which caused you to write complicated logic to manipulate calculations, manage union rules and deductions, and so on. Now, thanks to schemas, rules, and wage types in SAP Payroll, you don't have to write and maintain complex legacy code. While the payroll driver serves as the engine to run your payroll, the schema gives you the flexibility of "configuring" the rules. Figure 4.2 presents a concept diagram to explain the various parts of a schema. This is almost like a "Bill of Materials" for a schema with all its subassemblies and parts. You will notice that the schemas can contain subschemas and subschemas in turn can contain more subschemas. However, subschemas can be generally referred to as schemas as well. Figure 4.2 helps you understand the relationships between schema-subschemas, functions, rules, and operations. Do not get concerned about the actual examples used in Figure 4.2; for now, it's more important that you understand the basic concepts and relationships.

> **Note**
>
> SAP has provided a specific schema for the US Public Sector. We will keep our discussion to the generic US schema; however, differentiators of the US Public Sector schema are listed in Section 4.1 of this chapter.

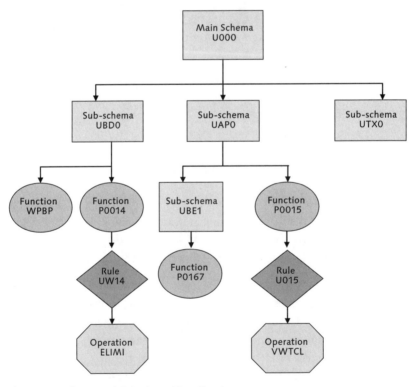

Figure 4.2 Schema and Subschema Tree Structure

Figure 4.2 presents a tree structure to show how the main schema, subschemas, functions, rules, and operations relate to each other. Treat it as an *ecosystem* of the payroll schema and you will notice that the ecosystem depends on its elements to function properly. The relationships shown in in Figure 4.2 are:

▶ Main schema consists of many subschemas

▶ Subschemas consist of many rules

▶ Rules consist of many operations

▶ Schemas and subschemas consist of many functions

Together, they form the schema ecosystem, as mentioned earlier. Now, use transaction **PE01**, and open US schema **U000**, as shown in Figure 4.3. You will learn more about the Schema Editor and transaction **PE01** later in this chapter. For now, it's important for you to develop some familiarity with the look and feel of the schema.

Edit Schema: U000

Line	Func.	Par1	Par2	Par3	Par4	D	Text
000010	COPY	UIN0					US Payroll: Initialization of payroll
000020	COPY	UODP				*	On-demand regular (no need after 4.5A)
000030	COPY	UBD0					Basic data processing
000040	COPY	UPR0					Read previous result of current period
000050	COPY	XLR0					Import previous payroll results
000060	COPY	UM00					Determine payroll modifiers
000070	COPY	UT00					Gross compensation and time evaluation
000080	COPY	UREI				*	Travel expense
000090	BLOCK	BEG					Gross cumulation and tax processing
000100	IF		NAMC				if non-authorized manual check (*)
000110	COPY	UMC0					Process Non authorized check (*)
000120	ELSE						else if non authorized manual check (*)
000130	COPY	UAP0					Process add. payments and deductions
000140	COPY	UAL0					Proration and cumulation gross
000150	COPY	UTBS					Save tables for iteration
000160	LPBEG						Begin of iteration
000170	COPY	UTBL					Load saved tables
000180	COPY	UDD0					Process deductions, Benefits
000190	COPY	UTX0					Calculate taxes
000200	COPY	UGRN					Calculate garnishments
000210	COPY	UNA0					Calculate net
000220	COPY	UDNT					Deductions not taken during loop ?
000230	LPEND						End of iteration
000240	ENDIF						to: if non authorized manual check (*)

Figure 4.3 Schema U000

Figures 4.2 and 4.3 use technical terms, including *rules*, *operations*, and *functions*. Before proceeding with the detailed discussion about schemas, it's important for you to understand the definitions of these three terms. We will first look at the definitions of schema and subschema and then examine the definitions for functions, rules, and operations.

4.2.1   Schema

The schema, or main schema, consists of many subschemas. For example, US schema **U000** contains subschemas **UAP0, UAL0, UTX0**, etc. Each schema has a four-character name. As noted earlier, the *U* character *is* the US country code. Schemas that start with the letter *X* are international and can be used for many countries. The statements and code shown in Figure 4.3 are for the main schema **U000**. Table 4.1 presents the meaning of different columns presented in Figure 4.3.

Column in Schema Screen	Explanation
Line Numbers	Are sequential and you can insert or delete lines.
Func.	Stands for Functions. Have an ABAP code in the background and carry out specific instructions, such as reading infotypes.
Par1, Par2, Par3, Par4	Functions have parameters and depending on the value of the parameters, functions can behave differently. There can be up to 4 parameters as shown in Figure 4.4.
D	When you have an asterisk (*) in this column, it means the line is commented and will not get executed. You use commenting when modifying schemas.
Text	Free form text to describe the purpose of the schema line.

Table 4.1 Schema Editor Columns

4.2.2   Subschemas

Subschemas form part of the main schema, and each subschema performs specific functions. For example, **UNA0** is used for net calculations, while **UTX0** corresponds to tax calculations. In Figure 4.4, you can see that **UIN0, UBD0, UPR0** are subschemas. You use the **COPY** function to copy subschemas into the main schema. At any given point in time, there will be one main schema and many subschemas; however, the term *schema* can be generically used for both the main and subschemas.

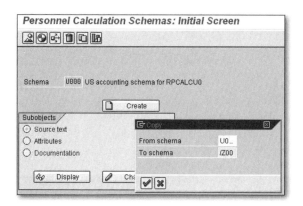

Figure 4.4 Copying a Delivered Schema

Functions

Functions are typically used to read infotypes in schemas and subschemas. They also perform other tasks, such as printing and rule execution. For example, see the **COPY** and **BLOCK** functions in Figure 4.4.

Rules

Rules are used to calculate and manipulate wage types. You'll learn more about rules as you explore the subschemas in this discussion. You'll need to expand the schema or subschema further to make the rules visible. Just like schemas, rule names can start with a *U* (for US) or an *X* (for international). Later in this chapter, you will create a custom rule following custom naming specifications.

Operations

Rules use operations for mathematical and logical processing. For example, operations can perform tasks such as multiplication, division, percentage calculation, wage type writing, and so on. You will learn more about operations in Section 4.5, later in this chapter.

SAP includes schemas, subschemas, rules, and operations, and you should copy and modify the schemas and subschemas as needed. All these objects are accessible by using their respective editors. The transactions to access the editors are listed in Table 4.2. When working with these editors in a transport-enabled SAP system, the editor generates the transports.

Editor transaction	Objects to edit
PE01	Schemas, subschemas
PE02	Rules
PE03	Features
PE04	Functions and Operations

Table 4.2 Editor Transactions for Schema and its Children

Tip

Don't forget the golden rule of SAP configuration: *Never modify SAP-delivered objects*; always copy and create new ones in a customer name space. SAP typically displays warning messages if you try to create objects in SAP's namespace rather than using customer specific names, such as those starting with Z.

To understand schema **U000**, you will also need to learn about its many sub-schemas. The next few sections explore those subschemas in depth.

4.2.3 US Subschemas

In Figure 4.3, you have already seen that subschemas form part of the main US schema, **U000**. Table 4.3 presents a simple list of all applicable US sub-schemas and a brief description of their functionality.

Subschema name	Description of subschema functionality
U001	ADP schema for RPCALCU0. For Gross to Net with ADP (third-party payroll processing).
U500	Used during Third-Party Remittance processing for taxes and benefits
UAC0	Personnel calculation schema for month-end accruals
UAL0	Gross calculation
UAP0	Reading in further pay and deductions
UBD0	Basic data
UBE1	Process benefits (1st time); health and insurance plans
UBE2	Process benefits (2nd time); savings and flex spending plans
UBEN	Process benefit infotypes

Table 4.3 US Subschema List

Subschema name	Description of subschema functionality
UCLM	Standard schema used during claims processing (overpayments)
UDBS	Deduction-based calculation
UDD0	Gross calculation
UDP0	Processing of deductions/donations, their balances and totals
UEND	Final processing
UGRN	Garnishments
UGRR	Garnishments (retro-calculation)
UIN0	Initialization of accounting
ULK0	Transfers payroll results from Table 558A/5U8A (US-specific) to the payroll results tables. This is used if the payroll system is going live in the middle of the year. You will learn more about this schema in Chapter 8.
ULK9	Transfers payroll accounts from Table 5U8C (US-specific) to the payroll results tables. This is used if the payroll system is going live in the middle of the year.
UMC0	This schema processes manual checks and is used during off-cycle payroll. In Chapter 7, we will refer to this schema for year-end off-cycle payrolls.
UNA0	Net calculation
UNN0	Net payments/deductions and transfers
UT00	Processing of time data for payroll accounting
UTX0	US tax processing

Table 4.3 US Subschema List (cont.)

You will need to copy and modify some of the schemas listed in Table 4.3 so you can insert new customized rules of your own. There is no fixed guidance about commonly modified subschemas; it depends entirely on your requirements. However, if you decide to add or change a rule in any of the subschemas, you will have to copy and modify the subschema as necessary. The following sections closely examine each subschema to help you learn about their individual functionality. They won't be analyzed line by line; however, important features of each are highlighted. In SAP configuration (IMG), these subschemas appear at different places as they are relevant. For example, the tax subschema appears under US tax configuration while the month-end accrual schema appears under month-end accrual configuration. However, it is easy to access any subschema using the **PE01** editor transaction. As you are reading any subschema through its main schema, it is easy to understand the flow of the logic and how the control is passed from one subschema to another. After you start the main schema in the editor, **double-click** each subschema in the editor to open it.

In each schema, functions, rules, and tables are the three most important dimensions you need to know. Please refer to Appendix A for detailed **U000** schema lines, as discussed here.

UIN0: Initialization of Payroll

This schema manages the status of a payroll control record. You can comment the function **CHECK** if you want to bypass the check for control record. The function description is as follows:

Functions

▶ Function **CHECK** (parameter ABR) checks the payroll control record status. During the testing stage of the project, you might want to comment this line in the schema so that, regardless of the payroll control record's status, you will be able to test-run your payroll. In a production payroll system, you should never comment this line.

UBD0: Basic Data Processing

After the initial checks on the control record are carried out, this schema checks for the existence of basic infotypes from the employee master data. Many of the infotypes discussed earlier in Chapter 2 will now be processed in the schema. The main features of this schema are:

Functions

▶ Function **WPBP** (Work Place/Basic Pay) manages any splits in an employee's infotype **0001**, **0007**, **0008**, or **0027**. For example, if an employee joined the organization in the middle of a pay period or if an employee has taken a new position in the middle of a pay period, you will see the impact of this function. In addition, if an employee's work schedule changed in the middle of a pay period, this function creates a table **WPBP** in payroll results.

▶ Functions **P0002**, **P0006**, **P0207**, and **P0014** read respective infotypes. For example, if infotype **0207** (residence tax area) is missing from your employee master data, the schema will cause an error when it reaches this subschema. Also, if you are interested in finding out the "internal" processing of data from infotype **0014**, you can drill down into the schema here. The drill down (*drill down* is a general term used to explode the schema to subschemas and rules Various employee master data or transaction data infotypes discussed earlier in Chapter 2 are processed in the schema using these functions. In Appendix A, you will notice similar functions referring to **P2010**, **P0221**, etc., and they process the respective infotypes.

Rules

► Rule **UW14** is used to process data from infotype **0014** with function **P0014**.The wage types from infotype **0014** will form input and output to this rule. For example, a recurring deduction for The United Way is maintained in infotype **0014**, and is processed by this rule.

Tables

► **WPBP**
Is created by function **WPBP** and is visible in payroll results

► **IT (Input Table)**
Contains wage types with their amounts, numbers, and rate information

► **NAME**
Is created from infotype **0002**

► **ADR**
Is created from infotype **0006**

► **TAXR**
Contains residence tax authority and is created from infotype **0207**

Tip
At this point, it might be a good idea for you to visit and review SAP's documentation on payroll tables and their usage.

UT00: Gross Compensation and Time

UT00 is probably one of the most important subschemas. This subschema deals with time management and also gross compensation along with rate calculations. It is appropriate at this point to remind you about the integration between the Time Management and Payroll sub-modules. You might be asking yourself: *Is my implementation using time evaluation?* If it does, then time evaluation results (B2 time clusters) are read by this subschema. Alternatively, if your system is not using time evaluation, then infotype **0007** and **0008** will govern the calculations.

This schema handles many important functions such as **ZLIT,** where the time management and payroll processes come together. The schema also has key rules such as **X010** and **X012** for valuation of wage types. In addition, the schema processes tables, as discussed here:

Functions

▶ Function **PARTT** acts if an employee joins in the middle of the month or in situations where the schema has to perform partial-month calculations. When a partial-month calcualtion is performed, a table **PARX** is generated, as listed later in this section.

▶ Function **P2003** processes the substitution infotype. Since infotype **2003** falls under the Time Management module in SAP, it is naturally processed in this time subschema.

▶ Function **P2010** relates to the employee remuneration infotype. Many SAP customers use infotype **2010** either to load time data from external time systems or to manually enter time data in the absence of any time clocking systems. Therefore, if you need to write any rules related to data in infotype **2010**, **UT00** is the subschema to use.

▶ Function **DAYPR** checks the time processing with or without clock times.

▶ Function **ZLIT** brings the hours from time management (either time evaluation or normal working hours) together with the dollar rates from payroll. For example, if an employee needs to get paid overtime by 1.5 times the normal rate, the schema needs to know the number of hours and the employee's hourly rate. The **ZLIT** function brings the two together: hours and rate.

Rules

▶ Rule **X013** performs the valuation. For example, if an employee is salaried, you may need to calculate that employee's derived hourly rate for partial-month calculations. In Chapter3 you saw wage types /001, /002.They are the valuation technical wage types that are generated in this subschema.

▶ Rule **X020** collects the wage types using operation **ADDCU**. See Appendix F for a list and description of this and other operations.

Tables

▶ **PARX**

Is generated if the function **PARTT** finds a partial period processing case during payroll processing. For example, this would be the case if a pay period is from Aug 8 through Aug 22, and an employee joined the company on Aug 14.

▶ **C1**

Is generated when an employee has worked across different cost centers in a single pay period. In a normal scenario, if an employee is salaried and always works in the home cost center, you won't see the impact on this table.

▶ **ZL**

Contains time wage types. Time wage types in this table contain hours, but not amounts. As discussed earlier with the **ZLIT** function, hours from the **ZL** table are used with rates from the **IT** table to arrive at amounts.

▶ **IT (Input Table)**

Once again flows through the schema building additional wage types as the table is passed through more subschema and rules. Therefore, the **IT** table you see in this schema will look different for contents and wage types compared to the earlier schema **UBD0**. As mentioned earlier, function **ZLIT** brings the **ZL** and **IT** tables together.

UMC0: Non-Authorized Check

In payroll processing, you can have two major payroll types: *normal* and *off-cycle*. In Chapter 7, we'll look at the year-end adjustment payrolls using infotype **0221**. This subschema addresses off-cycle payroll processing and therefore, the logic from this subschema will again repeat for normal payroll processing in schema **UDD0**. The functions, rules and tables in this schema are:

Functions

▶ Function **P0221** reads infotype **0221**, which is normally used in year-end adjustments as well as manual checks. For more examples using infotype **0221**, see Chapter 7.

Rules

▶ Rule **UNAM** processes infotype **0221** wage types.

▶ Rules **X023**, **X024**, and **X025** are related to gross calculations. Please note that the respective processing classes 20, 41, and 4 (**P20**, **P41**, and **P04**) for the wage types are used in these rules.

▶ The rules with processing class 66 (**P66**) are related to the wage types that have a goal/deduction scenario. Infotypes **0014** and **0015** carry these wage types as discussed in Chapter 2 and Chapter 3 (related to master data and wage types), respectively. These rules generate the payroll results wage types associated with deduction as well as balance.

▶ Rules **UD11** and **UD21** are related to retroactive calculations. During retroactive calcualtions, the payroll schema needs to keep track of intermediate wage types. These wage types are referred to as *inflow wage types*. In Appendix C you will find wage types **/X02** and **/Z02** at the end of the list of technical wage types.

Tables
▶ **IT (Input Table)**
This table continues to build further with wage types getting updates from the rules in the schema. New wage types are added to **IT** table (e. g., goals and deduction processing). Throughout the schema processing, the **IT** table gets updated with additional wage types as they get processed.

▶ **ARRRS (arrears)**
If the payroll processing does not have enough money in the current pay period, then depending on the configuration of the wage type, it can go into arrears. Which means that in the next pay period, if the payroll has enough money, this deduction is taken out of that payroll. If any of the wage types go into arrears processing, the payroll result tables will have an **ARRRS** table generated in this schema.

▶ **DDNTK (deductions not taken)**
As the name suggests, this table contains the deduction wage types that the payroll could not deduct in the current pay processing. This situation occurs as a result of not having sufficient earnings for an employee. Depending on your configuration, the wage type can be in both the Arrears and Deductions not taken tables.

UTX0: Tax Processing
If you refer back to the payroll concept diagram (see Figure 1.2 in Chapter 1), you might recall that SAP uses the Business Software Inc (BSI) tax factory to calculate taxes for US payroll. Almost everyone is familiar with the defini-

tions of *Gross Payroll* and *Net Payroll*. If you are running the net payroll, then the taxes are calculated within the payroll schema by this subschema. This subschema processes taxes and creates tax wage types by different tax authorities. Chapter 7 discusses tax processing and tax authorities at greater length. As with schemas before, the functions and rules are discussed as follows:

Functions

▸ Function **UPAR1** with parameter **BSI** controls the BSI version. (At the time of this writing, the BSI product is at version 7.0.). BSI tax factory is a third-party product that is integrated with SAP US Payroll and takes care of Federal, State and Local tax calculations. Tax policies, tax rates and any annual changes are handled by BSI. The same way that SAP sends out support packs on regular basis, **BSI** sends **TUBS** (Tax Update Bulletins) to their customers on a regular basis.

▸ Function **USTAX** passes control to **BSI** and brings back the tax wage types from BSI. The tax wage types (**/401**, **/402**, **/403**, etc.) discussed in Chapter 3 are generated in BSI and are sent over to the payroll schema when processing this function.

Rules

▸ Rule **UPTX**. As discussed in Chapter 2, infotypes **0207** and **0208** have multiple tax authorities and levels (Federal, State, and Local). This rule separates the tax amounts for each of the tax authorities. You will learn about rules and review typical changes to rule **UPTX** later in this chapter.

Tables

▸ **IT (Input Table)**

▸ **RT (Results Table)**
The table that is eventually visible in an employee's payroll history; the schema starts building them now.

▸ **TCRT**
Tables for cumulative tax results.

▸ **TAXR**
Tables that contain tax authorities.

▸ **V0**
Are also called *split tables*, as they contain tax authorities.

UAP0: Process Additional Payments/Deductions

As discussed in Chapters 2 and 3, the payroll process will have different deduction and earning types. These earnings and deductions are fed to the payroll process through infotypes in employee data. In Chapter 5, you will learn about the integration between the US Benefits and US Payroll modules. This subschema also has another subschema (**UBE1**) nested within it, which processes the US benefits for health and insurance plans.

Later in this chapter, you will find a section on modifying schemas. There you will see the steps necessary to copy and modify a schema in that section to, for example, modify subschema **UAP0**. The features, rules, and tables in this schema are as follows:

Functions

▶ Functions **P0014** and **P0015** process infotypes **0014** and **0015**. Also note that rules **U011** and **U015** are used in the processing.

▶ Function **P0267** handles off-cycle/bonus payments with rule **U012**.

▶ Function **COPY UBE1** copies subschema **UBE1** for benefits processing. The statements between **BLOCK BEG** and **BLOCK END** correspond to sub-schema **UBE1**.

▶ Functions **P0167** and **P0168** process health plans (infotype **0167**) and insurance plans (infotype **0168**), respectively. Therefore, if you need to drill down and examine the benefits amount or calculations, this is the place to do so.

Rules

▶ Rule **ZRU1** is a custom rule, created for this schema. This rule is examined more in-depth later in the chapter (see Section 4.3) during the discussion on customized rules.

Tables

▶ **IT (Input table)**

▶ **V0**
  Split tables for different benefit plans.

UAL0: Proration and Cumulation

In Chapter 3, you learned about wage type cumulation as well as prorated wage type calculations. This schema processes wage type cumulations as controlled by processing class **20**.

Functions

▸ Function **GEN/8** and Rule **XPPF** are used to generate wage types **/801**, **/802**, respectively. If a wage type needs to be prorated for the pay period (proration is the factoring of a wage type for partial pay period calculations), then this function and rule should be used.

Rules

▸ Rule **XPPF** generates wage types **/801**, and **/802**.

▸ Rule **X023** uses processing class **20** (**P20**) and the wage types in result tables of payroll.

Tables

▸ **IT (Input Tables)**

UDD0: Process Deduction and Benefits

The **UDD0** subschema plays an important role in retroactive accounting. It also handles intermediate wage types during retroactive calculation as the payroll schema runs multiple times, depending on the number of retro periods.

For example, if, during payroll period 17, retroactive accounting demands adjusting period 15, the schema will run for periods 17, 16, and 15. In that situation, subschema **UDD0** handles the intermediate flow of wage types. It has two nested subschemas: **UBE2** for US benefits, and **UDP0** for handling deduction goals and totals. Earlier in subschema **UAP0**, the benefits subschema **UBE1** processed health and insurance deductions; now the subschema **UBE2** processes savings, flexible spending, and miscellaneous benefit plan-related deductions. You will also notice that some logic from schema **UMC0** has repeated again. In case of **UMC0**, the logic was related to non-authorized manual check off-cycle payroll processing and now for **UDD0**, the same logic relates to normal payroll processing. The functions, rules, and tables in this schema are:

Functions

▸ Function **COPY UBE2** processes savings plans and flexible spending accounts in benefits through subschema **UBE2**.

▸ Function **P0170** processes flexible spending account plans.

▸ Function **P0169** processes savings plans (401(k)).

► Function **P0377** processes miscellaneous benefit plan deductions. If you need to know more about this or any of the earlier functions, please use transaction **PE04** to access these functions. The same transaction (**Menu Goto**) also offers you access to documentation for these functions.

► Function **COPY UDP0** manages a subschema to process infotype **0014-** and **0015**-based deductions with goal amounts wage types.

► Function **LIMIT** checks if the amounts in certain wage types exceed a limit. This function works in conjunction with arrears processing to ensure that deductions that went into arrears do not exceed the arrears amounts.

► Function **PRDNT** works with the **DDNTK** table. Just like arrears processing, **DDNTK** processing has a deeper impact in retroactive accounting calcualtions.

Rules

► Rules **UD11** and **UD21** are related to retroactive calculations. During retroactive calculations, the payroll schema needs to keep track of intermediate wage types. These wage types are referred as inflow wage types. In Appendix A3, which lists the technical wage types, you will find wage types **/X02** and **/Z02** at the end of the list; these are the wage types handled by these rules.

► Rules **UD****. Rules using processing class **66** (**P66**) manage goals and deduction wage types. (These rules changed to P50 in newer versions of SAP)

► Rules **X024** and **X025** manage cumulation of wage types using processing class **41** and **04**, respectively.

Tables

► **IT (Input Table)**

► **ARRRS**
(See the discussion for schema **UMC0**.)

► **DDNTK**
(See the discussion for schema **UMC0**.)

UGRN: Garnishments Calculation

Chapter 6 specifically focuses on garnishments, covering this topic in depth. While using the discussion points from that chapter and running your tests in the payroll, this subschema forms an important part of the equation. Various functions and rules related to garnishments are discussed here. Also note that the tables generated in this schema are different than those generated in other schemas, and are naturally oriented to garnishments.

Functions

▶ Function **IF** with the parameter **GREX** checks for active garnishments. Active garnishments will have their status set using infotype **0194**. Garnishments that are inactive and are in released status won't be processed in the schema.

▶ Function **UGARN** performs calculations of garnishments.

Rules

▶ Rule **UGRT** with processing class **59** (**P59**) processes all earnings that have garnishability. This rule is read by function **PRT**. (Just as **PIT** helps rules to read **IT** tables, **PRT** helps rules to read **RT** tables.)

▶ Rule **UGDN** calculates disposable net income, which is discussed in Chapter 6.

Tables

▶ **GRDOC**
Contains garnishment documents.

▶ **GRREC**
Contains the garnishment record.

▶ **GRORD**
Contains the garnishment order.

▶ **IT**
Are generated just like with all other subschemas.

In Chapter 6, we will see the contents of these tables in subschema **UGRN**.

UNA0: Calculate Net Pay

As we get closer to the end of schema **U000**, the net pay is calculated with this schema. If you need to write rules before final result tables are written, this is the subschema to use. You will mostly be concerned with the **IT** and **RT** tables in this subschema, which by now have completed the logic and calculation portions of schema.

Tables

▶ **IT**

▶ **RT**

UNN0: Net Processing Bank Transfer

The payroll processing isn't complete until it processes check payments or bank transfers, as chosen by the employee in infotype **0009**, which is discussed in Chapter 2. Schema **UNN0** uses the infotypes to create bank transfers or check payment tables.

Functions

► Function **P0011** is used if your implementation is using infotype **0011** (external bank transfer).

► Function **P0009** processes infotype **0009**; bank/check data using details such as the bank routing number, account number, and so on.

► Function **P9ZNC** is used by the schema if any of the employees have to receive checks with an amount of zero. It is also recommended that you run the wage type reporter or payroll journals for such cases.

Tables

► **BT (Bank Table)**
Contains information for bank transfer/checks printing

► RT

UEND: Final Processing

Final processing with schema **UEND** serves a single, very important purpose: presenting you with the payroll results table that will be available in the payroll clusters. These tables will be used for all subsequent processing, such as finance posting, accounts payable posting, checks processing, tax processing, and payroll reporting in general (as seen in Figure 1.1). These tables contain an individual employee's payroll results for each pay period. When running the schema using the log option, this is where you will drill down to check the results with the following tables:

Tables

► RT

► **CRT (Cumulative Results Table)**
Contains MTD and YTD (Month to Date and Year to Date) accumulations

Now that you have an overview of subschema functionality, you're ready to learn how to modify schemas using simple examples.

4.3   Why, When, and How to Change the US Schema

By now you have seen many subschemas, and you might feel that they will meet all of your payroll processing needs. If that's the case, you're probably asking: *Why do I need to modify the included schema and subschemas?* To assist with answering this question, Table 4.4 presents some practical US Payroll requirements and solutions.

Your Requirement	Suggested Solution	Impact on Schema Modification
Part of your benefits are out-sourced, and you don't want SAP payroll to calculate those deductions.	Modify subschemas **UBE1** and **UBE2**.	Copy and modify subschemas **UBE1** amd **UBE2**.
You have a customized formula to calculate your union deduction.	Build the formula in a rule.	Copy the appropriate delivered subschema and insert the new rule in it.
You need to generate a wage type for certain groups of employees, using a specific base amount for calculation.	Create a new rule that checks the employee grouping and creates a wage type. This rule needs to be inserted in the appropriate subschema.	Copy the appropriate delivered subschema and insert the new rule in it.
You calculate per-pay-period payroll service costs based on an employee's base salary and post them to a General Ledger (GL) account.	Create a new rule that generates the wage type and is mapped to a particular GL account for posting.	Copy the appropriate delivered subschema and insert the new rule in it.
You have not yet installed BSI, and still want to continue other testing.	Comment out the **USTAX** function in schema **UTX0**.	Copy **UTX0** to **ZTX0** and comment out the line.
You have to post the tax wage types for different tax authorities to different GL accounts.	Modify the **UPTX** rule.	Copy **UTX0** to **ZTX0**, comment out the **UPTX** line, and then insert a new line for the **ZPTX** rule.

Table 4.4 Sample Payroll Requirements that Drive Schema Modifications

These are just a few of the many requirements that can drive rule modifications, and therefore subschemas. Each industry can have their own requirements and can sometimes demand very unique situations that can be handled through custom rules and custom subschemas. Next, you will learn how to modify schemas using the Schema Editor.

4.3.1 Copy and Modify U000 using the Schema Editor

Using a step-by-step approach, we'll use the Schema Editor to copy and modify transaction **PE01**.

1. **Open the Schema Editor and copy schema U000**

   To start working with the schema, first copy the **U000** schema and create your own version named **/Z00**. Using editor transaction **PE01**, create schema **/Z00,** as shown earlier in Figure 4.4. When creating new schemas, it is best to keep the naming convention in mind. Do not use SAP's name space; it is safer to use **Z** or **/ (slash)** as the starting letter.

2. **Modify new copies of schema /Z00 using the editor**

   After you copy and create the **/Z00** schema, the Schema Editor's Change option takes you to the screen shown in Figure 4.5.

Edit Schema: /Z00

Line	Func.	Par1	Par2	Par3	Par4	D	Text
000010						*	My New Schema 12/25/2006
000020	COPY	UIN0					US Payoll:Initialization of payroll
000030	COPY	UODP				*	On-demand regular (no need after 4.5A)
000040	COPY	UBD0					Basic data processing
000050	COPY	UPR0					Read previous result of current period
000060	COPY	XLR0					Import previous payroll results
000070	COPY	UMO0					Determine payroll modifiers
000080	COPY	UT00					Gross compensation and time evaluation
000090	COPY	UREI				*	Travel expense
000100	BLOCK	BEG					Gross cumulation and tax processing
000110	IF		NAMC				if non-authorized manual check (*)
000120	COPY	UMC0					Process Non authorized check (*)
000130	ELSE						else if non authorized manual check (*)
000140	COPY	UAP0				*	Process add. payments and deductions
000150	COPY	ZAP0					Added 12/25/2006
000160	COPY	UAL0					Proration and cumulation gross

Figure 4.5 Modifying the New Schema /Z00

You should follow the same process to copy and modify any subschemas. The following changes were made to schema **/Z00,** as shown in Figure 4.5:

▶ **Line 00010:** Added a comment line at the beginning of the schema.

▶ **Line 00140:** Commented the line for standard schema **UAP0,** which means **UAP0** isn't processed by the **/Z000** main schema. It is a good practice to keep the original line commented rather than deleting it. This eases maintenance and it is also helpful to know what the schema looked like before and after changes were made.

▷ **Line 00150:** A new line is added, containing the copied and modified subschema **ZAP0**. To add a new line in the Schema Editor, place the cursor at a line number and insert the letter *i*. The Schema Editor adds a new blank line at the cursor's position. Similarly, to delete a line, place the cursor at a line number and press the letter *d*.

3. **Drill down to subschema ZAP0 from the main schema /Z00**

Next, place the cursor at line **00150** and double-click to expand the subschema **ZAP0**. Figure 4.6 presents the subschema ZAP0 in an exploded or detailed fashion. Add a new rule called **ZRU1** at line number **000040**. Don't worry about the rules and why **ZRU1** is in the subschema. At this stage, just focus on copying and modifying the US schema to your own version **/Z00**. You will learn the steps to create rules later in the chapter.

Edit Schema: ZAP0

Line	Func.	Par1	Par2	Par3	Par4	D	Text
000010	BLOCK	BEG					Processing further deductions/payments
000020	P0014	U011	GEN	NOAB			Process reoccuring deductions/payments
000030	P0015	U015	GEN	NOAB			Process additional payments
000040	PIT	ZRU1					Rule for My Test
000050	P0057	Z014	GEN	NOAB			Process Membership Fees/Union Dues
000060	P0267	U012	GEN	NOAB			Process one time payments off-cycle
000070	P0165						Process individual limits
000080	COPY	UBE1					Process Benefits (1st time)
000090	BLOCK	END					

Figure 4.6 Explosion of Subschema ZAP0

After you have made changes to any of the subschemas, it is a good idea to generate the main schema. This helps you catch any syntax errors before running the schema through the payroll driver. You will find the Generate button in the Schema Editor screen itself. You are now ready for a trial run of the schema. As discussed at the beginning of this chapter, you will need the US Payroll driver **RPCALCU0** to run the schema.

4.3.2 Running an Error-Free Schema

Using the US Payroll driver **RPCALCU0**, now run schema **/Z00**. Make sure to turn the log button *ON* for testing and, as shown in Figure 4.7, an error will be visible. Note that we're testing the schema with just one employee. Of course, you would normally schedule a **RPCALCU0** batch run for all employees. If your schema encounters a run-time error, the error will be clearly visible on your SAP screen in red, as shown in Figure 4.7. You will need to analyze and fix the error and then run the driver again. In this example, there seems to be an error with wage type **0750** with an operation in the rule. Take note of the error message (**Termination in operation ERROR**) that identifies the error. This also means that you need to focus on checking the specific rule where the termination has occurred for wage type **0750**.

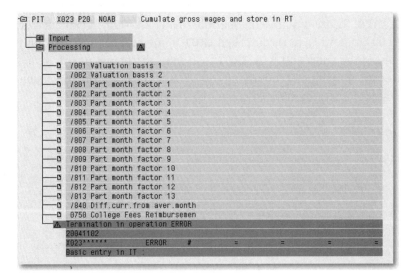

Figure 4.7 Error While Running the Schema

If the schema ran without errors, you will also see statistics at the end, listing the number of employees included in the run, as shown in Figure 4.8.

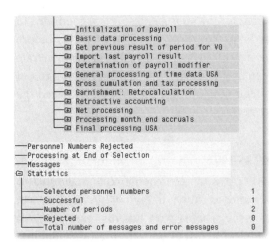

Figure 4.8 An Error-Free Schema Run

The next obvious question is: *What are the typical conditions that will cause the schema to error out?* Table 4.5 presents a sample list of errors and possible resolutions, but this is by no means a complete list as every situation can have different error types.

Error Category	Example of Error Condition	Resolution
Employee master data	Missing employee master data infotypes.	If any of the mandatory infotypes, such as infotype 0008, 0207, or 0009 are missing, the schema will error out.
Rules and operations	You might have added a new custom rule to the schema that has operation errors.	Rules normally will have errors related to wage types and/or operations.
Wage type	Missing specifications of wage type processing class in a rule.	Many rules use processing class specification values for wage types as decision criteria. If the wage type has a missing value for a particular specification, the schema will error out.
Employee master data	Infotype **0003** has improper dates.	The employee's master data dates and payroll run dates do not match.
Garnishment data	Missing master data for garnishment.	Garnishment infotype **0195** master data can cause errors in the payroll schema.
Rules and operations	In the rules editor, you need to follow a certain indentation convention for operations, which you will learn more about in the next section when writing rules. If the operation in a rule is coded at the wrong place, then the schema will have an error.	The operation does not give an error, because it doesn't perform the desired tasks specified by the rule.

Table 4.5 Sample Error Conditions During a Schema Run

After all errors are cleared and you have performed an error-free run of the schema (shown in Figure 4.8), you're ready to drill down into the schema (explode the schema). The drill down has a simple structure, and although it looks intimidating at first, it is not difficult to work with. Before we start the drill down of the schema, Table 4.6 lists the different possible tables you will see during and after the payroll processing. Only tables relevant to the discussion are listed.

> **Note**
>
> If you require additional information, or an expanded list, you should visit SAP's standard documentation (*http://help.sap.com*) for a discussion on all available tables. You will find this documentation under generic (not country-specific) payroll components (PY-XX-BS).

Table	Decription of Table	Used during processing	Available after processing
IT	Input Table. Used during processing and passes data to the RT tables. Your rules will typically write wage types to these tables.	✓	
RT	Results Table. Final table where payroll results are stored.		✓
CRT	Cumulative Results Table. Contains Month-to-Date (MTD) and Year-to-Date (YTD) details.		✓
ARRRS	Contains the deductions that are carried over to the next payroll period. See UMC0: Non-Authorized Check, in Section 4.2.3, for additional information.		✓
DDNTK	Contains the deductions not take during the current pay period. See UMC0: Non-Authorized Check, in Section 4.2.3, for additional information.		✓
ACCR	Month-end accrual tables, discussed further in Chapter 8.		✓
WPBP	The Work Place/Basic Pay (WPBP) table is created due to changes to infotypes **0001**, **0027**, **0007**, and **0008**. See UBD0: Basic Data Processing, in Section 4.2.3, for additional information.		✓

Table 4.6 Payroll Tables

Now let's follow the drill-down steps to check the table contents as well as the processing of the schema.

1. **Drill down into the schema and get to the exact subschema or rule location**
   Figure 4.9 presents the schema at function **P0014** and rule **UW14**. Explode the schema in the same way you would click and open folders in Microsoft Windows Explorer.

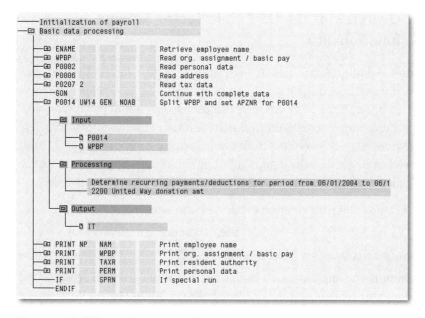

```
──────Initialization of payroll
──⊟ Basic data processing

    ──⊞ ENAME                    Retrieve employee name
    ──⊞ WPBP                     Read org. assignment / basic pay
    ──⊞ P0002                    Read personal data
    ──⊞ P0006                    Read address
    ──⊞ P0207 2                  Read tax data
    ───GON                       Continue with complete data
    ──⊞ P0014 UW14 GEN  NOAB     Split WPBP and set APZNR for P0014

        ──⊟ Input

            ──◻ P0014
            ──◻ WPBP

        ──⊟ Processing

            ──────Determine recurring payments/deductions for period from 06/01/2004 to 06/1
                  2200 United Way donation amt

        ──⊟ Output

            ──◻ IT

    ──⊞ PRINT NP    NAM          Print employee name
    ──⊞ PRINT       WPBP         Print org. assignment / basic pay
    ──⊞ PRINT       TAXR         Print resident authority
    ──⊞ PRINT       PERM         Print personal data
    ──IF            SPRN         If special run
    ──────ENDIF
```

Figure 4.9 Drill Down Schema and Rule

2. **Click on Input, Output, or Processing for the rule**
   You can click on any of the tables visible under Output. In many rules and functions, you will see the IT tables, but as we have seen in subschemas before, you can also check other tables such as **WPBP**, **RT**, **ARRRS**, etc.

3. **Getting into the speciality functions, such as USTAX processing**
   Aside from normal rules and standard functions, it also helps to drill down into special areas such as tax processing. If you drill down at the **USTAX** function in the tax processing subschema (as shown in Figure 4.10), you will be able to see detailed tax calculations by each tax authority that is processed. Figure 4.10 shows the Federal tax authority-related calculations within the USTAX function. The figures are for reference only.

Tax result for payment type Regular payment					
Regular income taxes					
Tax authority FED Federal					
Tax Category	Tax.inc	Tax-free	Inc.Declare	Tax.earning	Tax
03 Employee Social Security Tax (REG)	2628.34	0.00	2628.34	2628.34	162.96
04 Employer Social Security Tax (REG)	2628.34	0.00	2628.34	2628.34	162.96
05 Employee Medicare Tax (REG)	2628.34	0.00	2628.34	2628.34	38.11
06 Employer Medicare Tax (REG)	2628.34	0.00	2628.34	2628.34	38.11
10 Employer Unemployment Tax (REG)	2628.34	0.00	2628.34	0.00	0.00

Figure 4.10 Drill Down to the USTAX Function

4.4 Overview of the US Public Sector Schema functionality

Since the US Public Sector has its own unique requirements, SAP has provided additional functionality through a US Public Sector schema, titled as **USPS** (US Public Sector). The schema, and its associated functionality, is visible when you implement **IS-PS** (Industry Solution-Public Sector). This section provides a quick overview of the functionality of this schema. It is not our intention to get into the details about public sector requirements. Public sector-related information is available from multiple resources, including:

▶ SAP's standard documentation (*http://help.sap.com*)

▶ The IRS web site for non-resident alien taxation (*http://www.irs.gov*)

▶ Savings bonds (*http://www.treasurydirect.gov*)

▶ In addition, the implementations that use **IS-PS** will give you access to the Public Sector schema and the documentation associated with it.

4.4.1 NRA: Non-Resident Alien Processing

An *alien* is a person who is not a citizen or national of the United States. A *non-resident alien* (NRA) is someone who is allowed temporary entry in the country for a specific purpose, and for a limited amount of time. The IRS has published specific instructions for NRAs. The purpose of this discussion is not to tell you about various forms and instructions regarding NRA processing; instead, the section will highlight SAP's overall functionality for this topic.

Employee master data for NRA

▶ Infotype **0094**: Work permit and residence status that needs to be maintained in the employee record.

▶ Infotype **0048**: Visa status that needs to be maintained in the employee record.

▶ Infotype **0556**: Tax treaty infotype that maintains the treaty groups based on the NRA's home country.

▶ Infotype **0235**: Other taxes infotype. Can maintain exemptions by the type of taxes based on eligibility and visa status.

Payroll

▶ Subschemas **UPNR** and **UPPT** are provided by SAP.

▶ A statutory reporting **1042S** needs to be peformed using Tax Reporter.

▶ Wage types in wage type group **1042** which allow for payroll processing of scholarships, etc.

4.4.2 Savings Bonds Processing

Savings bond deductions and purchases are an important US Public Sector topic. Savings bond deductions are carried out as per the employee's choice. Typically, the payroll system sends the details via an interface to the US Treasury for savings bond purchases, which are then mailed directly to the employee. Once again, it starts with the employee master data and ends with interfaces from the payroll system. The savings bond life cycle steps are listed here:

Employee master data for savings bonds as per the following infotypes:

▶ Infotype **0103**: Bond purchase amount and deduction amount details.

▶ Infotype **0104**: Bond denomination and name details.

Payroll schema for processing savings bond deductions:

▶ In the US Public Sector schema, after benefits subschema **UBE2**, you will find a statement which uses function call **P0103** to process savings bond deductions.

▶ When an employee decides to leave an organization, you can have a situation where there is a remaining balance. For example, if an employee has choosen to buy a $100 savings bond with a per-pay-period deduction of $25. After accumulating $50 over the course of two pay periods, the employee decides to leave the company. As a result, the payroll process needs to refund the $50 to the employee. As you delimit the savings bond infotype **0103**, the refund process kicks in and a refund wage type gets created in payroll. This wage type will have no tax impact because the employee had already paid tax on this amount before it was taken out as a post-tax deduction.

4.4.3 Public Sector Savings Plans: 403(B), 457(B)

The public and education sectors have different retirement plans than the normal 401(k) plans. These plans are referred by the related tax bills. They are processed in a similar way to 401(k) plans through benefits infotype **0169**. The schema can process them as any other savings plan. You need to write custom rules in schemas to handle the investments and accumulation of wage types associated with 403(b) and 457(b) plans.

4.4.4 Employer Benefits and Tax Allocation Rules

A subschema **QPCD** (with rules **QP10**, **QP12**, **QP14**, **QP16**, **QP18**, and **QP20**) is provided by SAP to handle the employer (ER) benefits and tax distributions.

4.5 Writing Rules in US Payroll

In Figure 4.1, you saw that rules are related through functions in the schema, and they use operations to execute the logic. Rules provide tremendous flexibility to SAP payroll configurators for managing business requirements. In fact, rules make it very easy to fulfill payroll requirements, which typically depend on industry-specific issues or union agreements. Rules (also referred to as *Personnel Calculation Rule*, or PCR) are defined by SAP as a *"Statement for the execution of defined tasks in time management and payroll."*

While the discussion here is limited to payroll rules, the philosophy is applicable to both time management and payroll rules. Rules manipulate wage types using operations. Appendix F lists many useful operations for rules. Although we will be learning about many operations in the examples in this section, it is not possible to cover all of the operations delivered by SAP. Use the examples in Appendix F and practice writing rules using other operations.

As you read the examples in this section, you will notice that rules are purely based on logic and arithmetic. Once you have figured these two out, you will be able to code error-free rules. Figure 4.11 presents the simple concept around processing the rules, which has input, processing, and output. The three basic elements of wage types seen earlier in Chapter 3 (**RTE** (rate), **NUM** (number), and **AMT** (amount)) are used heavily in many rules. Table **T511K** in Figure 4.11 maintains various constants, and you can also create your own constants in this table and use them in rules.

Let's now move on to rules editing, where you'll learn how to create and maintain rules.

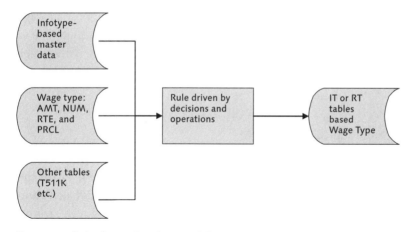

Figure 4.11 Rules Processing, Input and Output

4.5.1 The Rules Editor

Transaction **PE02** allows you to access the Rules Editor. When you start this transaction, you will notice that each rule has three important dimensions:

▶ Attributes: Name and creation date for the rule.

▶ Source Text: Actual logic, with operations.

▶ Documentation: Documents the functionality.

These three dimensions contain all of the information about a particular rule. As mentioned earlier, do not modify SAP-delivered rules and always follow the *copy and modify* approach. You can also access rules from the Schema Editor, **PE01**. For example, explode the subschema and double-click on the rule to open **PE02**, the rule editor. The rule source text is always valid for a combination of wage types and employee subgroup groupings. Before proceeding to create a rule, it's important to understand the combination of employee subgroup and wage types.

> **Note**
>
> You can use the rules editor with one of two display options—table display or structure graphics display. The examples that follow use the table display option.

Wage Types

You are already familiar with wage types from discussions in Chapter 3. You can code rules for any valid wage type (i. e., the logic in the rule will only work when payroll processing finds that wage type). You can use the wildcard characters ******** in this field to specify that the rule will work for all wage types. For example, if you insert a rule into the schema and the input table to the rule reads the wage type, then the rule logic checks to see if the wage type is valid for processing. If you have used ********, then all wage types are processed.

Employee Subgroup Grouping (ESG)

Let's detour in the IMG menu to **Personnel Management • Personnel Administration • Basic Pay • ESG** for the PCR node and refer to Figure 4.12 for the employee subgroup grouping for PCR. PCR refers to Payroll Calculation Rules. You will notice that the HR enterprise structures (employee groups, employee subgroups) have an impact on the grouping. For example, hourly employees have a different grouping compared to salaried employees. Therefore, if you need to write certain rules in payroll and differentiate between certain employee types, you can either do it through these groupings or you need to have separate wage types. Another example might be where drivers receive a special allowance and the calculation of this allowance depends on the group of employees called Drivers. In this case, if you want the rule to apply to all types of employees, then you can use the wildcard ***** in the ESG field in rules editor.

Change View "EE Subgroup Grouping for PCR/CollAgmtProv.": Overview

EE group	Name of employee ...	Emp...	Name of EE subgro...	ESG for PCR	ESG for CAP
1	Active	U1	Hourly rate/labor	1	1
1	Active	U2	Hourly rate/staff	1	1
1	Active	U3	Pay scale salary	2	2
1	Active	U4	Salaried staff	3	3
1	Active	U5	Senior staff	3	4
1	Active	U6	Hourly rate/trainee	1	1
1	Active	U7	Non-payscale staff	2	4
2	Salaried	06	Hourly		
2	Salaried	A4			
2	Salaried	U8	Retirees	3	3
4	Contractors/3rd prty	U9	Contractor Pay	1	1
5	Terminated	U4	Salaried staff	1	1

Figure 4.12 Configuration for Employee Subgroup Grouping

In US Payroll, you will find many situations dealing with unions and different employee groupings that require using this field. As such, it is a good idea to check the payroll processing requirements while finalizing your enterprise structures. The best way to learn about rules is to create one, as discussed in the next section.

4.5.2   Creating a Simple Rule

This section follows a step-by-step approach to creating a simple rule with basic operations:

1. **Use transaction PE02 to access the rules editor, as shown in Figure 4.13**
   Enter the name of the rule and click the Create icon; the editor takes you to the Attributes screen.

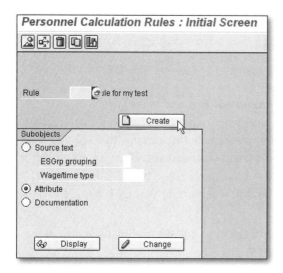

Figure 4.13 The Rules Editor

2. **Create the rule's attributes as shown in Figure 4.14, using the following steps:**
   Create the attribute fields listed here:

   ▷ **Program class** = C, for payroll rules

   ▷ **Country grouping** = 10, because we are working with US Payroll

   ▷ **Text:** Provide a useful description for the rule. Sometimes, four-character naming is not enough because most of the common rules start with Z and so you are left with three characters to use for the name.

   ▷ **Flag:** Changes only by person responsible. If possible, do not check this so other configurators are able to modify your rule, if required. In this example, we are creating a rule called **ZRU1**, which is used in this payroll run. The name **ZRU1** has no significance. You can use your own innovative naming scheme so the four-character name meets your needs.

Edit Rule: Attributes

📄 Documentation

Rule   ZRU1 Rule for my test

Attributes
Program class   C   Payroll
Country grouping   10 USA

Person responsible   🔾
☐ Changes only by person responsible

Figure 4.14 Rule Attributes

3. **Access the editor for a combination of ESG and wage type**

Section 4.5.1 discussed ESG and wage types, the two key fields used to write your source code for the rule. Create this rule for **ESG = 3** and **wage type = 0750**. This means that the rule only works when an employee in payroll processing falls in **ESG = 3** and has a wage type **0750** coming in for processing. Later in the chapter you will learn how wage types are read by the rule for input processing.

When you enter ESG (**3**) and wage type (**0750**), the blank editor screen appears as shown in Figure 4.15.

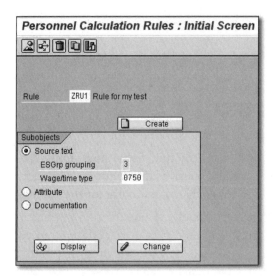

Figure 4.15 Creating a Rule for ESG-Wage Type Combination

4. **Create source code statements in the rule**

   Figure 4.16 shows the blank editor screen in which you create the statements. Note the heading for the rule editor at this stage; it shows that you are writing code for a particular combination of ESG and Wage Types.

   Next, start coding the lines in the editor screen. Remember, the only way to learn different styles and logics of the payroll rules is to try different examples. You might feel somewhat lost at the beginning, but don't worry too much. When you complete the coding and run the rule, you will get a feel for the process. Before you start coding (as you already know from the discussion of fields in the Schema Editor), you need to become familiar with the rules editor fields as explained here:

   ▸ **VARKEY** (Variable Key): This field is used to send the logic of the rule to different routes based on the decisions you make in the rule.

   ▸ **NL** (Next Line): In case your logic exceeds one line, you can go to the next line. (There will be more examples of this later in the chapter.)

   ▸ **T**: Type of rule.

   ▸ **D**: Decision on the variable key.

   ▸ **P**: Rule for which processing continues to the next operation on the line.

   ▸ **Z**: Rule for which processing does not continue to the next operation and logic jumps. Later, you will see an example to clarify the type **P** and **Z**.

   ▸ *****: Comment line.

   ▸ **OPERATION**: Each operation has to start at the correct indentation, where you see a plus (+) sign on the top line.

   ▸ **Line numbers**: As was the case with the Schema Editor, rules also have line sequencing for the code.

5. **Source Code of the Rule**

   Figure 4.17 shows that a few lines have been added to the source code. In the first line, a decision is made on the field **NUM** to check if the number is non-zero. In subsequent lines, depending on the value of **NUM**, certain operations will be performed. If the number is greater than zero, then line **000030** logic will work; if the number is less than zero, then rule line **000020** will work. Please refer to Appendix F for a list and description of various operations you can use in rules. Operation **MULTI** is used to multiply **NUM (N)** with **AMT (A)**, which moves the result into field **AMT (A)**.

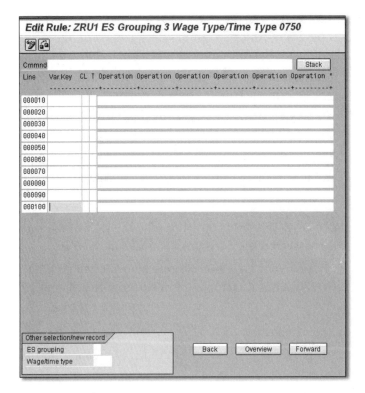

Figure 4.16 Editor Screen for ESG=3, Wage Type=0750

At the end of the code, click on the balancing icon to see if there are any syntax errors; if not, save the rule. Please note the *Rule OK* message on the last line. The message shows that there are no syntax errors and the rule can be used in the schema.

Line	Var.Key	CL	T	Operation	Operation	Operation	Operation	Operation	Operation	*
000010			D	NUM?0						
000020	<			NUM=0	MULTI NAA ADDWT *					
000030	>			AMT=10	MULTI NAA ADDWT *					

Figure 4.17 Adding Source Code Lines to the Rule

> **Note**
>
> Always use ADDWT * logic in the rules, otherwise, you will run a risk of loosing wage types during the rule processing. Wage types which are not explicitly referred by the rule, are not written to **IT** table, if you do not have the ADDWT * logic.

4.5.3 Creating Complex Rules

It's now time to move on to coding more complex rules. In the interest of time, let's keep the source code and logic part unchanged, to avoid having to explain the routine elements of rules we have already worked with. Instead, we will discuss different scenarios with rules. By no means is this a complete list, but it will definitely help you build confidence as you create new rules of your own. For a list of additional operations available to you, see Appendix F.

The payroll rules and some of the complex operations contained in them are required in many day-to-day situations. These situations broadly fall into the following categories:

▶ Calendar-based manipulations in payroll. For example, with certain payroll periods during the year.

▶ Employee type-based manipulations. For example, with certain employees having special calculations.

▶ Creating new wage types in payroll based on calculations. For example, take 10 % of gross earnings and create a wage type as the base for other subsequent calculations.

Example 1: Enterprise Structure Driven Requirement

The enterprise structure driven requirements are typically based on location, employee groupings, or union differentiators (if unions are separated in enterprise structures). Here are some examples that drive these rules:

▶ Salaried and hourly employee separation for calculations.

▶ Different unions have different rates for calculations.

▶ Different locations are treated differently.

▶ Different types of employees (executives vs non-executives) are treated separately.

Figure 4.18 presents one such example, using the operation **OUTWPPERSG**, which reads the employee group and separates the logic for calculation. The operation **OUTWP** has around 30 different variations to read different elements of enterprise structure, payroll structures, and organization structures to make the decisions in the rule.

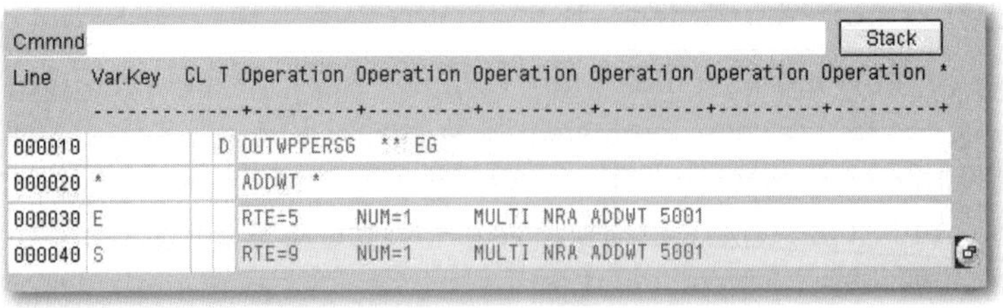

```
Cmmnd                                                              [ Stack ]
Line    Var.Key   CL T Operation Operation Operation Operation Operation Operation *
        --------------+---------+---------+---------+---------+---------+---------+
000010            D OUTWPPERSG  ** EG
000020  *           ADDWT *
000030  E           RTE=5     NUM=1     MULTI NRA ADDWT 5001
000040  S           RTE=9     NUM=1     MULTI NRA ADDWT 5001
```

Figure 4.18 Enterprise Structure Decision

Table 4.7 presents a line-by-line analysis for the rule shown in Figure 4.17. Employee groups E and S are used only as examples and could have any meaning from project to project.

Line Sequence Number	Operation/Logic Explanation
000010	Decision on employee group. Note that you can write a comment if you skip the operation indentation, as shown by the "** **EG**" comment in this line.
000020	If employee group = "*", which means any value, do not do anything. Operation **ADDWT *** writes back the wage type.
000030	If employee group = "E", then set Rate = 5, Number = 1. Multiply Number with Rate and move the result to the Amount field. Specify wage type 5001, which means wage type 5001 will have RTE = 5, NUM = 1, and AMT = 5.
000040	Same as above, except that when employee group = "S", RTE = 9.

Table 4.7 Rule Logic Using the OUTWP Operation

Example 2: Wage Type Driven Requirement

Many requirements are driven by a certain wage type and its processing classes. As discussed earlier in the chapter, processing classes can be used to determine many different dimensions of a wage type. As such, SAP-delivered rules, customized rules, and processing classes form popular decision making criteria. Figure 4.19 shows a decision based on processing class 90. The operation **VWTCL** reads the processing class of any wage type that may be getting processed in this rule. Similarly, you can write a rule to make a decision on other processing classes using the operation **VWTCL**. It is also possible to create new specifications for any processing class and then use that value in a rule.

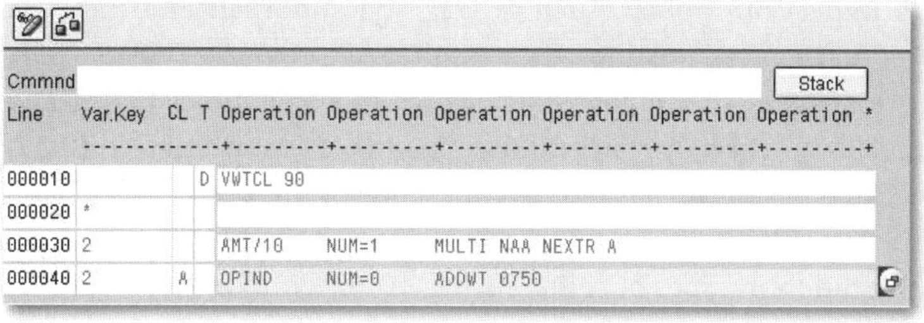

Figure 4.19 Processing Class Decision

Table 4.8 presents the line-by-line analysis for the rule shown in Figure 4.18. Depending on the specification value of a processing class, the rule logic routes to different lines. Please remember that an asterisk (*) is used as a wildcard character in all areas of rule writing.

Line Sequence Number	Operation/Logic Explanation
000010	Decision based on processing class 90. Note that the rule only works for wage type = 0750 and employee sub group grouping = 3 (which is typically reserved for salaried employees).
000020	If employee group = "*" (meaning "any value"), don't do anything. This should have been **ADDWT *** operation. If you leave this value blank, you will discover that the wage type gets "dropped" when the rule is processed; if the condition is met, the wage types need to be written back into the table.
000030	If the specification for processing class 90 = 2, divide the **AMT** field by 10 and multiply **NUM** with **AMT** and move the result into **AMT**.
000040	Because of the **NEXTR** operation from an earlier line, the logic continues in this line. The **OPIND** operation changes the sign for the amount. NUM = 0 sets zero in the Number field and writes wage type **0750** with the **ADDWT** operation. As such, wage type **0750** will have NUM = 0, and **AMT** will be divided by a factor of 10 from the original amount in wage type 0750.

Table 4.8 Rule Logic Using the VWTCL Operation

Example 3: Adjusting Splits of Wage Types

As shown earlier in function **WPBP**, there could be splits to the wage types if there are changes to infotypes **0001**, **0027**, **0007**, and **0008** in the middle of a pay period. When the wage type has split, you will see two, three, or as many occurrences as the number of splits for the wage types. Wage type splits have an impact on reports, such as wage type journals and they can have an impact on financial postings. As a result, SAP provides some popular operations to manage splits. Figure 4.20 shows the operations **ELIMI** and **SETIN**; together they will help you eliminate and reset appropriate splits. A discussion on the types of splits is beyond the scope of this book. If you need to learn more about them, see the documentation for the **ELIMI** operation. There are many different types of splits, such as A for work center, K for cost center, and so on. You should use transaction **PE04** and access the documentation for operation **ELIMI** to read more about splits.

```
Cmmnd                                                    [ Stack ]
Line   Var.Key  CL T Operation Operation Operation Operation Operation Operation *
       ----------+---------+---------+---------+---------+---------+---------+
000010              ELIMI *    SETIN 1=01ADDWT *                              ⏎
```

Figure 4.20 Eliminating Wage Type Splits

Example 4: Checking if Payroll Run has Retro

Retroactive accounting during payroll processing is a very common phenomenon. Figure 4.21 presents an example to see whether retroactive accounting is taking place in the payroll process, and then drives the logic based on the result. Operation **RETRO** uses *YES* or *NO* decisions to drive the logic, as shown in Figure 4.21.

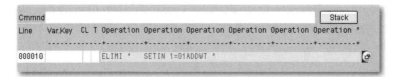

```
Cmmnd                                                    [ Stack ]
Line   Var.Key  CL T Operation Operation Operation Operation Operation Operation *
       ----------+---------+---------+---------+---------+---------+---------+
000010            D RETRO
000020 N            ADDWT *
000030 Y            XMES RETRO                                                ⏎
```

Figure 4.21 Checking a Retro Run

Example 5: Managing Rounding of Values

In payroll, you will most likely run into situations where you need to round items, such as salary amounts, hours, or other numbers associated with wage types. There is a very simple operation, **ROUND**, that handles rounding. Figure 4.22 uses the **ROUND** operation to round off the numbers and then writes the wage type after the calculation. You can read more about the **ROUND** operation using transaction **PE04**.

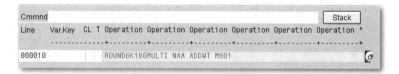

```
Cmmnd                                                            Stack
Line     Var.Key  CL  T Operation Operation Operation Operation Operation Operation *
         --------------+---------+---------+---------+---------+---------+---------+
000010                   ROUNDGK100MULTI NAA ADDWT M001
```

Figure 4.22 Rounding Wage Types

Example 6: Using Payroll Periods

Some industries have unique requirements that, in a particular pay period, are used to manage certain earnings or deductions. As far as deductions are concerned, you have learned about payment models in Chapter 3. Payment models manage the deductions by a pre-defined pay period-based calendar. However, payment models also have their own maintenance based on calendar years. There is a lesser-known operation, **CMPER**, which you can use to check payroll periods. Figure 4.23 presents the rule that checks for payroll period 13. If the current period is 13, the rule gives $50 through wage type **7001** to all employees. Table 4.9 lists the line-by-line analysis of this rule.

```
Cmmnd                                                            Stack
Line     Var.Key  CL  T Operation Operation Operation Operation Operation Operation *
         --------------+---------+---------+---------+---------+---------+---------+
000010               D  CMPER MM13
000020   <              ADDWT *
000030   =              AMT=50     NUM=1      MULTI NAA ADDWT 7001
000040   >              ADDWT *
000050
```

Figure 4.23 Using the Payroll Period for a Decision

Line Sequence Number	Operation/Logic Explanation
000010	Decision on payroll period value. The operation **CMPER** can be used in more than one way to read the current period or a retro period. This line is reading current period.
000020	If the value of the payroll period is less than 13 (i.e., if payroll is running for period 11), then the rule won't do anything and will just write back the wage types by using the **ADDWT** operation.
000030	If the period = 13, then the rule is creating a wage type 7001 with the amount = $50, which is created with the **MULTI** operation.
000040	If the period is greater than 13, then just like line 20, the rule won't do anything.

Table 4.9 Rule Logic to Compare the Payroll Period

Example 7: Using Rules to Identify Wage Types or Occurrences of Conditions

The **XMES** operation helps you print small messages in the payroll log, depending on the decision the rule makes. You can use this operation in many different situations, such as:

▶ You want to find out if an employee is processed with a certain local tax authority, which is normally not a routine in master data.

▶ You would like to know when a certain wage type has a negative value, and it may be almost impossible to identify this situation in a large employee population.

In Figure 4.24, if the rule finds wage type **0100** in payroll processing, the payroll log prints a message *WT100* in the log.

Cmmnd									Stack
Line	Var.Key	CL	T	Operation	Operation	Operation	Operation	Operation	Operation *
000010			D	WGTYP?					
000020	0100			XMES WT100					
000030									

Figure 4.24 Message in Payroll Log When Wage Type is Found

Example 8: Calling One Rule from Another

You can also send the logic from one rule to another. You can either send the logic so that the control is passed to the other rule or you can bring the control back to the same rule after executing the second rule. In the decision logic, if you use rule type **P**, then the processing logic will come back to the next line in the rule. If you use rule type **Z**, then the processing will jump to the other rule.

Now that you have seen a few examples about rule writing, we'll show you how to run them in a schema and perform a drill down to check results. The process is the same as shown earlier with schema runs.

4.5.4 Running Error-Free Rules

After coding the rules you want to use, you need to add them to the correct subschema and test the schema for the desired effect. The obvious question is: *How do I decide where to add the rule in schema?* The answer is straightforward, and depends on the answers to the following questions:

▶ What is the wage type I am processing in this rule?

▶ Has the wage type entered through an employee infotype? If yes, have we processed the infotype yet?

▶ Does this have an impact on taxation? If that is the case, do I need to process it before tax processing?

▶ Does this have an impact on retroactive accounting? If so, how do I position it?

▶ Is this related to an earning, deduction, or tax wage type?

For you to get a better understanding of how to run the rules, let's walk through the process step-by-step:

1. **Add rules to the subschema**

   Add the *PIT* function to the schema's rule. Figure 4.25 shows how the *PIT* function is used to add the rule *ZRU1* to the schema.

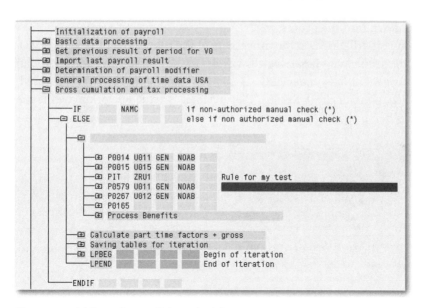

Figure 4.25 Adding a Custom Rule to the Schema

2. **Check if the input IT table is sending the correct wage type to the rule**

   The drill down when the schema is run is shown in Figure 4.26. As seen earlier in the discussion about writing rules, input, processing, and output are the three elements on which you need to focus.

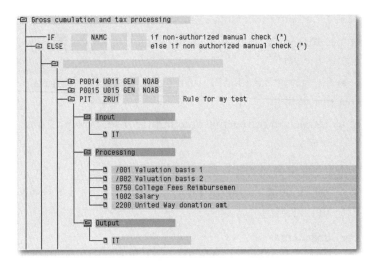

```
-⊟ Gross cumulation and tax processing
    ┌──IF        NAMC           if non-authorized manual check (*)
    ├─⊟ ELSE                    else if non authorized manual check (*)
               └─⊟
                  ┌─⊞ P0014 U011 GEN  NOAB
                  ├─⊞ P0015 U015 GEN  NOAB
                  ├─⊟ PIT   ZRU1           Rule for my test
                     ┌─⊟ Input
                        └─□ IT
                     ├─⊟ Processing
                        ┌─□ /001 Valuation basis 1
                        ├─□ /002 Valuation basis 2
                        ├─□ 0750 College Fees Reimbursemen
                        ├─□ 1002 Salary
                        └─□ 2200 United Way donation amt
                     └─⊟ Output
                        └─□ IT
```

Figure 4.26 Drill Down Custom Rule in Run-Time

3. **Drill down into the processing**

When you drill down at the processing of the rule (shown in Figure 4.27), the line sequencing-based logic is visible. In the example in Figure 4.27, an employee that falls under **ESG = 3** and has wage type = **0750** is processed. As such, you can check to see if the rule logic is actually working while the rule is being executed in the schema.

```
⊞ Processing

⊞ /001 Valuation basis 1
   Rule   ESGPCR VaKey    Operation

   Calculation rule not processed for wage type

⊞ /002 Valuation basis 2
   Rule   ESGPCR VaKey    Operation

   Calculation rule not processed for wage type

⊞ 0750 College Fees Reimbursemen
   Rule   ESGPCR VaKey    Operation

   ZRU1   3               AMT=100
   ZRU1   3               NUM=2
   ZRU1   3               MULTI NAA
   ZRU1   3               ADDWT 0750

⊞ 1002 Salary
   Rule   ESGPCR VaKey    Operation

   Calculation rule not processed for wage type

⊞ 2200 United Way donation amt
   Rule   ESGPCR VaKey    Operation

   Calculation rule not processed for wage type
```

Figure 4.27 Inside the Rule during Run-Time

4. Verify whether the ouput IT table has the correct values

This step shows you the wage types with rates, number, and amount as processed by the rule. Figure 4.28 shows the IT table from a rule. IT tables have wage types with **RTE**, **NUM**, and **AMT** values.

```
Table IT

A Wage type        APC1C2C3ABKoReBTAwvTvn One amount/one number    Amount
3 /001 Valuation b01                       38.46
3 /002 Valuation b01                       38.46
3 0750 College Fee                                  2.00           200.00
3 1002 Salary     01                                             3,333.33
3 2200 United Way 01                                                10.00-
```

Figure 4.28 Input Table (IT)

This concludes the chapter on schemas and rules.

4.6 Summary

You have learned a lot about schemas, subschemas, rules, and operations in this chapter. You can now try to build your own rules as you further explore this topic. The sections on the runtime environment will help you debug your rules and make changes to schemas.

In this chapter, we talked about benefits processing in schemas. In the next chapter, you will learn more about how to integrate benefits with your payroll. The earlier discussion on wage types, along with the current discussion on schemas, and the following discussion on benefits will make the discussion on benefits processing almost complete. Subsequent chapters related to garnishments (Chapter 6) and tax processing (Chapter 7) will continue to reference schemas and discuss rules.

US Benefits and US Payroll are almost inseparable from each other. Benefits deductions are processed in Payroll before being sent to Benefit Providers for data transfer and remittance of money. This Chapter discusses the three angles to Benefit-Payroll integration: Employee, Employer, and the Benefit Provider. The Chapter covers key issues around each type of Benefit Plans, including health, life, savings, and Flexible Spending Accounts.

5 Benefits Integration

Any US Payroll discussion would not be complete without talking about US Benefits. Due to the nature of different types of benefits in the US, benefits bring a unique perspective to payroll deductions. US employees are always equally as concerned about the benefits component their employer offers as they are about the base salary or cash components. There are many different benefit plans: health insurance, savings, flexible spending, and even stock investments. This chapter focuses on the integration aspect between benefits and payroll and touches on the appropriate US benefits functionality as needed.

5.1 Integration of US Benefits with US Payroll

Let's start with Figure 5.1, which shows the overall benefits-payroll integration. An employee will have benefits enrollment details (in the form of infotypes) in his/her master record, while the benefits module provides data on the benefits plans, cost, and coverage details (which ultimately have an impact on costs). In addition, the third-party processing module in US Payroll maintains the benefit provider linkage to all vendors.

> **Note**
>
> In the interest of focusing on the topic of integration, please refer to SAP's standard documentation on the benefits module wherever applicable.

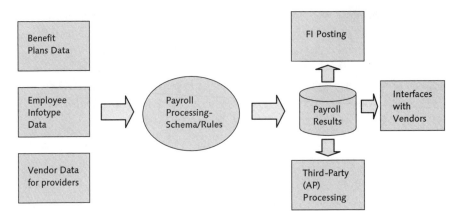

Figure 5.1 Benefits-Payroll-Finance Integration Process

Figure 5.1 shows you that integration starts before payroll, in the employee master data (as seen in Chapter 2), and continues through payroll to post-processing for finance and accounts payable posting. Those of you who may have worked in benefits departments will also know that there are many interfaces sent from a payroll system to the benefit providers. In addition to getting the money, the benefit provider/insurance company needs to know the enrollment date and any life event changes of an employee so the appropriate coverage adjustments can be made. This data is sent to the benefit provider using these interfaces.

Using the *Input-Processing-Output* approach we followed in earlier chapters, the following list will help you better understand Figure 5.1. Inputs to the payroll-benefits integration are from multiple sources, as listed here:

▸ Employee data using infotypes:

- ▹ Infotype **0167** (health plans)
- ▹ Infotype **0168** (insurance plans)
- ▹ Infotype **0169** (savings plans)
- ▹ Infotype **0170** (flexible spending account plans)

▸ Benefits plan configuration details (from the Benefits module):

- ▹ Plan cost rules and variants
- ▹ Coverage details

▸ Benefits wage types configuration details (from the Payroll module):

- ▹ Deduction wage types for the employee, employer, and provider

- ▸ Vendor details (from the Accounts Payable module):
  - ▹ Map benefit providers
  - ▹ Link wage types to providers for remittance

These inputs are provided to the *processing* and are handled by schemas and rules.

5.1.1 Processing

Payroll schemas and rules provide the processing engine to benefits. As noted in Chapter 4, there are specific subschemas (**UBE1** and **UBE2**) that SAP has provided for processing benefits.

5.1.2 Output

Output of the payroll-benefits processes payroll results, which are further integrated with SAP Financials. The list of output activities is as follows:

- ▸ Benefit deduction wage types are written to payroll results tables, such as **RT** and **CRT**.
- ▸ Postings are carried out to General Ledger (GL) as well as Accounts Payable (AP).
- ▸ Actual money is remitted by AP to vendors.
- ▸ Interfaces read payroll and benefits data to send data files to vendors.

Table 5.1 presents an overview of US Benefit plans. Visit *http://help.sap.com* for additional resources on these benefit types.

Benefit Plan Type	Impact on Payroll
Health (medical, dental, vision)	▸ Employee and employer cost calculations ▸ Different costs depending on coverage ▸ Employee-only, employee and spouse, etc. ▸ Different options resulting in different costs ▸ PPO with lower or higher deductible ▸ Pre-tax deductions handling
Insurance (life, accidental death and dismemberment, dependent life)	▸ Imputed income calculation ▸ Post-tax deductions for accidental death and dismemberment (AD&D)

Table 5.1 Overview of Various US Benefit Plans

Benefit Plan Type	Impact on Payroll
Savings (such as 401(k), 403(b), 457)	▶ Pre-tax deduction ▶ Base for percentage calculations ▶ Catch-up contribution based on age ▶ Deciding annual limits as mandated by regulations
Flexible Spending Accounts (health care, dependent care)	▶ Pre-tax deduction ▶ Annual goal amount vs per-pay deduction ▶ Claims processing

Table 5.1 Overview of Various US Benefit Plans (cont.)

In Chapter 2 you saw many different infotypes that affect employee earnings, deductions, taxes, and benefits. So far, however, we have skipped over infotype **0041**, which indirectly affects benefits calculations. Figure 5.2 shows infotype **0041** along with possible dates that can affect the benefit calculation amounts. For example, if benefit coverage starts on a date different from the employee's actual hire (or starting) date.

Date Specifications

Date type	Date	Date type	Date
01 Techn. date of entry	01/01/2007	03 Pension fund entry	03/31/2007
40 First working day	01/01/2007	50 Service year entry	02/01/2007

Figure 5.2 Infotype 0041 Impact on Benefits

Infotype **0041** is used during benefit configuration for hire and termination dates, or any other date types. Each of the plan types, along with applicable details for the types that are relevant to payroll integration, will be discussed in the next section.

5.2 Health Plan Integration

Health plans are always more important to US employees due to the nature of the US healthcare system and its associated processes. Employees are often interested in knowing more about their health plan before accepting a job than they are about any of the job's other possible benefits (with the possible exception of stock options). Health plans have pre-tax deductions and offer different options and coverage levels. In the sections that follow, you will learn about health plans through infotype **0167** used with the employee master data.

5.2.1 Health Plans

Health plans are of three different sub-types: health, dental, and vision. Figure 5.3 shows infotype **0167** (Health Plans) with many tabs for the infotype. Focus on the *Plan data* tab. This tab shows that the employee can choose the plan type, options for the plan, and include coverage for dependents. Cost of the coverage depends on the options and dependent coverage the employee chooses; for example:

▸ If an employee chooses an option with coverage for themselves, their spouse, and two children, and another employee selects benefits only for themselves, the costs for the second employee will be far less than that for the employee with dependents.

▸ If one employee chooses a Health Maintenance Organization (HMO) plan and another employee chooses a Preferred Provider Organization (PPO) plan, they also may be paying radically different amounts.

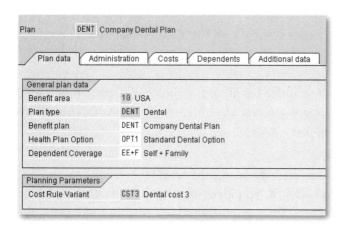

Figure 5.3 Infotype 0167 Health Plan Data

Plan rates are decided by the benefits configuration, and they appear on the Costs tab of infotype **0167**, as shown in Figure 5.4. The Costs tab shows different employee costs depending on the employee's choices. As such, the deductions for each employee will have different amounts; for example:

- ▸ Some employers may provide a health plan to their employees at no cost to the employee. In that case, *Employee costs* would be 0.00.

- ▸ Some employers may pass a portion (typically a percentage) of the benefit costs to their employees:

  - ▹ An employee pays $75 for choosing an option that covers themselves, a spouse, and two children.

  - ▹ The employer pays $600 for that option.

  - ▹ The provider charges (and gets paid) $675 from payroll for the benefits coverage.

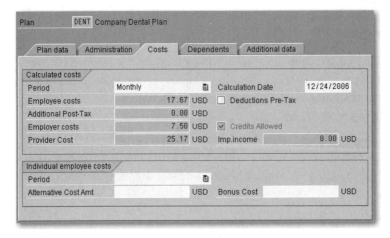

Figure 5.4 Infotype 0167, Costs Data

While benefit deductions differ based on the choice of plans, options, and dependent coverage, there are typically three costs involved. This means there are the following three wage types:

- ▸ **Employee cost (EE)**
  These are dependent on agreements between the employer and the employee. In some cases, the employer might offer a "free" plan, where employees don't have to pay any portion of the cost. In some cases, the employee pays for a portion of the health plan costs as a payroll deduction. The payments made by the employee through payroll are typically taken as a pre-tax deduction (known as Section 128) because the amount is applied toward a qualified health plan. The employee depicted in Figure 5.4 pays $17.67 per month for their dental coverage (as noted in the Plan field at the top).

▶ **Employer cost (ER)**

Employers will always have costs related to health plans and once again, they will be lower or higher depending on what the employee choices are for dependent coverage. The example in Figure 5.4 shows an employer cost of $7.50 per month.

▶ **Provider cost**

If you add the employee and employer costs, the result is the provider cost, which is the overall cost of that benefit (per month). However, in rare cases, some implementations use a tricky formula and set of rules to calculate the provider cost; it may not be as simple as adding the EE and ER costs.

Now let's look at how wage types are linked with these three costs so you can better understand how they are eventually processed in payroll.

Wage Types for Health Plans

The three costs described in the previous section translate to the following three wage types in payroll (see Appendix D for a complete listing):

▶ Wage type **BE14** for pre-tax HMO EE costs

▶ Wage type **BR14** for HMO employer costs

▶ Wage type **BP14** for HMO provider costs

You can use this set of wage types to copy and create custom wage types for HMO plans in your own implementation. (You will find model wage types for PPO plans as well.) As you learned in Chapter 3, you should use the SAP wage types table **T512W** to check the processing classes and cumulations for custom wage types after you create them.

In the IMG, you will be able to find the wage type creation node at **Payroll USA • Benefits Integration • Create Wage Type Catalog** to copy and create custom benefit wage types. When you use this IMG menu path, you will notice that the model benefits wage types appear in the list, as shown in Figure 5.5.

After you **COPY** and create your own wage types, you need to assign them to the health plan. After you do that, all employees who are enrolled in that health plan (and who have infotype **0167**) will generate these wage types in the payroll results. The menu path **Payroll USA • Benefits Integration • Enter wage types for plans** enables you to assign wage types to the plans. Figure 5.6 shows an example for a dental plan, along with its associated wage types.

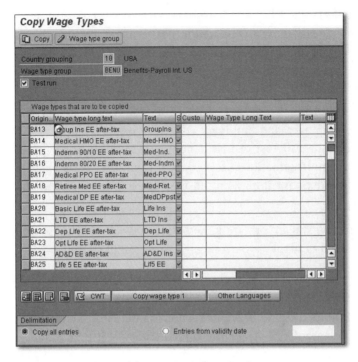

Figure 5.5 Benefits Model Wage Types from Catalog

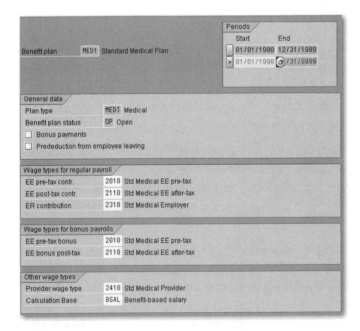

Figure 5.6 Assigning Wage Types to a Health Plan

Savings plans bring slightly different challenges to US Payroll integration, as you'll discover in the next section.

5.3 Savings Plan Integration

As the name suggests, *savings plans* are related to an employee's retirement savings. While different countries use different terminology and concepts for retirement savings, this book focuses on the popular US savings plans: 401(k), 403(b), and 457's. Savings plans have their own characteristics (thanks to IRS rules) regarding annual limits as well as certain age-based contributions, known as *catch-up contributions*.

5.3.1 Savings Plans

Most of you will know savings plans as 401(k) plans. However, the term savings plan also refers to other retirement plans such as 403(b) and 457. Similar to 401(k) retirement plans, 403(b) plans are offered by higher education and non-profit organizations. Similarly, 457 plans are offered by many government entities as qualified deferred compensation plans.

Note
401(k), 403(b), and 457 refer to tax code sections. For additional information about these retirement plans and their regulations visit the IRS web site at *http://www.irs.gov*.

Many public sector and higher education implementations of SAP US Payroll use 403(b) and 457 savings plans, while 401(k) is a general US retirement plan in the commercial and private sector. The structure of infotypes and wage types is somewhat similar to health plans, as we have seen in earlier sections. However, due to the nature of these plans, deduction handling is different and the various tabs on the infotype screen are different as well.

Figure 5.7 shows infotype **0169** with the *Regular Contribution* tab for a 401(k) plan selected. You can have two types of contributions in 401(k) plans: pre-tax and post-tax. The limits for per-tax-year contributions are as defined by the IRS. Contributions are generally a percentage of an employee's base pay; employees can also specify a fixed amount, as shown in the Amount fields of Figure 5.7. In the discussion on health plans, you saw that there are three sets of wage types for health plans. With retirement savings plans, however, there are four sets of wage types as listed in Appendix D and shown in the following list:

- **BA31**, for after-tax contributions.
- **BE31**, for pre-tax contributions.
- **BR31**, for employer contributions.
- **BP31**, for providers.

The typical equation for savings plans is:

BA31 + BE31 + BR31 = BP31

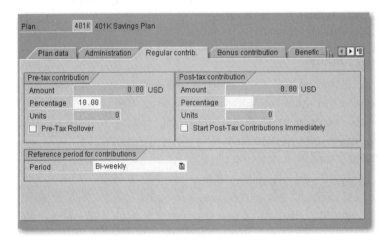

Figure 5.7 Infotype 0169, Savings Plan Data

Deductions that are taken in savings plans are typically invested in mutual funds, based on the employee's choice. The provider who manages the retirement funds offers a variety of mutual funds from which employees can choose when allocating their resources. With health plans, the money is sent to the provider and the provider ensures that the employee, (and any sub-scribed dependents), are provided with health care coverage. Money for sav-ings plans, however, is placed into an account employees can access when they retire. Typically, employers work with investment companies such as Fidelity, Vanguard, T Rowe Price, etc., to manage retirement plans.

SAP's infotype **0169** has a provision for capturing investments, as shown in Figure 5.8. However, most employers together with the investment compa-nies create a web-based tool where employees can manage their investments and change their contribution allocation to different funds. In these cases, the web-based tools need to interface with SAP appropriately. Normally this integration is achieved using SAP's EP (Enterprise Portals) and XI (Exchange Infrastructure) technologies.

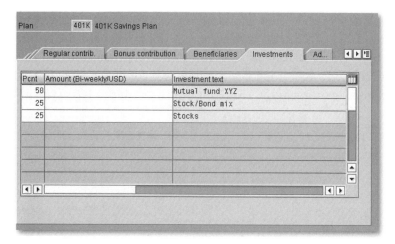

Figure 5.8 Infotype 0169, Investments Options

The following sections examine some of the additional features of 401(k) plans you need to know so you can better integrate them with your US Payroll system.

Annual Limits

As noted in Chapter 3 (*Wage Types*), all qualified retirement plan deductions are pre-tax, and there are annual limits to these contributions. For example, the maximum an employee can contribute in 2006 is $15,000 per year, while in 2007 that limit is $15,500. An employee will be able to contribute pre-tax dollars within those limits in that particular tax year. If an employee chooses to maximize their contribution for 2006 ($15,000), and if the employee is paid a monthly salary of $10,000, then the percentage of their monthly contribution will be 12.5 % in infotype **0169**.

Let's take a brief detour to talk about the constants table; we will come back to the current topic of savings plans after discussing constants. *Constants*, as the name suggests, are the numbers or amounts that are maintained in a table and are used from that table. The annual limit we talked about earlier in this section, for example, is maintained annually as a constant. Constants, as their name implies, remain constant throughout the year until a change is announced.

SAP US Payroll has two tables to hold constants: tables **T511K** and **T511P**. These tables are used to maintain benefits constants, which in turn are used by SAP and can also be used by users in custom payroll rules. In legacy systems, you had to hard-code these constants in the payroll system, and maintain them annually, which was cumbersome. It was a real pain. SAP's support packs update these constants, allowing you to maintain them in one central location, and without the need to update them on an annual basis. Figure 5.9 shows a portion of the **T511P** maintenance table.

Constant	Info	Payroll constant	From	To	Amount	Crcy	
401CL	**ℹ**	Catchup Contribution Limit	01/01/2006	12/31/9999	5,000.00	USD	▲
401KL	**ℹ**	Combined lim for DEFERed plans	01/01/2006	12/31/9999	15,000.00	USD	▼
401KS	**ℹ**	401(k) Base Salary Limit	01/01/2004	12/31/9999	205,000.00	USD	
402GL	**ℹ**	402(g) lim for pretax elective	01/01/2006	12/31/9999	15,000.00	USD	
415CL	**ℹ**	415(c) lim for defined contrib	01/01/2004	12/31/9999	41,000.00	USD	
457CL	**ℹ**	457 catch-up contrib. limit	01/01/2006	12/31/9999	30,000.00	USD	
457KL	**ℹ**	457 combined contrib. limit	01/01/2006	12/31/9999	15,000.00	USD	
EE41A	**ℹ**	EEO-4 Salary Range: $ 0.1-15.9	07/01/1195	12/31/9999	100.00	USD	
EE41B	**ℹ**	EEO-4 Salary Range: $16.0-19.9	07/01/1995	12/31/9999	16,000.00	USD	
EE41C	**ℹ**	EEO-4 Salary Range: $20.0-24.9	07/01/1995	12/31/9999	20,000.00	USD	
EE41D	**ℹ**	EEO-4 Salary Range: $25.0-32.9	07/01/1995	12/31/9999	25,000.00	USD	
EE41E	**ℹ**	EEO-4 Salary Range: $33.0-42.9	07/01/1995	12/31/9999	33,000.00	USD	
EE41F	**ℹ**	EEO-4 Salary Range: $43.0-54.9	07/01/1995	12/31/9999	43,000.00	USD	
EE41G	**ℹ**	EEO-4 Salary Range: $55.0-69.9	07/01/1995	12/31/9999	55,000.00	USD	
EE41H	**ℹ**	EEO-4 Salary Range: $70.0 PLUS	07/01/1995	12/31/9999	70,000.00	USD	
GLIDP	**ℹ**	Maximum Dep. GLI Tax-free amt	01/01/1800	12/31/9999	20,000.00	USD	
GLIEE	**ℹ**	Maximum EE GLI Tax-free amt	01/01/1800	12/31/9999		USD	
GLIOP	**ℹ**	GTL: max. tax-free cov. child	01/01/1800	12/31/9999	2,000.00	USD	
GRUEB	**ℹ**	Minimum for transfer	01/01/1800	12/31/9999		USD	
HASAL	**ℹ**	HCE Post-tax 401(k) Amt. Limit	01/01/1800	12/31/9999	10,000.00	USD	
HCEER	**ℹ**	HCE ER contribution	01/01/1800	12/31/9999	1.00	USD	
HCSLC	**ℹ**	HCE EE Catch-up contribution	01/01/1800	12/31/9999		USD	▲
HCSLM	**ℹ**	HCE EE Post-Limit contribution	01/01/1800	12/31/9999	1.00	USD	▼

Figure 5.9 Maintaining Benefits Constants in Table T511P

Some experienced configurators have used a shortcut to maintain the benefits constants table. They use transaction **SM31** to directly access this table. If you use this transaction and access the table in maintenance mode, you will see the screen shown in Figure 5.9. If you instead follow the IMG path **Payroll USA • Benefits Integration • Constants for Benefits Processing**, you will only get to the savings- and insurance plan-related constants and you can only maintain their applicable constants. Also note that the entries in this table are date-sensitive, which means you will be able to delimit old entries and create new entries.

In Figure 5.10, you will notice a constant with the name **401KL**. This constant, as delivered by SAP, maintains the annual limit for 401(k) plans (determined by the IRS). As you maintain this limit from year to year, the earlier records get delimited. For example, the annual limit for 2007 is announced sometime during 2006. The limit for 2007 needs to be valid from 01/01/2007 until 12/31/9999. When the year 2008 limits are announced, the year 2007 record is delimited. As such, you will see multiple records for this constant. If you want to create your own constants in this table, SAP allows you to use a customer name space starting with the letter **Z**. You might do this, for example, when you need to maintain a number that is used during payroll calculations for certain union employees.

401CL	ⓘ	Catchup Contribution Limit	01/01/2006	12/31/9999	5,000.00	USD
401KL	ⓘ	Combined lim for DEFERed plans	01/01/1980	12/31/1997	9,500.00	USD
	ⓘ		01/01/1998	12/31/1999	10,000.00	USD
	ⓘ		01/01/2000	12/31/2000	10,500.00	USD
	ⓘ		01/01/2000	12/31/2001	10,500.00	USD
	ⓘ		01/01/2002	12/31/2002	11,000.00	USD
	ⓘ		01/01/2003	12/31/2003	12,000.00	USD
	ⓘ		01/01/2004	12/31/2004	13,000.00	USD
	ⓘ		01/01/2005	12/31/2005	14,000.00	USD
	ⓘ		01/01/2006	12/31/9999	15,000.00	USD
401KS	ⓘ	401(k) Base Salary Limit	01/01/2004	12/31/9999	205,000.00	USD
402GL	ⓘ	402(g) lim for pretax elective	01/01/2006	12/31/9999	15,000.00	USD

Figure 5.10 Date Delimiting the Constants in Table T511P

Now let's go back to the original discussion on savings plans.

SAP US Payroll automatically tracks the year-to-date 401(k) plan deductions and compares those deductions with figures in table **T511P** for the annual limits. SAP's support packs normally update these limits. SAP releases the support pack based on a predefined schedule on the SAP Service Marketplace (*https://websmp104.sap-ag.de*), which requires a log-in based access. Support packs are delivered two or three times a year, especially around year-end, to ensure correctness of tax calculations. If an employee exceeds the annual limit for pre-tax contributions, the system will send the deductions post-tax to the 401(k) plan with the aid of flags in infotype **0169**, as shown in Figure 5.7. (The pre-tax rollover flag sends pre-tax contributions to post-tax wage types after the annual limit is reached.) For example, you will see wage type **BA31** (or the copied wage type) in an employee's payroll results. At the same time, if you check the **CRT** tables in payroll, you will see that the **YTD** amount for wage type **BE31** is equal to $15,000, which is the applicable annual limit for the tax year.

Catch-Up Contributions

The IRS also allows an age-based additional "catch-up" contribution to qualified savings plans. The IRS allows an additional $5,000 pre-tax contribution to your qualified 401(k) plans if you are 50 years or older. Starting in 2007, that amount was increased to $5,500. In Figure 5.9 shown earlier (which relates to benefits constants), take a close look at the first row; you'll see a catch-up contribution limit of $5,000.

Many SAP implementations set up a separate savings plan and attach additional payroll wage types for the catch-up contribution. As such, there will be two plans as well as two deduction wage types for normal and catch-up contributions. To configure catch-up contributions in the system, use the IMG menu path **Payroll USA • Benefits Integration • Set up catch up contributions**. Figure 5.11 shows the age-based (50 years) wage types for catch-up contribution.

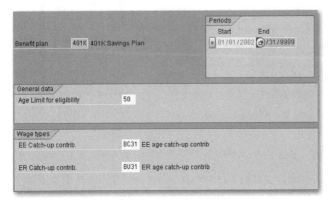

Figure 5.11 Wage Types for Catch-Up Contributions

So, how do normal wage types attach to the appropriate savings plans? And, if your company offers more than one plan, how do you differentiate between the wage types for each plan? Let's find out.

Wage Types

As seen earlier with health plans, you'll use the same menu path to copy and create wage types for savings plan deductions. As always, you need to follow an appropriate model wage types to copy and create your own custom wage types for savings plans. In Appendix D, *Model Wage Types* refer to the wage types that start with the letter *B*; these are the model wage types for benefits. For example, **BE31** and **BA31** are pre-tax and post-tax deductions for 401(k) savings plans. You can copy them and create your own custom wage types. Figure 5.12 shows the 401(k) plan wage type assignment. The wage types are copied and created by using the same steps we discussed earlier in the health plans section.

Figure 5.12 Wage Types for Savings Plan

To better understand the different wage types in Figure 5.12, take the time to review Table 5.2. This table explains the different wage types used in Figure 5.12. Unlike health plans, savings plans have additional wage types, as described in the table.

Wage Type	Used For
EE pre-tax contribution, regular payroll	This is the deduction wage type for employee contributions during regular payrolls.
EE pre-tax contribution, bonus payroll	This can be the same wage type that is used during normal payrolls. Employees can also contribute the same percentage as bonus payrolls.
ER contribution regular payroll	When employers offer a 401(k) plan with an employer contribution.

Table 5.2 Savings Plans Wage Types

Wage Type	Used For
ER contribution bonus payroll	Can be the same as a regular payroll contribution wage type from the employer.
EE post-tax contribution, regular payroll	When an annual pre-tax limit is exceeded or when the employee chooses to contribute additional post-tax amounts.
EE post-tax contribution, bonus payroll	Can be the same as a regular payroll post-tax contribution wage type.
Calculation base	SAP uses a delivered wage type (**BSAL**) for the calculation base. However, you can create your own custom wage type for the base calculation. For example, you can create a cumulation wage type **/123** and cumulate the earnings in that wage type. You can then use the cumulation wage type in the calculation base.

Table 5.2 Savings Plans Wage Types (cont.)

After reviewing health and savings plans, next up are insurance plans and how to check the payroll integration points for them.

5.4 Insurance Plan Integration

Employers in the US often offer life insurance plans for their employees through a benefit provider such as Prudential or AIG. Employees get better rates for insurance through such group life plans and they typically don't have to undergo a medical examination either. Employers also extend such group life plans to employee's spouses. Of course, there are tax implications for such life insurance plans. As you recall from the *Imputed Income* discussion in Chapter 3, employers in the US offer Group Term Life Insurance (**GTLI**) and a few other plans to their employees. The insurance plans in US Benefits cover the following:

▶ Life insurance for employees

▶ Dependent life insurance

▶ Accidental Death and Disability (AD&D)

▶ Long-term care

Different employers might have different policies and regulations for their GTLI plans. As noted here, the list describes how such policies affect your benefits constants table **T511P**; you may have to write custom rules in schemas to handle some of these:

- Employers typically have a minimum number of hours rule for coverage. For example, an employee must work a minimum of 20 hours per week to be eligible.

- Premiums are fully-covered by the employer for coverage up to a certain amount. For example, the employer pays for coverage up to twice an employee's annual salary; employees pay the difference for coverage higher than that.

- Under IRS regulations, employer-covered GTLI plans in excess of $50,000 are considered taxable income. This concept is known as *imputed income*, and was discussed in Chapter 3 in a sample US paystub.

- Premiums are based on an individual's age and coverage amount.

- Many employers let their employees continue coverage during an unpaid leave of absence by having employees pay the required amount to the employer during the absence.

Similar to health plans, employees can have options with insurance plans as well. Figure 5.13 shows infotype **0168** for choosing plan options. With insurance plans, the employee's age and coverage amount are the deciding factors for the cost of the insurance. Because of this, SAP provides a tab in infotype **0168** (shown in Figure 5.14) for the insurance coverage. Coverage can be twice the annual salary or three times the annual salary. The costs are calculated based on the configuration rules in the benefits module as per-coverage and age-based factors. The deduction in the payroll results varies from employee to employee.

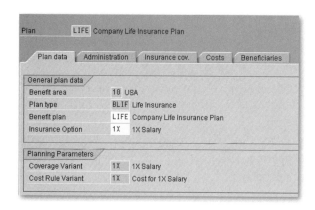

Figure 5.13 Infotype 0168, Insurance Plan Options

Table **T511P** also maintains the constants for insurance plans. These constants are mainly for tax-free amounts, as per IRS guidelines. Figure 5.9

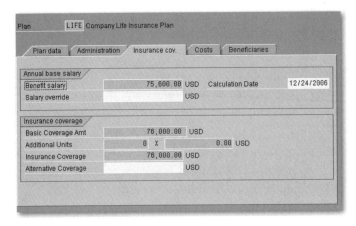

Figure 5.14 Infotype 0168, Coverage Options for Insurance

shows a portion of table **T511P**, which displays some of the constants for insurance plans. In Chapter 3, we defined *imputed income* as follows: When an employer extends group life insurance coverage of more than $50,000 to employees, then (per the IRS rate tables), an imputed income is calculated and is subject to Federal Insurance Contribution Act (FICA) taxes. This is the place where the concept of imputed income gets applied in SAP Payroll. For example, when an employee elects to enroll in a life insurance plan, the imputed income is calculated in payroll. To learn more about how imputed income gets calculated, see Figure 5.15. Also, in Figure 5.16, you can see wage type **/BT1**, which shows the employee's taxable income due to the group term life plan enrollment. The amount of $3.15 is the taxable amount generated in payroll. Based on IRS regulations, SAP maintains age-based factors for imputed income calculations.

> **Note**
>
> It is a good idea to confirm the tables with IRS tax publications, since SAP sometimes includes a disclaimer about the rates in these tables.

As with health and savings plans, SAP also provides model wage types for insurance plans. Consult Appendix D for a complete list, but here are the model wage types for insurance plans:

- ▶ Wage type **BA13** for after tax deductions
- ▶ Wage type **BE13** for pre-tax deductions
- ▶ Wage type **BR13** for employer contributions
- ▶ Wage type **BP13** for provider contributions

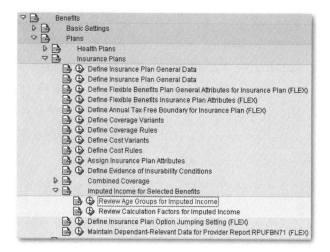

Figure 5.15 IMG for Imputed Income Calculation

These model wage types are similar to those for health and savings plans, where the provider wage type is used to send money to the provider. Figure 5.16 presents the payroll result table **RT** showing various benefits deductions. A technical wage type **/109** totals the **ER** (Employer) portion of benefits. As discussed in Chapter 3, if you follow a routine of wage type numbering where **EE** and **ER** wage types fall in different ranges, the reporting and reading of payroll results will be much easier.

```
Table RT - Results Table (Collapsed Display)

A Wage type       APC1C2C3ABKoReBTAwvTvn One amount/one number      Amount

* /101 Total gross                                             1,750.00
* /102 401(k) Wage                                             1,750.00
* /104 NQP Eligibl                                             1,750.00
* /109 ER benefit                                                453.97
* /110 Net payment                                               177.37-
* /114 Base wage f                                             1,750.00
* 2030 401k EE pre01              B 04                            157.50-
* 2110 Std Medical01              B 02                             11.04-
* 2117 Dental EE a01              B 01                              8.83-
* 2310 Std Medical                                               159.96
* 2330 401k Employ                                               105.00
* 9C35 Pension Com                                             1,750.00
2 /001 Valuation b01                          20.19
2 /002 Valuation b01                          20.19
2 /003 Valuation b01                       2,019.15
2 /844 Paid holida01                                    86.67
2 /BER Benefits ER01                                             269.55
2 /BT1 EE GTLI Tax01                                               3.15
2 1002 Salary     01                                    86.67   1,750.00
2 1090 Base Salary01                                            1,750.00
2 2317 Dental Empl01              B 01                              3.75
2 2320 Basic Life 01              B 03                              0.84
```

Figure 5.16 Benefits Deductions in the Payroll Results RT Table

Table 5.3 presents the wage types and amounts for the deduction wage types shown in the payroll results in Figure 5.16.

Wage Type	Use	Amount
2030	For employee 401(k) plan contributions (pre-tax)	$157.50
2110	For employee medical plan contributions plan (pre-tax)	$11.04
2117	For employee dental plan contributions (pre-tax)	$8.83
2330	For employer 401(k) plan contributions	$105.00
2310	For employer medical plan contributions	$159.96
2317	For employer dental plan contributions	$3.75
2320	For employer life insurance contributions	$0.84

Table 5.3 Explanation of Benefits Deductions in Payroll Results

In Figure 5.16, you will notice that wage types in the series 2000–2199 relate to EE deductions, while those in the 2300 range are for **ER** deductions. Also, if you total the **EE** deductions, the total will be $177.37; the total of the **ER** contributions is $269.55. If you check Figure 5.16, you will find the appropriate **EE** and **ER** totals wage types matching these amounts.

Now let's discuss one of the lesser-known plans: Flexible Spending Accounts (FSA).

5.5 Flexible Spending Account Integration

To better understand the process flow for a Flexible Spending Account (FSA), let's start with the diagram in Figure 5.17. This figure shows the lifecycle of an FSA deduction starting with annual goals and ending with employee claims.

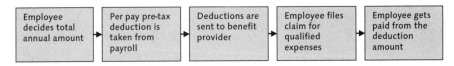

Figure 5.17 FSA Concept Diagram

The facts you need to know about FSA plans are:

▶ There are two types of FSAs: Health Care Account (HCA) and Dependent Care Account (DCA). In Figure 5.18, you can see the Benefit Plan field that captures these plans.

- The IRS allows you to contribute up to $6,000 into an HCA and up to $5,000 into a DCA (at the time of this writing). The amount also depends on your tax filing status. Figure 5.19 shows infotype **0170** with the contribution field that captures the target amount chosen by the employee.

- Depending on the payroll frequency (weekly, biweekly, or monthly), you will have a per-pay deduction. For example, if you choose to contribute $1,000 to an HCA and you get paid monthly, you will see a pre-tax deduction of $83.33 each pay period. Contributions can be made only up to the December 31st payroll.

- You file claims for qualified health care expenses, such as co-pays, prescriptions, or over-the-counter drugs. Claims can be filed anytime during the year, and up to March 31st/April 15th (the dates have changed in the past few years) of the following year.

- You receive reimbursements from the HCA account for the claims you submitted.

Although many employers outsource FSA management, SAP provides you with infotype **0170** (sub-types HCA, DCA) for the target amount, and infotype **0172** for claims so you can handle the full lifecycle of the FSA.

> **Note**
>
> In Appendix D, refer to model wage types **BE40** and **BE41** for HCA and DCA pretax deductions.

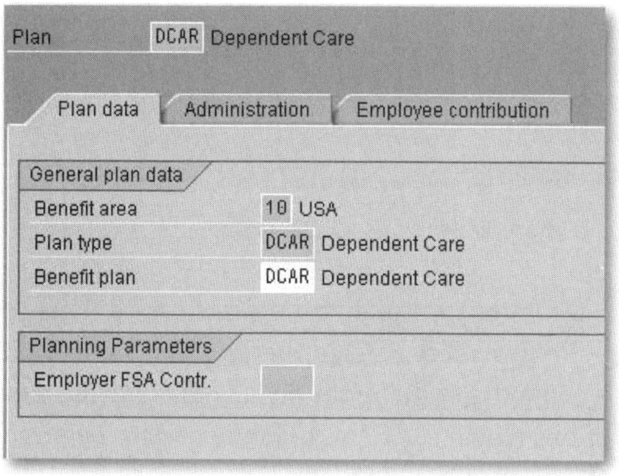

Figure 5.18 FSA Plan

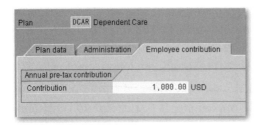

Figure 5.19 Infotype 0170 Shows an Annual FSA Contribution of $1000

As with health and insurance plans, FSA plans also need a wage type, which you can create by using the IMG path **Payroll USA · Benefits integration · Enter wage types for plans**. Figure 5.20 shows the link of the wage type with the benefit plan.

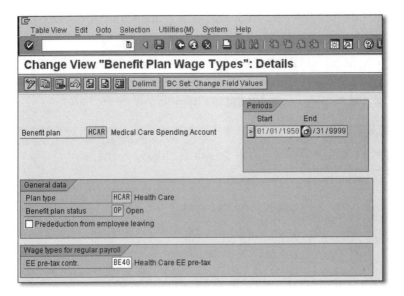

Figure 5.20 Linking the Wage Type to the FSA Plan

It is important to ensure that accurate and timely data transfers are done to the benefit providers. Unless the providers receive the data and money on time, your employees are not going to get the required coverage for the various plans. The final section of this chapter reviews the type of data required by each type of plan discussed earlier in the chapter.

5.6 Sending Data and Remittance to Benefit Providers

Enrolling employees in benefits and running the payroll to generate benefits deductions is only half the battle. The remaining half of the work involves sending the data and money to benefit providers. Let's first look at some examples before discussing SAP's functionality for sending payments to providers.

5.6.1 Health Plans

Typically, big insurance companies (such as Aetna, United Health Care, Blue Cross/Blue Shield, etc.) work with employers to offer a group health plan. Depending on the size of the company and the number of employees, employers are offered one or many different health plans. Typically, employers offer once-a-year benefit enrollment period. The exception to this rule is when an employee experiences a life event (such as a marriage, child birth or adoption, divorce, death in the family, etc.). In these cases, employees are permitted to make the necessary changes to their benefits coverage at that time. As noted here, some typical employee events in the US that you need to send to benefit providers (insurance companies) include:

▶ Data for newly hired employees, including benefits enrollment information

▶ Details about dependents of newly hired employees

▶ Regular per pay deductions

▶ Employee life events:

　▸ Marriage or divorce

　▸ Births, adoptions, or deaths

　▸ Dependent age out. (Typically, children lose the health coverage under a parent or legal guardian on their 19th birthday. However, there are some US states which have exceptions to this rule.)

　▸ Retirement or termination of employment

▶ Annual enrollment

5.6.2 Insurance Plans

Unlike with health plans, insurance plan data won't have a big impact on life events. Mostly, it is the regular employer deduction amounts that need to be sent to the benefit provider after employees have chosen their plan during the open enrollment period.

5.6.3 Savings Plans

Savings plan data consists of:

▶ Employee and employer deduction amounts

▶ Selection of investment funds by the employee (in most of the cases, 401(k) providers have a web site where these selections can be maintained)

▶ Changes to the 401(k) deduction amount (either a percentage of the base pay, or a set dollar amount)

5.6.4 Sending Remittance

Third-party remittance to benefits providers is covered in Chapter 8. However, it is worth noting a few useful SAP reports under the menu path **Benefits • Administration • Payment List**, which can be run to check the payments. Figure 5.21 shows the output of this report. You should make it a standard practice to run this report after every payroll run, and to send a copy of this report to your finance department. They can use the information in this report to help them to reconcile when the third-party remittance postings hit accounting from payroll.

BAr.	Benefit plan	Name	Long text	Σ Amount	Crcy
USA	Company Life Insurance Plan	AIKMA...	Basic Life Provider	0.71	USD
		ANDE...	Basic Life Provider	0.73	USD
		BRAXT...	Basic Life Provider	1.55	USD
		FOUT...	Basic Life Provider	0.57	USD
		LARSE...	Basic Life Provider	0.60	USD
		LAWS...	Basic Life Provider	0.68	USD
		METZ...	Basic Life Provider	0.50	USD
		PARRI...	Basic Life Provider	1.09	USD
		RENE ...	Basic Life Provider	0.73	USD
		ROBE...	Basic Life Provider	0.85	USD
	Company Life Insurance Pl...			▪ 8.01	USD
	Dependent Life	AIKMA...	Dep Life Provider	0.27	USD
		ROBE...	Dep Life Provider	0.11	USD
	Dependent Life			▪ 0.38	USD
	Long Term Disability	AIKMA...	LTD Provider	3.48	USD
		METZ...	LTD Provider	2.44	USD
		ROBE...	LTD Provider	4.18	USD
	Long Term Disability			▪ 10.10	USD
	Spousal Life	AIKMA...	Spousal Life Pro...	1.06	USD
		METZ...	Spousal Life Pro...	0.43	USD
	Spousal Life			▪ 1.49	USD

Figure 5.21 Payment List Report from the Benefits Module

5.6.5 Sending Data

SAP provides several standard IDocs you can use to send benefit data for all types of benefits and plans. You can run these IDocs by using the menu path **Personnel management · Benefits · Administration · Data transfer to provider**. However, because of specific requirements of some providers, the implementation team may need to modify these IDocs or create custom data transfer programs.

5.7 Summary

This chapter has provided you with a good sense the tight integration of benefits plans with US payroll wage types and schemas. Benefits contribute to both pre- and post-tax deductions in payroll, and since your employees depend on these benefits to be there when they need them, it is important for the payroll system to not only be accurate, but to process payments to benefits providers on time. Working with benefits and payroll integration requires current and updated knowledge of tax rules and IRS mandates to ensure that various tables have accurate values for calculations and limits for deductions.

The next chapter focuses solely on how to set up and handle garnishments in US Payroll. As with benefits, garnishments also introduce many new concepts.

Garnishments is a senseitive topic since, most of the time, it involves a child support payment. As much as the timing and accuracy of processing is crucial, understanding, the calculations in SAP US Payroll is also very important. This chapter discusses the configuration aspects, and talks about disposable net income as well as the garnishment schemas. The Chapter uses calculation-based examples, which will make it easy for you to understand the concepts.

6 Garnishments

A garnishment is a court-ordered collection of debt directly from an employee's pay. Normally child support payments are collected through garnishments (or garnishing the wages), however there are other debts and payments such as tax levy and credit card debts that can also be collected through garnishments. Typically, an HR department receives the court orders and then, during the payroll process, the employer is supposed to take the deduction and remit to the garnishment authorities immediately. SAP has provided US Payroll with a robust garnishment functionality that takes care of garnishment input through infotypes, processing during payroll and the post-payroll process to remit the deductions to authorities. Figure 6.1 presents a very simple process flow for garnishments.

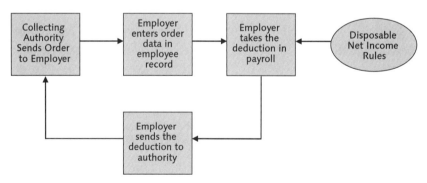

Figure 6.1 Garnishment Process Flow

The applicable SAP US Payroll as well as HR functionality that plays a role in this process flow is as follows:

- The employer enters the garnishment order data in **SAP • Infotypes 0194 and 0195 maintenance**.

- The employer calculates the deduction in **US Payroll • Payroll schema**, The Payroll rules along with the disposable net income models assist the Payroll schema to calculate the correct deduction amounts.

- The employer sends the deduction to **Authorities • Third-party remittance processing**, which is integrated with **Accounts Payable**.

Let's begin with infotypes **0194** and **0195** because they are the starting points to enter the order details from the court or other garnishment authority.

6.1 Configuring Garnishments

There are three garnishment-related infotypes in SAP US Master Data for employees. Reviewing these infotypes will help with your understanding of the configuration required for garnishments.

6.1.1 Garnishment Infotypes

There are three major garnishment infotypes you need to know about:

- Infotype **0194** – Garnishment document
- Infotype **0195** – Garnishment order
- Infotype **0216** – Garnishment adjustment

Figure 6.2 presents infotype **0194** where garnishment details are captured. You don't need to carry out any major configuration for this infotype.

Table 6.1 lists the fields from Figure 6.2 about which you need to know more for the configuration and to understand their impact on the garnishment process flow.

Infotype 0194 Field	Description
Status	Garnishments with a status of Activeare processed in payroll. Garnishments with a statuf of Pending or Released will not be deducted in payroll.
Category	Child support (also referred to as an Order to Withhold Income, or OWI), Federal or State tax levy, credit card debts.

Table 6.1 Infotype 0194, Field Details

Infotype 0194 Field	Description
Remittance	In most cases, the remittance rule for garnishments will be "Immediate," which means after deducting it from payroll, the employer should send the money to authorities without delay.
Priority	If there is more than one garnishment, the priority decides which one is deducted first.

Table 6.1 Infotype 0194, Field Details (cont.)

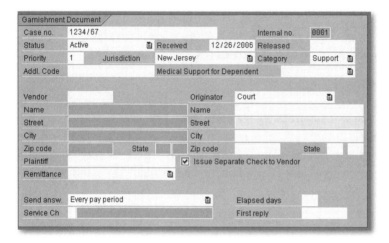

Figure 6.2 Infotype 0194, Garnishment Document

After you create and save infotype **0194**, infotype **0195** appears and prompts you to enter the required data, as shown in Figure 6.3. In infotype **0195**, the order details regarding the deduction amount and frequency are entered. Depending on the type of garnishment, the order details can have just the deduction or both the balance and the deduction. For example, child support payments have a regular deduction while a credit card payment or tax levy will have a balance and a deduction amount. It is possible for an employee to have more than one garnishment, and as such, multiple instances of infotypes **0194** and **0195**.

As noted earlier, these infotypes do not require much configuration. There are, however, other topics such as disposable net income rules and remittance rules that will require additional configuration. Also, even if you decide to use SAP's garnishment types, you still need to configure and attach the wage types for the deductions. Using Figure 6.4 as a guide, let's review the steps required to configure garnishments:

Garnishment Order					
Case no.	1234/67			Internal no.	0001
				Sequence no.	01
Order Type	CS	Child Support			
Rule Non-exempt	000	Sup-Specify Exmpt% on Splmtl Scrn, exc U			
Initial Balance		USD			
Deduction	215.00	Pay period amount			

Limit 1		Limit 2		Additional Amount	
● Non-exempt ○ Exempt		● Non-exempt ○ Exempt		● Non-exempt ○ Exempt	
Value		Value		Value	
Unit		Unit		Unit	

Fields for Special Rule		
Special Rule	04	Federal Rule - Support
Fed.exempt (35%-50%)	50.00	%

Figure 6.3 Infotype 0195, Garnishment Order

1. **Configure the Document Category and Order Types:**
   You won't be doing each step from the IMG, but rather focus on the important or key aspects around garnishments. The goal here is to share the information that generally might not be available in standard documentation.

2. Check or create the document category using **Create document category** in the IMG.

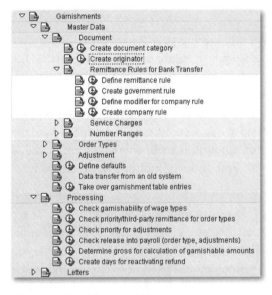

Figure 6.4 Garnishments IMG

3. Figure 6.5 shows the included *Document category*. You can create new categories by copying existing categories or by creating new entries. The Document category field in infotype **0194** was shown earlier in Figure 6.2.

Document Category	Text
C	Creditor
F	Federal Tax
S	Support
T	State Tax
V	Voluntary

Figure 6.5 Garnishments Document Category

4. Configure the order type and attach it to a category. In the example shown in Figure 6.6, the order type for *Child Support* is attached to the order category for *Support*. If you refer back to infotype **0195** in Figure 6.3, you will notice that many of these fields are configured using the garnishment order type, as shown in Figure 6.6.

Later in this chapter, you will learn more about garnishment-related wage types. However, please note that the wage type is attached to the order type, as shown in Figure 6.6.

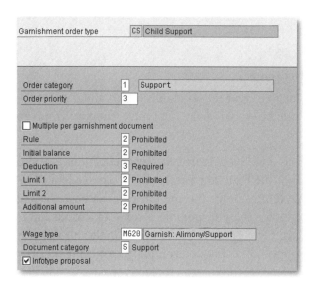

Figure 6.6 Configuring an Order Type

175

6.2   Disposable Net Income

SAP allows you to configure rules to manage disposable net income. These rules in turn determine garnishable amounts, which are controlled by processing classes. In particular, processing class **59** controls the wage types and disposable net income amount calculations.

6.2.1   Definition of Disposable Net Income

Disposable net income is not the same as net pay. There are two types of disposable incomes: disposable net income and allowable disposable net income. The *allowable disposable net income* counts towards child support payments, because child support has the highest priority. This garnishment has additional rules for disposable net income, calling it allowable disposable net income.

Disposable Net Income

Disposable net income is equal to gross earnings minus compulsory deductions. Compulsory deductions are typically federal and state taxes. Each state has their own tax laws to determine compulsory deductions. Because the equation talks of compulsory deductions, disposable net pay is not same as normal net pay.

Allowable Disposable Net Income

Allowable disposable net income is meant for child support and decides the maximum amount that can be taken away for child support from an employee's pay.

There is an act which protects employees from excessive deductions and also helps the employee based on their current family status. The Federal Consumer Credit Protection Act (**CCPA**) limits the amount that can be garnished (deducted) from an employee's weekly disposable income to various limits based on the conditions listed here. These restrictions are applicable only for child support and do not apply to tax levy or voluntary garnishments. The restrictions are as follows:

▶ 50 % when an employee supports a second family and has no arrears, or the arrears are less than 12 weeks.

- 55 % when an employee supports a second family and has arrears for more than 12 weeks.

- 60 % when an employee is single and has no arrears, or the arrears are less than 12 weeks.

- 65 % when an employee is single and has arrears for more than 12 weeks.

- Using these restrictions, the formula for calculating the allowable disposable net income is:

Allowable disposable net income = Disposable net income * CCPA % limit

The US Department of Health and Human Services web site offers detailed resources on **CCPA** as well as current disposable net income rules. You can visit this site at *http://www.acf.hhs.gov/programs/cse/newhire/employer/publication/opm_iw_guidance.htm*. Please note that individual states have their own web sites and describe the rules as applicable in the state.

In most cases, the garnishment order ensures that the amount to be deducted or withheld will be less than the total disposable net amount. However, the CCPA act and the limits specified there take precedence. Let's review the steps for disposable net income and the standard models that SAP has provided. If you check the configuration, you will notice that SAP has supplied most of the garnishment-related rules for the individual states.

1. *Disposable net income configuration:* Figure 6.7 shows the IMG path to the garnishment Disposable Net and Non-Exempt Amount nodes.

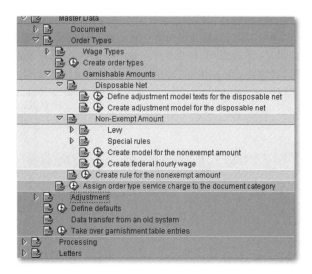

Figure 6.7 Configuring Disposable Net Income

2. The example in Figure 6.8 shows how a rule is attached to an order type. Also note the CCPA checkbox in the figure. When checked, SAP compares the CCPA rules with the rule you have established and applies the most favorable of the two rules to the garnishment calculation.

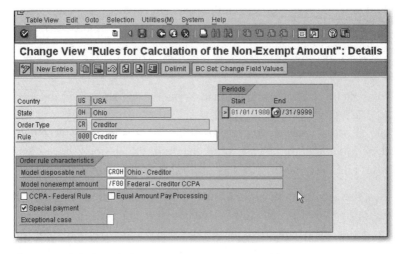

Figure 6.8 Rule for Calculating Amounts

If you select the checkbox for the **CCPA** Federal Rule (shown in Figure 6.8), the **CCPA** rule takes precedence when payroll is calculated.

6.2.2 Example

Rather than discussing the theory, Table 6.2 presents an example with actual figures to help you relate to the concept of disposable net income. Table 6.2 uses simple round figures to keep the example simple. The amounts in brackets represent a negative sign (or a deduction). Please refer to the latest rules and regulations from Federal and Local authorities for your actual testing work.

Wage Type (Earning/Deduction)	Amounts
Total Earnings	$1,000
Federal Tax	($100)
FICA Tax	($50)
Medicare Tax	($20)

Table 6.2 Disposable Net Income Calculations for Child Support

Wage Type (Earning/Deduction)	Amounts
Health Insurance	($25)
United Way	($10)
Disposable Net Income	**$830**

Table 6.2 Disposable Net Income Calculations for Child Support (cont.)

If this employee has a $300 garnishment for child support and the employee is single with no spouse or children, the employee will be subject to the 60 percent **CCPA** regulation. In this case, 60 percent of the employee's disposable net income, or $498, is available for garnishment based on the following calculation:

$830 (disposable net income)

× 60 % (CCPA allowance for child support garnishments)

$498

Because $498 is greater than the $300 the employee is ordered to pay, the full $300 is deducted from the employee's pay.

To help you better understand the concepts, let's look at another example. In this example, the employee has two garnishments: one for child support ($500 per month), and a second, also for child support (a $75 deduction per pay period). In this scenario, the employee has a weekly payroll. In a particular pay period, the wage types are shown as listed in Table 6.3.

Wage Type	Amounts
/101 – Total Gross	$810
/5U0 – Total EE Taxes	$140
/G00 – Disposable Net Income	$670
First garnishment geduction (weekly)	$125
Second garnishment available limit	$545
Second garnishment deduction	$75
/G03 – Garnishment Deductions	$200

Table 6.3 Example with Two Garnishments

6.3 Managing Wage Types for Garnishments

The topic of garnishment wage types spans two broad areas:

▶ Deduction wage types for garnishments.

▶ The impact of other earnings and deductions on garnishments.

For example, you need to decide on a base income for garnishment calculations and you need to decide on the priority of garnishment deductions when compared to other deductions. Let's start the discussion with garnishment deduction wage types.

6.3.1 Garnishment Deduction Wage Types

Figure 6.9 presents payroll results that include garnishment-related wage types. You will notice a deduction of $125 using wage type **MG20** in these results. Although in this example, I have used model wage type **MG20**, you will need to create different custom wage types, such as **3021** for child support, **3022** for federal tax levy, and so on.

In addition to the garnishment deduction, the garnishments subschema generates a few technical wage types in the payroll results. (As discussed earlier, technical wage types start with a slash, /.) In Figure 6.9, you will notice the following facts about garnishment wage types:

▶ Wage type **/G00**, disposable net income is equal to total gross minus the EE taxes.

▶ Wage type **/G01** is the gross wage amount.

▶ Garnishment deduction wage type **MG20** is calculated based on the disposable net income calculation rules. In Figure 6.9, you can see that the disposable net income is $1,200.00, so the system takes a full garnishment deduction of $125.

In Appendix D, you will find wage types **MG20** through **MG50** as model garnishment deduction wage types. You should use them to copy and create new garnishment deductions following a procedure similar to the one you used to create wage types for earnings and deductions in Chapter 3. We won't repeat these steps again here, because the steps to create garnishment custom wage types are the same as for any deduction, as long as you use the correct model wage types in the **MG20** through **MG50** series. You will notice from Figure 6.9 that garnishment deductions are added to **/110** – Total

Deductions. Wage type **/110** is the total of **MG20** as well as **M740**; the two deductions shown in Figure 6.9.

* /102 401(k) Wag			1,200.00
* /110 EE deducti			149.00-
* /114 Base wage			1,200.00
* /550 Statutory			1,200.00
* /559 Bank trans	01		1,051.00
* /560 Amount pai			1,051.00
* /5UT Actual Wor		40.00	
* /700 RE plus ER			1,200.00
* /840 Diff.curr. 01		20.00-	400.00-
* /600 Disposable			1,200.00
* /601 Gross for			1,200.00
* /603 Garnishmen			125.00-
* 0750 College Fe			750.00
* M620 Garnish: A	6 01		125.00-
3 /001 Valuation 01		20.00	
3 /002 Valuation 01		20.00	
3 M803 Salary 01			1,200.00
3 M740 Union dues 01			24.00-

Figure 6.9 Payroll Results showing Garnishment Wage Types

6.3.2 Impact of Other Wage Types

Processing classes **59** and **60** directly affect garnishment calculations. In the next section, you will learn about garnishment subschemas and the rules that use these processing classes. Besides garnishment deductions, you will also need to look at other earnings and deductions that use processing classes **59** and **60**. Chapter 3 referred to the wage type utilization report (**RPDLGA20**). This report is useful to find the wage types that have processing classes **59** and **60** with valid specification values. This report is very useful for testing purposes, as well as for problem solving garnishment and disposable net income calculations.

6.4 Garnishment Subschema

In Chapter 4, you learned about subschemas and also heard about the garnishment subschemas **UGRN** and **UGRR**. However, you'll need to learn more about **UGRN** because it runs during every pay period for all employees with garnishments.

As noted earlier, Appendix A details the US schema, **U000**. After the tax sub-schema **UTX0**, you will see the garnishment subschema, **UGRN**, as shown in Figure 6.10:

```
Fct    Par1 Par2 Par3 Par4 L E Text

                                * END OF COPY UTX0
COPY   UGRN                     *    Calculate garnishments
BLOCK  BEG                      Garnishment calculation: Current period
COM                             * ****************************************
IF            0                 Actual period
IMPRT         L                 * Import results from last payroll period
UGARN  READ        3            Read garnishments (in IN-period)
UGARN  SETC  B     3            Set for check: Active garn., adjustments
IF            GREX              Active garn., adjustm.in current period?
COM                             *   There are garnishmnts in current per.
PITAB  S     AIT                Save IT in AIT
PIT    UGIT  P59  NOAB          Delete special wage types in IT
UGARN  RFND        3            Refund, wage types in IT
UGARN  SETC  A     3            Set for check: Active garnishments
IF           GREX               Active garnishments?
COM                             *   There are active garnishments
PRT    UGRT  P59  NOAB          Get necessary WT from RT in IT
UGARN  GETD        3            Get differences from recalculation
PRINT  NP    IT                 IT after get differences
XDECI  CONV  IT   2             * Convert to 2 decimal digits
PIT    UGDN  P59  NOAB          Disposable net
ACTIO  UGGR                     Gross
PORT   UGCL       NOAB          *   Net Garnishments from claims
PIT    UGNG                     *   Zero negative gross/net
UGARN  CALC        3            Calculate garnishments
ENDIF                           End: Active garnishments
COM                             *   Active garnishments, adjustments
PRINT  NP    IT                 IT before save wage types
PIT    UGSV  P60  NOAB          Save garnishment wage types
PITAB  L     AIT                Load IT from AIT
ENDIF                           End: Active garnishments, adjustmein IT
COM                             * Independent from active garnishments
```

Figure 6.10 Garnishment Subschema UGRN

Processing class **59** is used three times, in rules **UGIT**, **UGRT**, and **UGDN**, as shown in Figure 6.10. Out of the three, **UGDN** has special significance because it performs the disposable net income calculation. Let's review the rules which use processing classes **59** and **60** in subschema **UGRN** to understand the processing.

6.4.1   Rule UGIT

Figure 6.11 presents the input (**IT** table) to the rule **UGIT**. Please note wage types such as **/101**, **/110**, etc. If necessary, use transaction **SM31** to display wage type table **T512W (Vew V_512W_D)** to check processing class **59**'s values for the wage types in Table IT.

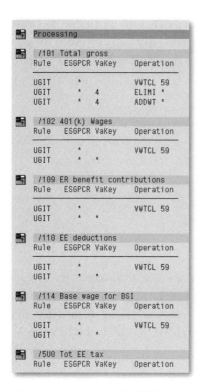

Figure 6.11 Input to Rule UGIT

Figure 6.12 shows the processing within the rule **UGIT**. Because wage type **/101** has the processing class **59** specification set to a value of 4 (Appendix E tells us that the value 4 means this is used for garnishments), this wage type is processed by the rule and written to output. All other wage types are dropped by the rule and not written to output because the logic does not find a value for processing class **59**.

A Wage type	APC1C2C3ABKoReBTAwvTvn	One amount/one number	Amount
* /101 Total gros			2,628.34
* /5U0 Tot EE tax			692.07
* /5UU Taxable Ho		80.00	

Table IT

Figure 6.12 Processing in UGIT Rule

Finally, Figure 6.13 shows the output of rule **UGIT**. It looks similar to **Table IT**, except that other wage types are dropped and only those relevant for garnishments are sent further. In this case, wage type **/101** is part of the output.

```
  M003 Salary
  Rule    ESGPCR VaKey     Operation

  UGDN      *              VWTCL 59
  UGDN      *    1         ADDWT *
  UGDN      *    1         ZERO= NR
  UGDN      *    1         ADDWT /600
```

Figure 6.13 Output of UGIT Rule

6.4.2   Rule UGDN

Figure 6.14 shows the rule **UGDN** and the creation of disposable net income wage type **/G00**. The wage type **M003** has its processing class **59** specification value set to 1 (which means transfer the amount to the disposable net amount with the same sign) and the **NUM** and **RTE** fields are set to zero. As such, **/G00** will only be written with **AMT**.

```
  M003 Salary
  Rule    ESGPCR VaKey     Operation

  UGDN      *              VWTCL 59
  UGDN      *    1         ADDWT *
  UGDN      *    1         ZERO= NR
  UGDN      *    1         ADDWT /600
```

Figure 6.14 Rule UGDN and Creation of Wage Type /G00

With the **UGDN** rule, processing class **59** has a value of 1 (transfer to the disposable amount with the same sign) and a value of 2 (transfer to the disposable amount with a reverse sign, from positive to negative). These are the significant values and will drive the disposable net income up or down. The output of the **UGDN** rule will be wage type **/G00** with the disposable income value. Figure 6.15 shows the payroll results for a sample case, where there are three wage types from the payroll results: **/101**, **/5U0**, and **/G00**. The **/G00** wage type is a result of subtraction of **/5U0** (Total EE taxes) from **/101** (Total Gross). As such, **/G00** has a value of $871.68 (as a result of subtracting $232.52 from $1105.20).

```
Table RT - Results Table (Collapsed Display)

A Wage type      APC1C2C3ABKoReBTAwvTvn One amount/one number      Amount
* /101 Total gross                                              1,105.20
* /102 401(k) Wage                                              1,105.20
* /104 NQP Eligibl                                              1,105.20
* /109 ER benefit                                                 220.65
* /5PY Good Money                                               1,105.20
* /5U0 Tot EE tax                                                 233.52
* /5U1 Tot ER tax                                                  85.93
* /5U3 Number of p                            1.00
* /600 Disposable                                                 871.68
* /601 Gross for g                                              1,105.20
* 2030 401k EE pre01            B 04                               110.52-
* 2112 Medical HM001            B 01                                14.66-
```

Figure 6.15 /G00 in RT Table

After **UGIT** and **UGDN** generate wage type **/G00**, the function **UGARN** uses wage type **/G00** to calculate garnishments. If an employee has more than one garnishment, then the priority of garnishments in infotype **0194** decides the calculation sequence. All garnishments will be dipping into the same disposable income bucket. For example, if **/G00** shows a disposable net income of $1500, and the first garnishment deduction is $300, then the second garnishment uses an amount of $1200 for its disposable net income amount. Of course, in this example, the employee has enough money.

Let's look at an example where the employee doesn't have enough money. (The amounts used are rounded for ease of understanding, as was done in the previous examples.) This example will help you understand how multiple child support payments are divided if there isn't enough allowable disposable net income. Table 6.4 presents these amounts and shows how the system will take a percentage portion based on the total of the garnishments.

Calculation / Explanation	Amount
Order # 1 for child support	$100
Order # 2 for child support	$75
Order # 3 for child support	$50
Total child support payments	$225
/101 – Total gross	$450
/5U0 – Total EE taxes	$100
Disposable net income	$350
Let us say that this employee is single with no arrears.	CCPA 60 %

Table 6.4 Mutiple Garnishments Example

185

Calculation / Explanation	Amount
Allowable disposable net income. This is less than the total deductions required ($225)	$210
Order # 1	(100/225) * 210 = 93.33
Order # 2	(75/225) * 210 = 70.00
Order # 3	(50/225) * 210 = 46.67

Table 6.4 Mutiple Garnishments Example (cont.)

6.4.3 Function UGARN

Function **UGARN** calculates garnishment deductions and creates wage types in the payroll results tables. Apart from the **IT** tables, this function also writes two additional tables. These two additional tables are **GRREC** (Garnishment Records) and **GRORD** (Garnishment Order), which are used for reporting as well as for remittance details. Figure 6.16 shows the tables from the payroll clusters. SAP uses these tables to keep track of total deductions as well as **MTD** amounts. In the example shown in Figure 6.16, the employee has two garnishments, so you will only see two records in each table. In this case, the payroll result will have two garnishment deductions, as shown in Figure 6.17.

Table GRREC

IntNo	195ID	OType	ActionDate	Recordtype	216ID	WageT	Amount deducted	RemainBalance	Month to date	Total to date
0004	01	CS	06/15/2004	1		3020	400.00	0.00	400.00	23,600.00
0005	01	FT	06/15/2004	1		3030	1,916.67	47,599.30-	1,916.67	52,599.30

Table GRORD

IntNo	195ID	OType	Prio	LimFederalMin	DispsblNet	Gross	NonExemptAmt	Starting limit	DedIType	DedVendor
0004	01	CS	003	3,333.33	3,333.33	3,333.33	2,000.00	0.00	400.00	400.00
0005	01	FT	009	2,775.00	2,775.00	3,333.33	2,316.67	400.00	0.00	1,916.67

Figure 6.16 GRREC and GRORD Tables

```
* 3020 Garnish: A1          G 01                    400.00-
* 3030 Garnish: Le          G 02                    867.75-
```

Figure 6.17 Two Garnishments in Payroll for Single Employee

Before wrapping up this chapter, Figure 6.18 shows the garnishment subschema during run time. This figure serves as a useful guideline for those of you who may be wondering about how and where to find the tables and rules from the earlier discussion.

```
┌─ Garnishment calculation: Current period
│   ┌─ IF          0              Actual period
│   │   ┌─ IMPRT    L               Import results from last payroll period
│   │   ┌─ UGARN READ         3     Read garnishments (in IN-period)
│   │   ┌─ UGARN SETC B       3     Set for check: Active garn., adjustments
│   │   ┌─ IF          GREX          Active garn., adjustm.in current period?
│   │   │   ┌─ PITAB S    AIT        Save IT in AIT
│   │   │   ┌─ PIT    UGIT P59  NOAB Delete special wage types in IT
│   │   │   ┌─ UGARN RFND        3   Refund, wage types in IT
│   │   │   ┌─ UGARN SETC A      3   Set for check: Active garnishments
│   │   │   ┌─ IF          GREX      Active garnishments?
│   │   │   └─ENDIF
│   │   │   ┌─ PRINT NP   IT         IT before save wage types
│   │   │   ┌─ PIT    UGSV P60  NOAB Save garnishment wage types
│   │   │   └─ PITAB L    AIT        Load IT from AIT
│   │   └─ENDIF
│   │   └─ UGARN TBAP          3     Take over unused garnishment orders
│   └─ENDIF
└─ENDIF
```

Figure 6.18 Run Time Garnishment Schema

Tip

Typically, you don't have to modify the garnishment subschema or add new rules in this subschema.

You will learn more about the Accounts Payable module and third-party processing integration aspects for garnishments in Chapter 8.

6.5 Summary

As with taxes, garnishments are impacted by various rules and laws pre-scribed by authorities. You need to configure the deductions as well as the disposable net income rules for garnishments to work properly. If an employee has multiple garnishments, the priority of those deductions and the disposable net income process work together to handle multiple garnish-ments. Although garnishment infotypes (**0194** and **0195**) aren't difficult to configure, the disposable net income topic is rather complex. As per our dis-cussion, other wage types with processing class 59 and 60 impact the dispos-able net income calculation process.

It's nearly impossible to discuss Payrollwithout also discussing taxes. SAP US Payroll uses an integrated tax calcualtion engine called BSI. This chapter discusses how BSI works with SAP Payroll and focuses on configuring the tax models that drive the tax calculations. You'll also get an overview of the different tax wage types generated in SAP Payroll. The Chapter briefly disccusses year-end tax processing and the Tax Reporter.

7   Tax Processing

The most interesting part of US Payroll is its tax models as well as its tax processing and tax reporting capabilities. As mentioned earlier, the BSI Tax Factory must be installed as well so you can calculate taxes. This chapter starts with an introduction to tax processing and the concepts around US taxes. It also covers tax model configuration in detail. The most hectic time for any payroll department is year-end, when companies calculate adjustments, overpayments, and tax processing prior to the end of December. You will learn about SAP's year-end workbench and related off-cycle payroll functionality to carry out year-end adjustments. The chapter concludes with a discussion on the Tax Reporter and some routine statutory tax reports.

7.1   Introduction to US Tax Processing

Tax processing gets its inputs from various sources, as shown in Figure 7.1:

- ▶ Tax infotypes from the employee record.
- ▶ Earnings, deductions, and benefits from relevant infotypes as well as from payroll calculations.
- ▶ Wage type processing classes relevant for tax processing from the configuration of wage types.
- ▶ Tax authorities and relevant tax models from tax configuration.

These input sources are used by the US payroll schema with the BSI Tax Factory. The output contains the results table with the tax wage types. So far in this book, you have learned about master data, wage types, and schemas. This should make it easy for you to extend your knowledge further into tax processing.

Let's recap some of the concepts you've already learned before moving on to the discussion of tax models.

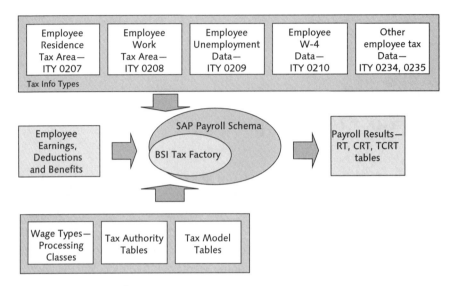

Figure 7.1 Overview of US Tax Processing

7.1.1 Tax Infotypes

In the master data and transaction data discussion in Chapter 2, you learned about infotypes **0207** (Residence), **0208** (Work), and **0210** (W-4). There are, however, additional tax-related infotypes you should know about. They aren't mandatory, but let's discuss them briefly.

Figure 7.2 shows infotype **0209**, which is used for Unemployment. This infotype is applicable to the US states where State Unemployment Insurance (SUI) is applicable. If your state does have SUI, your payrolls will have the relevant tax wage types for **SUI**. The infotype captures the worksite and in the configuration a rate for the calculation as prescribed by the state (or agreed with the state by employers) is maintained. Figure 7.3 shows the IMG for configuring the **SUI** rates for different worksites in infotype **0209**.

Figure 7.4 presents infotype **0234,** Withholding Overrides, which might be applicable in a few situations. This infotype is used along with infotype **0210**. Infotype **0234** records any override methods used for tax calculations for a particular tax authority. Such overrides are rare in a normal payroll. The majority of the configuration is maintained in **BSI**. However, if you have certain employees that require a special calculation treatment, you can create override groups. For example, you need to use supplemental rates for some payments to former employees. There are also special cases where you may need to turn-off the local tax authority reciprocity and instead use the tax override infotype.

Figure 7.2 Infotype 0209, Unemployment

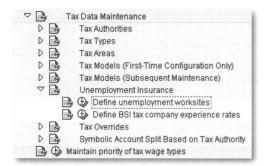

Figure 7.3 Maintain Unemployment Worksites and Rates in IMG

Figure 7.4 Infotype 0234, Withholding Overrides

Figure 7.5 presents infotype **0235**, Other Taxes, which is used for exempting employees from certain taxes. This infotype is used more frequently compared to infotype **0234**. For example, students might be exempt from certain tax types, such as Social Security and Medicare taxes, depending on the students' type of visa and residency status.

> **Note**
>
> The IRS web site (*http://www.irs.gov*) provides information on student tax treatment. Another commercial site, *http://www.istaxes.com*, is also a good source of information for non-resident and student taxes.

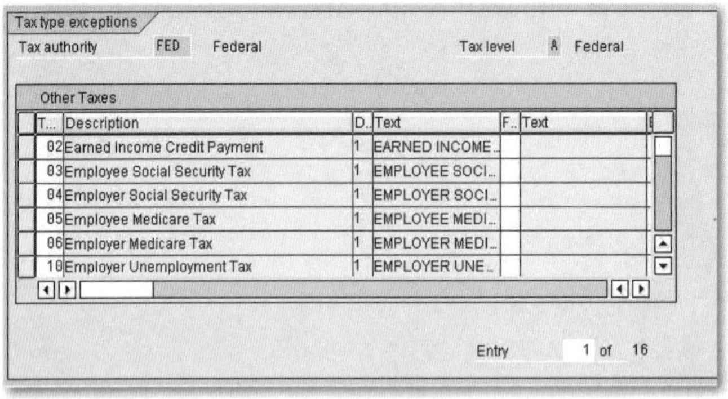

Figure 7.5 Infotype 0235, Other Taxes

Let's now revisit our earlier discussion about earnings and deductions.

7.1.2 Earnings and Deductions

Taxes are calculated based on earnings and primarily pre-tax deductions. Chapters 2 and 3 discussed earnings and pre-tax deductions as applicable in US Payroll. Table 7.1 recaps the tax-related explanations for the infotypes discussed in those chapters.

Infotype	Applicable Earnings/Deductions
0008 – Basic Pay	Basic pay is normally taxed according to tax-rate tables for Federal, State, and Local authorities. They depend on the income and tax filing status as per infotype 0210. (You can refer to these tables on the IRS and state government web sites.)
0014 – Recurring Payments	Any additional earnings wage types from infotype 0014 are added to the taxable income.
0015 – One-Time Payments	Any additional one-time payments are added to the taxable income. In some situations, if you are paying wage types which are taxed at supplemental rates (flat rates as prescribed by tax authorities), they are included in the calculations.

Table 7.1 Recap of Earnings and Deductions

Infotype	Applicable Earnings/Deductions
0167 – Health Plans	Health plan EE deductions are used for pre-tax calculations.
0168 – Insurance Plans	Imputed income will be handled as shown in Chapter 3.
0169 – Savings Plans	401(k) pre-tax deductions are taken up to the annual limits depending upon the percentage or amount chosen by the employee. Also, any additional catch-up contribution is taken out pre-tax, if the age limit condition is met.

Table 7.1 Recap of Earnings and Deductions (cont.)

These earnings and pre-tax deductions feed the payroll process through various subschemas, as discussed in Chapter 4. For example, benefits are processed in the benefits subschemas (**UBE1/UBE2**), while infotype 0014 and 0015 are processed in subschema **UAP0**. See Appendix A to learn more about the subschemas.

7.1.3 Relevant Processing Classes for Wage Types

Before we get into the discussion on tax models and tax types, it's important to know about the relevant tax processing classes. (Processing classes were discussed in Chapters 3 and 4.) As with the earlier recap for earnings and deductions, Table 7.2 revisits the relevant processing classes for taxes. Please refer to Appendix E for detailed specifications of these processing classes.

Processing Class Number	Tax Relevance
65 – Pre-tax or After-tax deduction	Pre-tax deductions, such as 401(k) contribution wage types will have this processing class.
67 – Work tax area override	Used to override any supplemental wages. In normal US Payroll, you might not use this class frequently.
68 – Payment type for tax calculation	Decides between regular (base pay) rate payments and supplemental rate (bonus) payments.
69 – Taxable and Non-taxable	Decides whether a wage type is taxable, non-taxable, or taxable but not reportable.
71 – Wage type tax classification	Processing class **71** controls the tax models and tax calculations for the wage types. You will learn more about this processing class in the next section.

Table 7.2 Recap of Tax Relevant Processing Classes

Processing Class Number	Tax Relevance
72 – EE/ER Tax	Employee (EE) or Employer (ER) tax. For example, taxes such as FICA and Medicare have both EE and ER wage types, while withholding taxes are only EE.
74 – 1042S processing	Refer to Appendix E to learn the different specifications for this processing class. The special nature of the 1042S processing class as it pertains to US taxes is beyond the scope of this book.
84 – Non-cash income	Is usually used for income received as tips, for employees such as waiters and waitresses, etc.
86 – Cumulate work hours	Cumulate hours worked: regular, overtime, or absence.

Table 7.2 Recap of Tax Relevant Processing Classes (cont.)

Now that we've recapped infotypes and processing classes, you are ready to learn more about tax models. There are many new concepts that will be introduced in the next section.

7.2   Tax Models

Tax models are a combination of tax authorities, tax classes, tax types, and tax combos. All of these concepts can be confusing and overwhelming, so let's take a step-by-step approach so you can understand one concept at a time and then bring all the pieces together.

7.2.1   Tax Authorities

SAP includes tax authority tables that you will very rarely need to maintain. These tables can be verified as shown in Figure 7.6. Tax authorities are a comprehensive list of all Federal, State, and Local tax authorities. Both infotypes **0207** (residence) and **0208** (work) use the tax authorities from this table.

In the US, there are multi-tier tax authorities, as detailed in the following list:

▶ **FED**
   Federal

▶ **NJ**
   New Jersey (or any other state authority)

► **PA01**

A specific local authority for the state of Pennsylvania (or any other local authority within that state)

► **OR01**

A specific local authority for the state of Oregon

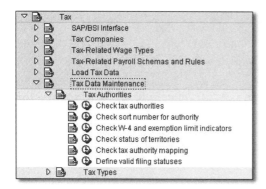

Figure 7.6 Checking Included Tax Authorities

Some states have more local authorities than others. For example, if you use the menu path for the previous list and check the tax authority tables for PA** (Pennsylvania), OH** (Ohio), IN** (Indiana), etc., you will notice that there are a lot more tax authorities in these states than there are in states like NJ (New Jersey) and NY (New York).

7.2.2 Tax Areas

Tax areas combine many different tax authorities. For example, when an employee lives in New Jersey, that employee is subject to both Federal and New Jersey state taxes. As such, a tax area consists of multiple tax authorities as applicable to that tax area. The tax area is decided by the employee's zip code, as mentioned earlier in Chapter 2. Figure 7.7 shows infotype **0207**, identifying the relationship for the tax area NJ (for the state of New Jersey) with tax authorities FED (Federal taxes) and NJ (state taxes). It is important that you do not confuse NJ as a tax authority and NJ as the tax area. Also in Figure 7.7, note the Tax Level column. SAP uses tax levels **A**, **B**, **C**, and **D** for Federal, State, Local, and school board tax authorities, respectively. We will refer to these tax levels later in the discussion.

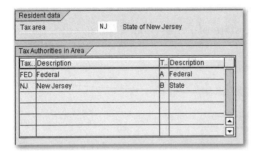

Figure 7.7 Tax Area-Tax Authority Relationship

Tax areas are configurable through the IMG. In the IMG, you will see the nodes to maintain the tax areas. They are included by SAP and you will very rarely need to maintain them. Figure 7.8 shows the IMG path to maintain both residence- and work-related tax areas using the tax authority table discussed earlier.

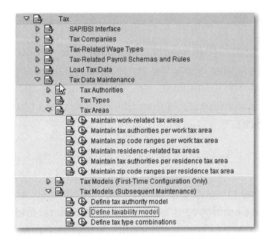

Figure 7.8 Maintain Tax Areas

The next concept you need to know more about is tax types. Each tax authority can have different types of taxes.

7.2.3   Tax Types

Tax types, as shown in Figure 7.9, refer to the different kinds of taxes for different authorities. For example, some states can have just withholding taxes while others can have withholding and unemployment taxes. Tax types have two-digit numbers, as shown in Figure 7.9.

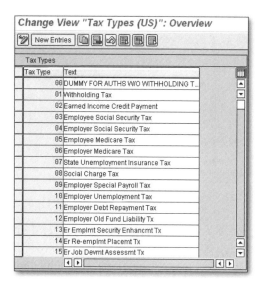

Figure 7.9 Tax Types

The final concept related to taxes is the *tax class*. We'll discuss that next before all of the concepts are brought together in a discussion of tax models.

7.2.4 Tax Class

A tax class is nothing more than the processing class **71** specifications for a wage type. Tax models refer to the processing class **71** value as a tax class. In Appendix E, you can see the long list of values for processing class 71 specifications. For example, the regular pay wage type in infotype **0008** will have a processing class **71** that's equal to **0**. However, with the 401(k) deduction wage type, processing class **71** is equal to **L**.

7.2.5 Tax Models

In the IMG, you will find two separate nodes: one for the first-time configuration and a second for the subsequent maintenance of tax models. The first-time configuration allows you to verify the SAP-delivered tax models in case they are suitable for your requirements. Figure 7.10 shows the appropriate nodes in the IMG that you need to configure for tax models. The Subsequent Maintenance node is used to create custom tax models. We will focus on the Subsequent Maintenance node since you'll need to learn about custom tax models.

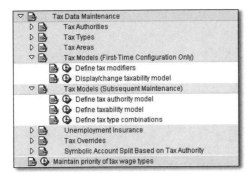

Figure 7.10 Tax Models Configuration

The three steps we are now going to discuss are interwoven and depend on each other. You may have to iteratively visit them in the IMG until you get it right. The three steps are discussed in next three sub-sections, and will show you how to build relationships to get tax models working properly.

Tax Authority: Tax Model Relationship

In the first step, you attach the tax model (a two-digit number; there is no significance to the number itself) to the tax authority, as shown in Figure 7.11.

Tax Authority	Tax model	Start Date	End Date
PA	052	01/01/1999	12/31/9999
PA01	053	01/01/1999	12/31/9999
PA02	053	01/01/1999	12/31/9999
PA03	053	01/01/1999	12/31/9999
PA04	053	01/01/1999	12/31/9999
PA05	053	01/01/1999	12/31/9999
PA06	053	01/01/1999	12/31/9999
PA07	053	01/01/1999	12/31/9999
PA08	053	01/01/1999	12/31/9999
PA09	053	01/01/1999	12/31/9999
PA0A	053	01/01/1999	12/31/9999
PA0B	053	01/01/1999	12/31/9999
PA0C	053	01/01/1999	12/31/9999
PA0D	053	01/01/1999	12/31/9999
PA0E	053	01/01/1999	12/31/9999
PA0F	053	01/01/1999	12/31/9999
PA0G	053	01/01/1999	12/31/9999

Figure 7.11 Tax Authority-Tax Model Relationship

The relationship has a date delimiting facility so you can change the tax models with an effective date.

Tax Model-Tax-Class-Tax Combo Relationship

As mentioned earlier, tax classes use the values of processing class **71**. Figure 7.12 shows the relationships between tax models, tax classes, and tax combos. (Tax combos are discussed in the next section.) In addition, Figure 7.12 also shows that the tax models will repeat for *R-Residence* and *W-Work* taxes, as indicated by the **R** and **W** in the Residence/Work tax column.

Tax Model							
Tax mod...	Res/Wrk...	Tax mod...	Tax class	End Date	Start Date	Tax Combo	
52	R	99	0	12/31/9999	01/01/1980	4	
52	R	99	1	12/31/9999	01/01/1980	4	
52	R	99	2	12/31/9999	01/01/1980	4	
52	R	99	A	12/31/9999	01/01/1980	4	
52	R	99	D	12/31/9999	01/01/1980	4	
52	R	99	E	12/31/9999	01/01/1980	4	
52	R	99	G	12/31/9999	01/01/1980	4	
52	R	99	L	12/31/9999	01/01/1980	4	
52	R	99	M	12/31/9999	01/01/1980	4	
52	R	99	P	12/31/9999	01/01/1980	4	
52	R	99	R	12/31/9999	01/01/1980	4	
52	R	99	S	12/31/9999	01/01/1980	4	
52	R	99	T	12/31/9999	01/01/1980	4	
52	R	99	U	12/31/9999	01/01/1980	4	
52	R	99	V	12/31/9999	01/01/1980	4	
52	R	U1	0	12/31/9999	01/01/1980	4	
52	R	U1	1	12/31/9999	01/01/1980	4	
52	R	U1	2	12/31/9999	01/01/1980	4	
52	R	U1	A	12/31/9999	01/01/1980	4	
52	R	U1	D	12/31/9999	01/01/1980	4	

Figure 7.12 Tax Models-Tax Class-Tax Combo Relationships

If you are checking a particular earning for a certain tax authority, you need to check the wage type's processing class **71**, and then find the appropriate tax model/tax combo record in this table. The same holds true while creating new tax models.

Tax Combo-Tax Types Relationships

The last of the three steps is to configure tax combos (which were used in the earlier discussion) using the appropriate tax types. Figure 7.13 shows the tax combos and tax types (refer to Figure 7.9, shown earlier). For example, tax combo **4** only has withholding taxes while tax combo **5** has type **10**, which is for employer unemployment tax.

If you're wondering how all of this translates to the tax calculations in payroll, the answer is presented in Figure 7.14, which shows the tax authorities and tax levels, shown earlier in the residence tax area of Figure 7.7. In the configuration, you will find different tax models for the tax authorities and that tax models use tax combos which in turn use tax types. The tax type number directly translates to the tax wage types **/4xx** in the payroll results, as shown in Figure 7.14. The example in this figure shows that tax type **01** is valid for all of the different tax authorities. As such, you will have wage type **/401** (tax type 01) with splits 01, 02, 03, and 04 for each tax authority in the payroll results. In the same example, you can see that the Federal tax authority has a tax combo which uses tax types **03** and **04**, giving rise to tax wage types **/403** and **/404**.

Tax Type Combinations					
Tax Co...	Tax type	End date	Start Date	Taxability Indi...	
4	1	12/31/9999	01/01/1980	Y	
5	10	12/31/9999	01/01/1980	Y	
5	16	12/31/9999	01/01/1980	Y	
5	19	12/31/9999	01/01/1980	Y	
5	41	12/31/9999	01/01/1980	Y	
5	48	12/31/9999	01/01/1980	Y	
6	19	12/31/9999	01/01/1980	Y	

Figure 7.13 Tax Combo, Tax Types Relationships

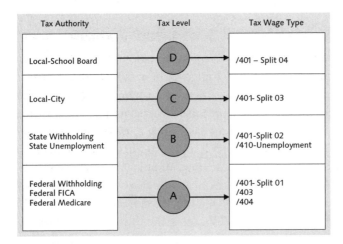

Figure 7.14 Results of Taxes

The **/4xx** wage types are calculated and generated in the **USTAX** function in subschema **UTX0** and the **RT** tables will show you results similar to the example in Figure 7.15. To find the taxability of a particular wage type, follow these steps:

▸ Go to table **T512W** and find the processing class **71** specifications. Write this down as a tax class.

▶ Go to the tax class-tax-model-tax combo relationship table and write down the residence as well as the work-tax-related tax model and tax combo.

▶ Go to the tax model and tax authority relationship table and write down which tax authorities are related to the tax class of the wage type.

▶ Go to the tax combo and find out which tax types are applicable.

The end result will be the appropriate **/4xx** wage types for those residence and work tax authorities using the taxable income as the wage type in question.

```
* /401 TX Withhol  01                    15.60-
* /401 TX Withhol  02                     3.41-
* /401 TX Withhol  03                     0.56-
* /403 TX EE Soci  01                     6.88-
* /404 TX ER Soci  01                     6.88-
* /405 TX EE Medi  01                     1.61-
```

Figure 7.15 Tax Wage Types in Payroll Results

The tax wage types generated in US Payroll are in series **/4xx**, and you need to be very familiar with them. Refer to Appendix C to check the list of all **/4xx** series wage types. Hopefully, the elaborate discussion on tax models has helped you understand the complex assembly of the tax models. In Chapter 3, we discussed tax wage types and also the **/3xx**, **/6xx**, and **/7xx** wage types. Along with the **/4xx** wage types, it is extremely important to keep an eye on **YTD** values for these wage types. In the following section, you will learn how the tax report output changes, based on the changes to the taxable base wage types. These wage types are maintained in **TCRT** tables in the payroll results. Figure 7.16 shows a portion of **TCRT** table from payroll clusters. This figure shows taxable gross **/301** series wage types for Federal taxes.

```
2004  05   M    US01   FED   /301   T6 Withholding Tax       2,808.00  05/01/2004  05/31/2004
2004  04   M    US01   FED   /301   T6 Withholding Tax       2,948.40  04/01/2004  04/30/2004
2004  02   M    US01   FED   /301   T6 Withholding Tax       2,808.00  02/01/2004  02/29/2004
2004  01   M    US01   FED   /301   T6 Withholding Tax       3,510.00  01/01/2004  01/31/2004
2004  02   Q    US01   FED   /301   T6 Withholding Tax       8,564.40  04/01/2004  06/30/2004
2004  01   Q    US01   FED   /301   T6 Withholding Tax       6,318.00  01/01/2004  03/31/2004
2004  01   Y    US01   FED   /301   T6 Withholding Tax      14,882.40  01/01/2004  12/31/2004
2004  06   M    US01   FED   /303   T6 EE Social Security Tax   2,808.00  06/01/2004  06/30/2004
```

Figure 7.16 TCRT Tables for Tax Wage Types Cumulations

We will now move our tax discussion to year-end activities. As important as regular payroll and taxes are, the discussion on year-end tax activities for US Payroll are crucial. If you refer to menu path **Payroll USA • Info system • Tax**, you will find many useful reports which can assist you when checking tax infotypes, tax authorities, and tax models.

7.3 Year-End Tax Adjustments and Workbench

In most US Payroll departments, the hectic year-end activities start around November and December and continue through the month of January, because W-2's have to be post-marked no later than January 31st. This ensures that employees have their W-2's in time to prepare their taxes by the April 15 filing deadline. To understand the purpose of the year-end workbench, let's list some scenarios which involve adjustments to employee payroll results, as follows:

▸ Employee overpayments (which are discussed in Chapter 8) resulting in wrong taxable incomes as well as taxes. This situation can arise for employees who are still with the company and for those who have left.

▸ Configuration errors resulting in wrong taxable incomes. For example, there could be an error in processing class **71**.

▸ You realize at some point in December that an employee was wrongly paid a sales commission earlier in the current tax year.

▸ An employee has resigned or was terminated while you completed the payroll and also did the post-processing, such as finance and third-party postings.

The majority of year-end adjustments revolve around infotype **0221** and running off-cycle payrolls using infotype **0221**. Figure 7.17 illustrates the lifecycle of the year-end workbench. The *year-end workbench* is a complete process, from analysis through master data maintenance and running off-cycle payroll. The process also involves carrying out financial postings and running the Tax Reporter in a test mode to verify tax figures. The year-end workbench is used with all other associated processes to correct the situations, as listed earlier.

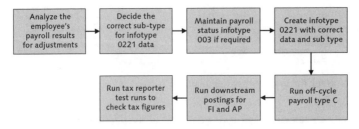

Figure 7.17 Concept of Year-end Adjustment Payroll

Using Figure 7.17 as a guide, here are the steps you need to follow for the year-end adjustment process:

1. Analyze the situation and decide whether or why you need to run adjustments for an employee. The reasons might include:

   ▶ Overpayments and claims

   ▶ Payroll errors caught by payroll analysts

   ▶ Employees reporting errors

   ▶ Delays or issues related to tax rate updates in your system

2. Adjust payroll status infotype **0003** dates as necessary in case the employee has left the organization. (For example, you may want to maintain the **Run payroll up to** date in infotype 0003 so that employee's last payroll or benefits calculations are managed appropriately.

3. Create infotype **0221** using transaction **PAUX/PAUY**. Later in this chapter, you will learn about the different subtypes and the transactions used to create infotype **0221**.

4. Run a payroll simulation to test the results. You will need a few iterations until you get the amounts in infotype **0221** right.

5. Run off-cycle payroll with an update.

6. Run the finance posting process for GL postings.

7. Run third-party remittance (AP) postings.

8. Run the Tax Reporter in test mode to verify sample tax reports (to be discussed later in this chapter).

Now let's move on to a detailed discussion of the subtypes for infotype **0221**, shown in Figure 7.18, which you'll need to use to make year-end adjustments.

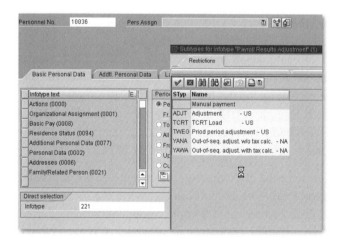

Figure 7.18 Year-End Adjustment, Infotype 0221 Subtypes

These subtypes are accessible when you use transaction **PAUX/PAUY** for the year-end workbench. The next section provides a step-by-step example of the year-end workbench.

7.3.1 Starting the Year-End Workbench

You access the year-end workbench with transaction **PAUX** through the menu path **Human Resources • Payroll • America • US • Subsequent Activities • Period independent • Payroll Supplement • Adjustment Workbench**. Then, use the **PAUX-Adjustment Workbench** option from the menu. Figure 7.19 shows the opening screen for the **PAUX** transaction.

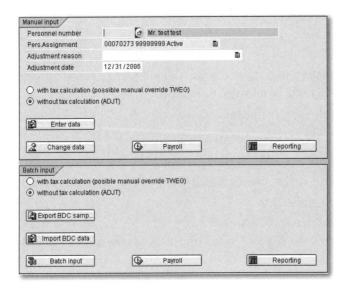

Figure 7.19 PAUX Opening Screen

The figure shows that you can use an option with or without a tax calculation. When you use the **ADJT** option (as shown in Figure 7.19) and click the **Enter data** button, the system opens the infotype **0221** screen shown in Figure 7.20. As represented in Figure 7.17, if you are sure about the subtype and develop a comfort level with this process, you can use normal **PA30** (the master data maintenance transaction) to create infotype **0221** as well.

Before going any further with the discussion on infotype **0221**, it's important to understand transaction **PAUY**, which you can access via the menu option **Human Resources • Payroll • America • US • Subsequent Activities • Period independent • Payroll Supplement • Adjustment Workbench (Special Retro Processing)**.

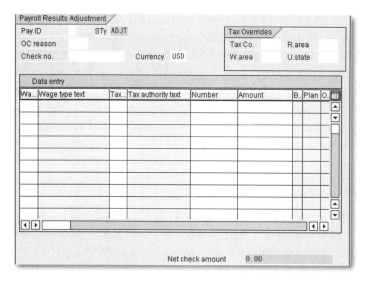

Figure 7.20 Data Entry through Infotype 0221

This second transaction is used for prior-year purposes. Remember, using the **PAUX** and **PAUY** transactions with infotype **0221** and its associated subtypes will impact the W-2 for the current year or the previous year, as needed. Table 7.3 shows a cross-reference for **PAUX**, **PAUY**, and the subtypes.

Year-end Transaction	Infotype 0221 Subtype	What can be adjusted
PAUX	ADJT	▶ Without tax calculation wage types including employee and employer taxes.
PAUX	TWEG	▶ With tax calculations and positive net only.
PAUY	YANA	▶ Without tax calculation. This allows both upward and downward adjustments; as such, both positive and negative adjustments are permitted. ▶ Use YANA when you know the tax figures. Chapter 8 shows how to use YANA to handle overpayments.
PAUY	YAWA	▶ With tax calculation. This increases the taxable wages and allows positive amounts. ▶ System calculates taxes that will be used for all missing taxable or non-taxable earnings. ▶ Taxable wages will increase.

Table 7.3 PAUX-PAUY Cross-Reference

In the examples listed in Table 7.3, payroll tables **RT**, **CRT**, and **TCRT** are updated. If you're trying to figure out what the difference is between **PAUX** and **PAUY**, or why you need to use the **YANA** and **YAWA** subtypes in infotype **0221**, the answer is pretty simple. **PAUY** is used for previous year adjustments. Remember that the W-2 deadline is Jan 31st, so you should run the adjustments to rectify the previous year's results on Jan 10th or 15th. The different subtypes are discussed further, along with actual examples, in the following sections.

Off-Cycle Payroll Concept

Since the discussion ahead will be referring to an off-cycle payroll, it may be a good idea to visit the off-cycle payroll concept. Off-cycle payroll allows users to run payroll on any day without waiting for a regular payroll run. Using SAP's off-cycle payroll workbench functionality, you can even run an off-cycle payroll for a single employee. In the payroll results table, off-cycle payroll results are maintained separately by SAP. The off-cycle payroll can be of different types, and typical SAP off-cycle payroll runs are used for:

▸ Replacement checks for lost or stolen paychecks

▸ Reversing payroll results

▸ Paying an employee on-demand ahead of a regular payroll

▸ Processing a manual check

▸ Bonus payments through a payroll run that isn't a regular run

Depending on the type of off-cycle payroll, SAP uses an off-cycle payroll indicator that's visible in payroll results. For example, Type **A** is an off-cycle bonus run, while Type **C** is a manual check run. In the sections that follow (as well as in the next chapter), we will refer to Type **A** and **C** runs when talking about year-end adjustments and overpayment processing. SAP's standard documentation provides detailed information on different types of off-cycle runs.

Now let's get back to the discussion on infotype **0221** subtypes.

Subtype ADJT: No Tax Calculation

Before we start the discussion on this subtype, it's important to define the meaning of a *Tax When Earned* calculation in SAP.

With this method, the payroll driver goes back to the previous pay period for a master data change and recalculates the taxes. In this scenario, an earning was changed in the past, so the system recalculates the taxable base and runs the tax calculations on the new taxable earnings. This also means that taxes paid in that period need to be changed as well. The taxes cannot be higher than they were withheld in the original period, and US Payroll performs that check as delivered. For example, the tax rate for a tax authority is changed retroactively and now the taxes are higher than they were originally. This causes an error in the system.

Now, let's look at an example where an employee was overpaid a certain taxable amount in the last pay period of the year 2006 (26/2006). Your payroll is already in the new year, in period 01/2007. Since the **ADJT** subtype is without tax calculations, you may need calculators and tax rate tables to perform this operation. Since you want to follow the taxed-when-earned method, you'll need to recalculate all taxable income in the period 26/2006 so that the 2006 W-2 is correct. If an employee was overpaid a sales commission of $2,500 in period 26/2006, you will need to create infotype **0221** (subtype **ADJT**) with figures that may look similar to the sample shown in Figure 7.21. (The numbers were rounded to make this easier to understand; typically they're not likely to be even.)

Payroll Results Adjustment								
Pay ID		STy ADJT			Tax Overrides			
OC reason					Tax Co.		area	
Check no.		Currency USD			W.area	U.state		

	Data entry							
Wa...	Wage type text	Tax...	Tax authority text	Number	Amount	B..	Plan	O.
1110	Bonus				2,500.00-			
/401	TX Withholding Tax	FED	Federal		200.00-		A	
/403	TX EE Social Securit...	FED	Federal		150.00-		A	
/404	TX ER Social Securit...	FED	Federal		100.00-		A	
/405	TX EE Medicare Tax	FED	Federal		100.00-		A	

Figure 7.21 Creating an Adjustment Using Infotype 0221 Subtype ADJT

Because the taxes were already paid by the employer, the employee will need to remit that amount to the tax authorities. Later in this chapter, you will see how the amount is calculated from the payroll results.

Subtype TWEG: With Tax Calculations

Let's look at an example similar to the **ADJT** subtype. The payroll for the last period (26/2006) is complete and you realize that a sales commission of $2,500 was overpaid to an employee. In this case, you want the system to calculate the taxes. To do this, create infotype **0221** with only the sales commission wage type; the taxes will be calculated by the payroll. This run will happen before the next payroll run of 01/2007, but after the last payroll run of the year 2006.

Subtype YANA: No Tax Calculations

If you are in the first payroll period of a new year (01/2007) and you need to make adjustments to the last payroll period of the previous year (26/2006), transaction **PAUY** with subtype **YANA** allows you to adjust the payroll results for payroll period 26/2006. Payroll tables **RT**, **CRT**, and **TCRT** will be updated with the amounts as entered with infotype **0221** (the figures can be positive or negative).

Subtype YAWA: With Tax Calculations

The philosophy here is similar to **YANA** and you can extend the same example; however, in this case, the tax calculations are performed. This is why the net amount cannot be negative. Because the taxes will be calculated, and because you will be running the third-party remittance process and taxes will get remitted to tax authorities, the employee typically needs to write a check to pay the taxes.

After selecting an appropriate subtype (depending upon the scenario), and after creating infotype **0221**, it is finally time to run payroll.

7.3.2 Running Payroll

After entering the data in infotype **0221** using the **Enter Data** button, the next step is to run the off-cycle payroll. The following lists some of the unique features of an off-cycle payroll Type **C** run:

▶ In Chapter 4, you saw subschema **UMC0** and the function **P0221** associated with the subschema. This subschema and function handle the processing of infotype **0221** when you run an off-cycle payroll. Also, this subschema is presented in Appendix A so that all subschemas and rules are visible.

▶ In Figure 7.19, you can see the adjustment date. You should use the date in this field that needs to fall in the tax year. For example, if the payroll end-date for the last payroll in 2006 is 12/26/2006, then this adjustment date should be equal to 12/31/2006.

▶ Wage type **/5U9** is generated as a result of the infotype **0221** off-cycle payroll. You need to plan a strategy around this wage type since this wage type translates to giving money to or recovering money from an employee. Also, the GL posting accounts for this wage type need to be planned properly so any receivables from the employee can be tracked and reconciled. Figure 7.22 shows the wage type **/5U9** in the payroll results. The negative amount for **/5U9** translates to the employee giving money back. The **/5U9** amount of $2,050 is calculated from $2,500 minus the total EE taxes of $450. Since the taxes were already remitted, the employee needs to reimburse the company a total of $2,050.

```
Table RT - Results Table (Collapsed Display)

A Wage type        APC1C2C3ABKoReBTAwvTvn One amount/one number    Amount

* /101 Total gross                                              2,500.00-
* /102 401(k) Wage                                              2,500.00-
* /104 NQP Eligibl                                              2,500.00-
* /114 Base wage f                                              2,500.00-
* /401 TX Withhold  01                                            200.00-
* /403 TX EE Socia  01                                            150.00-
* /404 TX ER Socia  01                                            100.00-
* /405 TX EE Medic  01                                            100.00-
* /550 Statutory n                                              2,050.00-
* /560 Amount to b                                              2,050.00-
* /5U0 Tot EE tax                                                 450.00-
* /5U1 Tot ER tax                                                 100.00-
* /5U9 Non-auth.ma                                              2,050.00-
* /700 RE plus ER                                              2,500.00-
1 1110 Bonus        01                                          2,500.00-
```

Figure 7.22 Wage Type /5U9

In the payroll driver (**RPCALCU0**) screen (shown in Figure 7.23), you can see the three fields for **Off-cycle payroll**. You can learn more about these fields in SAP's standard documentation; however, for a year-end adjustment, you should use off-cycle payroll Type **C** (as noted in the first field) and the from adjustment date, which matches the date in the workbench. The middle field (between the type and date) is used to enter a number in case you are running multiple Type **C** payrolls in a single day. For example, you can have three or four different payrolls with numbers ranging from 1 through 4.

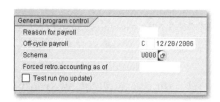

Figure 7.23 Payroll Driver- Off-Cycle Fields

Now it's time to verify the taxes for this off-cycle payroll run.

7.3.3 Verification

After you run the off-cycle payroll, the next thing you need to do is see the impact the adjustments had on taxes or taxable income. Although the payroll results tables (**RT**, **CRT**, and **TCRT**) show you the impact of the off-cycle run, the Tax Reporter is a better tool for verification. The W-2 audit report is one of the most useful reports from Tax Reporter for checking an adjustment's impact on the workbench. (Tax Reporter's functionality will be further discussed later in this chapter.) Figure 7.24 shows the W-2 audit report for the employee before running the off-cycle payroll from the previous section. Please note the wage base and tax amount columns. The amounts in these columns can be affected, depending upon the adjustment done to the taxable base and/or taxes.

----------Taxes----------				----------Earnings----------	
Jurisdiction	Wage Base	Tax Amount	Box	Description	Amount
FIT	14882.40	2177.08	7	Soc. Security Tips	0.00
Social Security	14882.40	922.71	8	Allocated Tips	0.00
Medicare	14882.40	215.79	9	Advance EIC	0.00
CA	14882.40	538.44	10	Dependent Care	0.00
NY	14882.40	125.09	11	Non-QualifiedPlans	0.00
			14	CA SDI Tax	94.24
			14	CA VDI Tax	94.24

Figure 7.24 W-2 Audit Report Prior to Adjustment Off-cycle Payroll

Figure 7.25 presents the W-2 audit report after the off-cycle payroll run. Notice that the taxes and the taxable base (as appropriate for tax authorities, depending upon processing class **71**) are reduced by the amounts entered through infotype **0221**.

----------Taxes----------		
Jurisdiction	Wage Base	Tax Amount
FIT	12382.40	1977.08
Social Security	14882.40	772.71
Medicare	14882.40	115.79
CA	14882.40	538.44
NY	12382.40	125.09

Figure 7.25 W-2 Audit Report After the Off-cycle Payroll

You will need to configure a suitable wage type for infotype **0221** with appropriate processing class **71** (tax classification), and then run the off-cycle payroll. Subsequently, you will need to run the W-2 audit report simulation again to see the impact. The IMG path to configure the wage types for infotype **0221** is **Payroll USA • Payroll Results Adjustment • Define Permissibility of wage types**. As discussed in Chapter 3, you can use transaction **SM31** and table **T512W** to check or maintain the processing class **71** value.

Your goal is to increase or decrease the taxable base and/or taxes, whichever the case may be. The W-2 audit report should show the appropriate impact on the amounts for the right tax authority.

Let us now find out how to run the W-2 audit report using the Tax Reporter.

7.4   Overview of Tax Reporter

Tax Reporter is a huge topic all by itself, and in SAP's world, there is plenty of information and documentation available on this topic. However, this section covers some of the commonly used US Tax reports and checks the usefulness besides filing with tax authorities. **PU19** is an easy transaction with which to start the Tax Reporter. Figure 7.26 shows the opening screen of **PU19** Tax Reporter. The Tax Reporter can be run in either test mode or production mode. Note that the W-2 audit report discussed earlier, which is used to verify the year-end adjustments, is normally run in test mode.

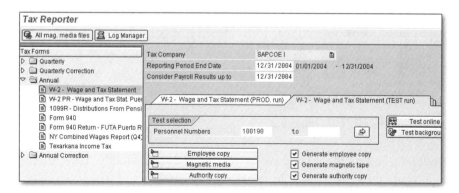

Figure 7.26 Tax Reporter

Before looking at the commonly used statutory tax reports, let's first learn about some of the necessary work for the Tax Reporter. The tasks listed in next section are not in any particular order, except for the fact that they should be completed prior to running the Tax Reporter.

7.4.1 Preparation Work

SAP recommends that you complete the following essential steps before running the annual Tax Reporter. You can run test runs at any time during the year; remember, however, that the results will be dependent on the payroll results as of that point. SAP's checklist includes the following items:

▸ Applying the latest support packs and Tax Update Bulletins (**TUBS**) for **BSI**

▸ Completing all payroll runs in case of final year-end run

▸ Clearing claims (see Chapter 8)

▸ Completing year-end adjustments using appropriate subtypes, as discussed earlier in this chapter

▸ Checking the configuration using the menu path **Utilities • Check Configuration**, as shown in Figure 7.27. This step helps you confirm that Tax Reporter is configured properly

▸ Running the Tax Reporter preparation step for employees transferred from non-SAP systems

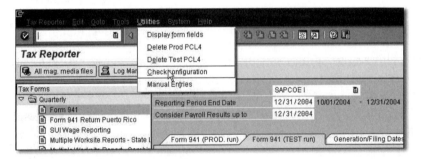

Figure 7.27 Checking Configuration

Now let's discuss the individual tax reports and their sample contents. Tax reports are typically divided by quarterly and annual submissions; let's start with quarterly reports.

7.4.2 Quarterly Reports

The most common quarterly reports are **Form 941** and State Unemployment Insurance (**SUI**). Later in Chapter 8, you'll learn about overpayments and claims, and you can use **Form 941** to check the impact of the claims clearing process for employees to ensure the correctness of tax results. Figure 7.28 shows **Form 941** for a single test employee.

Form **941** **Employer's Quarterly Federal Tax Return**

SAPCOE I 03/31/2004

94-1234588

469 Lincoln Street New York NY 08374

1	Number of employees			1	1.00
2	Total wages and tips, plus other compensation			2	6,318.00
3	Total income tax withheld from wages, tips, and sick pay			3	929.16
4	Adjustment of withheld income tax for preceding quarters of calendar year			4	
5	Adjusted total income tax (line 3 - line 4)			5	929.16
6	Taxable social security wages	6a	6,318.00X 12.4% (.124) =	6b	783.43
	Taxable social security tips	6c	0.00X 12.4% (.124) =	6d	
7	Taxable Medicare wages and tips	7a	6,318.00X 2.9% (.029) =	7b	183.22

Figure 7.28 Form 941 Output

So, how do you know if Form 941 has the correct output? After you run Form 941 in test mode, you should verify the figures for a few employees. You will be able to get the **QTD** results from payroll, or you can also run the payroll reconciliation report. For the example in Figure 7.28, refer to Figure 7.29 and check the total wages as well as total income tax withheld figures from the applicable wage types.

You can access the payroll reconciliation report, which is the most popular report for verification of tax results, through the menu path in payroll applications using **Payroll USA • Period-independent • Payroll Supplement • Payroll reconciliation report**. This report helps find differences between the actual payroll results and the Tax Reporter, as well as FI postings. This report is a great tool for catching any discrepancies, especially if an employee has retroactivity, adjustments, and in situations where users have missed posting any off-cycle runs to FI.

Table TCRT - Cumulated tax results

CalYr	CalNbr	CalTyp	Tax co.	TaxAu	Wage Type	Wage Type Text	Amount	From	To
2004	04	M	US01		/101	Total gross	842.40	04/01/2004	04/30/2004
2004	02	M	US01		/101	Total gross	2,808.00	02/01/2004	02/29/2004
2004	01	M	US01		/101	Total gross	3,510.00	01/01/2004	01/31/2004
2004	02	Q	US01		/101	Total gross	842.40	04/01/2004	06/30/2004
2004	01	Q	US01		/101	Total gross	6,318.00	01/01/2004	03/31/2004
2004	01	Y	US01		/101	Total gross	7,160.40	01/01/2004	12/31/2004
2004	04	M	US01	FED	/401	TX Withholding Tax	112.28	04/01/2004	04/30/2004
2004	02	M	US01	FED	/401	TX Withholding Tax	412.96	02/01/2004	02/29/2004
2004	01	M	US01	FED	/401	TX Withholding Tax	516.20	01/01/2004	01/31/2004
2004	02	Q	US01	FED	/401	TX Withholding Tax	112.28	04/01/2004	06/30/2004
2004	01	Q	US01	FED	/401	TX Withholding Tax	929.16	01/01/2004	03/31/2004
2004	01	Y	US01	FED	/401	TX Withholding Tax	1,041.44	01/01/2004	12/31/2004

Figure 7.29 Checking the QTD Cumulations

7.4.3 Annual Reports

The most commonly used annual report is the W-2. While Figure 7.30 shows a sample W-2, Figure 7.24 shows the W-2 Audit Report. The audit report is easy to read and quickly analyzed. If you are running tests and verifying figures, the audit report will be better than W-2's. In the case of W-2's, you need to know about the box numbers and what goes into each box of a W-2. The W-2 audit report is generated when you run W-2's.

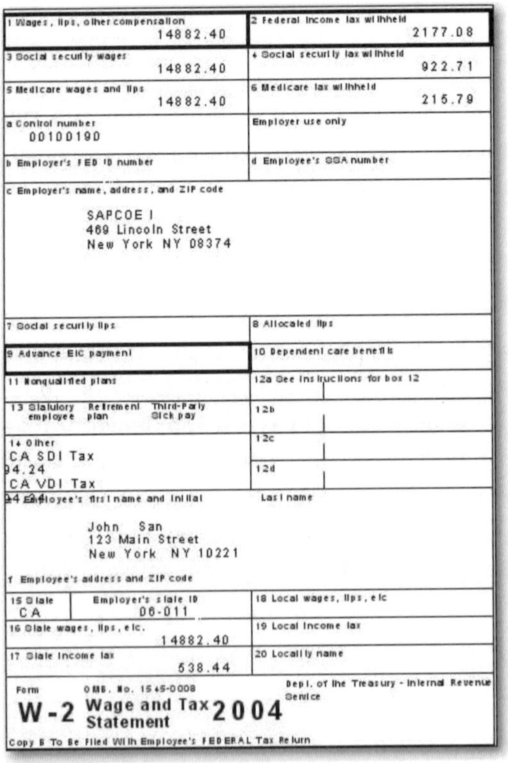
1 Wages, tips, other compensation: 14882.40
2 Federal income tax withheld: 2177.08
3 Social security wages: 14882.40
4 Social security tax withheld: 922.71
5 Medicare wages and tips: 14882.40
6 Medicare tax withheld: 215.79
a Control number: 00100190
Employer use only
b Employer's FED ID number
d Employee's SSA number
c Employer's name, address, and ZIP code
SAPCOE I
469 Lincoln Street
New York NY 08374
7 Social security tips
8 Allocated tips
9 Advance EIC payment
10 Dependent care benefits
11 Nonqualified plans
12a See instructions for box 12
13 Statutory employee / Retirement plan / Third-Party Sick pay
12b
14 Other
CA SDI Tax
94.24
CA VDI Tax
94.24
12c
12d
e Employee's first name and initial
Last name
John San
123 Main Street
New York NY 10221
f Employee's address and ZIP code
15 State: CA
Employer's state ID: 06-011
18 Local wages, tips, etc
16 State wages, tips, etc.: 14882.40
19 Local income tax
17 State income tax: 538.44
20 Locality name
Form W-2 Wage and Tax Statement 2004
OMB. No. 1545-0008
Dept. of the Treasury - Internal Revenue Service
Copy B To Be Filed With Employee's FEDERAL Tax Return

Figure 7.30 An Employee's W-2

7.5   Summary

Taxes—while not a very interesting topic—are a complex subject. However, the combination of SAP and **BSI** together create a logical and interesting subsystem for handling tax calculations in US Payroll. Earlier in this book, we talked about employee master data infotypes (Chapter 2), wage types (Chapter 3), and schemas (Chapter 4). The topic of tax calculation cuts across all of these areas. In addition, the discussion of tax types, tax combos, and tax models makes sure that the wage types and tax areas from employee master data infotypes help the system to arrive at the correct tax calculations for each employee. The year-end workbench is a powerful tool for users to adjust tax amounts and the taxable base to correct any erroneous situations during the year. You also learned how useful the Tax Reporter in SAP US Payroll is for handling net payroll; it is very useful when you need to complete the statutory and annual tax reporting for different tax authorities.

This Chapter discusses many advanced topics, which are useful during and after implementing SAP US Payroll. Although, it may not be practical for you to experience all the advanced topics in each of the SAP US Payroll installations, many of the topics will be of interest to you as you get more hands-on experience with SAP US Payroll.

8   Advanced Topics

In the world of US Payroll, it can be tough to choose a few advanced topics to cover within the constraints of a book. If you've worked on a US Payroll system implementation, you know from your own experience that there are many advanced topics to cover. I have chosen topics I'm sure you will quickly find practical in day-to-day operations, especially because they also tie in to the earlier discussions in this book. The first four topics presented here are purely operational, while the last provides you with useful implementation tips.

8.1   Overpayments and Claims Handling

An *overpayment claim* is an amount an employee owes an employer. The overpayment processing requires different treatment if the employee is still employed by the employer than if the employee has left the company. If the employee has left the company, the company may have to contact the employee and receive a personal check or payment from the employee. Such overpayments also have tax implications. Depending on the nature of the associated payments and taxes, some companies also use 1099's to adjust overpayments. Here are a few scenarios that might result in an overpayment in payroll:

▸ An employee leaves a company on a certain date, for example 12/15/2006. A data entry error is made and the termination is entered with a later effective date, for example 12/19/2006.

▸ Overtime hours are entered incorrectly for certain hourly employees and the mistake isn't realized until after a couple of payrolls have been run.

▶ A new rule is added in the payroll schema, resulting in incorrect calculations in payroll. As a result, excess payments are made to some employees.

These and similar situations will cause an overpayment. SAP US Payroll offers a very easy mechanism to identify claims in payroll. The diagram shown in Figure 8.1 shows the claims process from identification through planning to execution. You will learn the different steps of the process shown in Figure 8.1, and also about the claim that is generated in payroll. Immediately after you run the payroll, you need to identify the claims using SAP's standard claims report. Subsequently, you need a solution to clear the claims by adopting one of the three methods identified in the bubbles near the bottom of Figure 8.1.

Figure 8.1 Conceptual Process Flow for Clearing Claims

Let's start the discussion with why claims are generated in the first place.

8.1.1 Why Claims Are Generated

Most of the time, claims are generated as a result of retroactive calculations. Claims and retroactivity go together. To better understand the claim generation process, take the following example:

Scenario

Employee number 00099999 was paid up to period 09.2006. However, in period 10.2006, it is announced that the employee should have been terminated at the end of period 08.2006. The period begin and end dates are:

▶ Period 10: 04/17/2006 – 04/30/2006

▶ Period 09: 04/03/2006 – 04/16/2006

▶ Period 08: 03/20/2006 – 04/02/2006

The employee was terminated on 04/02/2006 and needs to get paid only up to the close of business on April 2, 2006.

User Actions

In this case, the user/HR department will typically carry out the following actions:

▸ The user retroactively creates a termination action for this employee.

▸ When the employee is processed in period 10.2006 (as per the period dates shown earlier), there will be a retroactive termination date of 04/02/2006.

What Happens in Payroll

Payroll will create a retroactive accounting back to the period 08.2006, since period 09.2006 should not have been paid to the employee. However, because the employee was paid during period 09.2006, the taxes and benefits were deducted from the pay, and remittances were sent to vendors. For this example, we'll use round figures (see Table 8.1) to keep the example simple; just remember that normally the figures will be more complex.

Wage Type in Payroll Result	Amount for Period 09.2006 in 09.2006	Amount for Period 09.2006 in 10.2006
1001 – Base Salary	$500	$0.00
/101 – Total Gross	$500	$0.00
/401 – TX NJ Withhold	$10	$10
/401 – TX FED Withhold	$30	$30
/403 – TX EE SS	$15	$15
/404 – TX ER SS	$15	$15
/405 – TX EE Med	$5	$5
/406 – TX ER Med	$5	$5
/560 – Amount Paid	$450	$450
/5PY – Good Money	$500	$500
/561 – Claim	No wage type	$60

Table 8.1 Claims Generation

Wage Type in Payroll Result	Amount for Period 09.2006 in 09.2006	Amount for Period 09.2006 in 10.2006
/563 – Claim from	No wage type	No wage type
/5U0 – Total EE taxes	$60	$60

Table 8.1 Claims Generation (cont.)

Table 8.1 presents the different wage types in each payroll period with retroactivity. Please refer to Figure 8.3 to see the output of the Claims Report. The EE taxes, and any EE pre-tax deductions, will impact the claims handling as discussed in the following sections.

8.1.2 Identifying Claims in Payroll

In Chapter 3, we reviewed wage type **/560** (Amount Paid). When **/560** is a negative number, it generates a claim and wage type **/561** in payroll. To identify claims in payroll, SAP suggests that you run a Claims Report each time you run payroll. The claims report (**RPCLMSU0**) is accessible from the Payroll menu, as discussed in the next section. It isn't enough to know that certain employees have claims, so let's examine a typical Claims Report for the information it provides.

Claims Report

Claims Reports use a payroll schema (**UCLM**) to run the report (**RPCLMSU0**). Behind the scene, the payroll driver runs schema **UCLM** in test mode. The menu path **Payroll USA • Subsequent activities • Period independent • Payroll supplement • Claims processing** leads you to run the Claims Report in US Payroll. Alternatively, if you have access to transaction **SE38,** you can directly run the **RPCLMSU0** program. Just like the normal payroll schema, you may need to modify the claims schema **UCLM** (as shown in Chapter 4) to create a custom claims schema. Figure 8.2 shows the Payroll USA IMG path for configuring the custom schema as well as linking the custom schema to the payroll driver. The three nodes under Claims Processing are simple and straight forward to configure.

When you run the Claims Report (shown in Figure 8.3), the output gives you a variety of information. The Claims Report shown in Figure 8.3 uses the same amounts shown in Table 8.1.

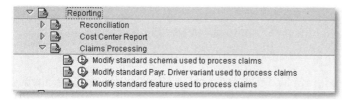

Figure 8.2 IMG for Claims Report

Claims Processing			
Pay Period – 10.2006 04/17/2006 – 04/30/2006		Run Date/Time: 12/10/2006 08:15:30	

00099999 Test Employee	SSN: 999-99-9999	Status: Withdrawn	
Pay Date: 05/14/2006	Pay Type:	Pay ID:	
Company Code: US01	Payroll Area: UW	Cost Center: 999999999	

Gross Claim Amount
Wagetype

/561 Claim		500.00
/5PY Good Money		500.00-

Taxable Repay Amounts

Wagetype	proc class 71	
1001 REGULAR SALARY	0 Regular Taxable Wages	500.00-

Tax Amounts

/401 TX Withholding Tax		10.00-	NJ
/401 TX Withholding Tax		30.00-	FED
/403 TX EE Social Security Tax		15.00-	FED
/404 TX ER Social Security Tax		15.00-	FED
/405 TX EE Medicare Tax		5.00-	FED
/406 TX ER Medicare Tax		5.00-	FED

Figure 8.3 Claims Report Output

SAP prints one page for each employee that has an outstanding claim in payroll. The report is divided into three or four different parts, as follows:

▸ Claim and Good Money

▸ Taxable salary or earnings

▸ Pre-tax deductions (if applicable)

▸ Overpaid taxes

You can use the contents of this report to decide the clearing process: once for payroll and a second time for accounts and taxes.

8.1.3   Strategy with Claims

After identifying a claim in payroll, the next step is figuring out what to do with it. Claims processing can go three ways, as discussed earlier with Figure 8.1:

▶ Forgive the claim and write it off.

▶ The employee reimburses the company in one lump-sum payment.

▶ The employee works out a payment plan to repay the debt.

Although the procedure may be slightly different, the end result is always the same: to clear the claim in payroll and set the accounts and tax records straight. Let's take the time to review the three different ways to handle a claim.

8.1.4 Clearing Claims: Payroll-Forgiven

If you have a claim that you want to forgive completely, the situation is the same as when the employee receives the payment, and hence no tax-related processing is necessary. You are just interested in clearing the claim from payroll and to post it correctly. The steps to follow are:

1. If the employee has left or was let go, set the payroll status infotype **0003** dates (run payroll up to date) correctly.

2. Make sure that you have used SAP's model wage type **MFT1** to create your custom wage type for claims clearing. For this example, use the **MFT1** wage type. You need to have as many custom wage types as you have earnings with variations in processing class **71** specifications.

   Earlier in the Claims Report, you saw that SAP prints processing class **71**-based earnings. For example, you may have wage type **1001** with processing class **71** specifications **0**, and you may have earning wage type **1002** with processing class **71** specifications **1**. If your Claims Report shows both of these wage types, then you need two copies of the **MFT1** wage type (let's call them **ZFT1** and **ZFT2**) with processing class **71** specifications **0** and **1**, respectively.

3. Create infotype **0267** with the correct wage type, as described in the previous step. The wage type's amount should be equal to the **/561** amount from the Claims Report. In this example, that amount is $500.00. The date for this infotype should be any date later than the date of the last payroll you ran.

4. Run off-cycle payroll Type **A** with the correct date (as noted in the previous step), and the schema you normally use for your payroll runs.

Because the employee already has the money, there is no impact on taxable wages or taxes, which means no subsequent actions are required.

8.1.5 Clearing Claims: Payroll-Not-Forgiven

If the employee is still actively employed by the company and a claim is generated, SAP's automatic process takes care of clearing and recovering money from future payrolls. For example, if the employee has a claim of $1,000 in payroll period 12/2006, and if the employee hasn't left the company, then $1,000 will be deducted in the next regular payroll (period 13/2006). However, if the employee has left the company or has been laid off, then you need to follow the process explained here. To clear the overpayment claim in payroll, you need to carry out an off-cycle payroll using infotype **0267**. The steps that follow apply to an employee who pays back the entire amount of the claim with one single payment.

1. Set the infotype **0003** dates (run payroll up to date) correctly, especially if employee has left or separated.

2. Make sure that you have used SAP's model wage type **MRP1** to create your custom wage type for claims clearing. For the purpose of this example, use **MRP1** wage type. You need to have as many custom wage types as you have earnings, with variations in processing class **71** specifications.

   Earlier in the Claims Report, you saw that SAP prints processing class **71**-based earnings. For example, you may have wage type **1001** with processing class **71** specifications **0**, and you may have earning wage type **1002** with processing class **71** specifications **1**. If the Claims Report shows both of these wage types, then you will need two copies of the **MRP1** wage type (let's call them **ZRP1** and **ZRP2**) with processing class **71** specifications **0** and **1**, respectively.

3. Create infotype **0267** with the correct wage type, as described in the previous step. The amount of the wage type should be equal to the **/561** amount from the Claims Report. In this example, that amount is $500.00. The date for this infotype should be any date later than the date of the last payroll run.

4. Run an off-cycle payroll Type **A** with the correct date (as noted in the previous step), and the schema you normally use for your payroll runs.

The payroll results table shows the following wage types and amounts:

- ▸ /101 $500.00
- ▸ /563 $500.00
- ▸ MRP1 $500.00

This process ensures that the payroll is clean of any claims, and that wage type **/563** clears the **/561** wage types. This payroll run has no accounts posting-related impact because there is no posting impact on expenses or balance sheet accounts. Now let's move to the slightly more difficult topic of clearing claims for accounting and taxes. It is important to keep accurate tax records, including W-2's.

8.1.6 Clearing Claims: Accounts Taxes (Employee Pays Single Check)

In Chapter 7, you learned about the year-end adjustment workbench. You use the workbench for the process of clearing claims as well. The following steps explain how a claim can be cleared for accounts and taxes if an employee makes a lump-sum payment to clear the claim:

1. Create infotype **0221** using the year-end workbench as shown in Figure 8.4.

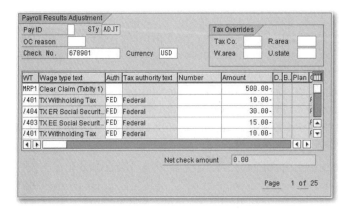

Figure 8.4 Infotype 0221 for Clearing Claims

2. Choose sub-type **ADJT**, without tax calculation.

3. Choose a date that is after the infotype **0267** date used in Section 8.1.2.

4. In this scenario, the employee is reimbursing the company for union dues owed. Some organizations can take a *foregiveness* stand and write-off the amount, but most prefer to get the money back. In Figure 8.4, refer to the field **Check No.**, which is used to capture the check received from the employee as payment for the debt.

5. Enter a negative amount for the claim using **MRP1** (copy with appropriate processing class **71**).

6. Note the negative amounts for taxes as well as deductions, which are taken from the Claims Report shown earlier.

7. Run a Type **C** off-cycle payroll from the workbench. Earlier, you saw how Type **A** was used to clear claims from payroll. Now you are using Type **C** for taxes and accounts posting.

8. The payroll results are presented in Table 8.2. Note wage type **/5U9** (Non-Authorized Manual Check). This is the wage type that will be used to post the employee payment to accounts. **/5U9** is the balance the employee pays back.

Wage Type in Payroll Result	Amount for Period 00.2006
MRP1 – Clear Claim-Base Salary	$500
/101 – Total Gross	$500
/401 – TX NJ Withhold	$10
/401 – TX FED Withhold	$30
/403 – TX EE SS	$15
/404 – TX ER SS	$15
/405 – TX EE Med	$5
/406 – TX ER Med	$5
/560 – Amount Paid	$440
/5U9 – Non-Auth Manual Check	$440
/5U0 – Total EE taxes	$60

Table 8.2 Payroll Results from ADJT Run

9. Run FI posting with the correct off-cycle date you used earlier for the infotype **0221** off-cycle payroll run.

10. Run AP posting with the correct off-cycle date you used earlier for the infotype **0221** off-cycle payroll run.

11. Process a W-2 with a test run for this employee to see the effect of this off-cycle run; ensure that the taxable base as well as the tax figures are correct.

The third method, presented next, shows how to set up a payment plan for the employee to repay a claim.

8.1.7 Clearing Claims: Accounts Taxes (Employee Pays by Payment Plan)

When the overpayment amount is too large, or if the employee cannot repay the debt in a lump-sum, some companies offer the employee an opportunity to repay the debt using installments or a payment plan. SAP provides model wage types to handle this situation. You will notice that wage types **MP10** and **MP11** are similar to the goal and deduction scenario we talked about in Chapter 3. Let's follow a similar step-by-step approach as we have earlier:

1. Create a copy of model wage type **MP10** for infotype **0014** permissible usage. (Appendix D lists this wage type.)

2. Create infotype **0014** in the employee's master data using this wage type and the amount the employee chooses as repayment per pay period.

3. Create a copy of model wage type **MP11** for infotype **0015** permissible usage. (Appendix D lists this wage type.)

4. Create infotype **0015** in the employee's master data using this wage type and the amount equal to the claim minus taxes (net check amount).

5. Process the employee through normal payroll and the claim payments will be taken out in the same manner as any other deduction.

The three different scenarios are complex and could be confusing. Table 8.3 recaps all of the steps discussed in the previous sections.

Claims Processing Step	How to Perform the step in SAP	Explanation
How to identify claims	Run the **RPCLMSU0** claims report using the **UCLM** claims schema.	Typically run after every payroll to verify any employees with claims. This step is done regardless of the strategy you adopt to clear the claim.
Payroll status infotype **0003** maintenance	Use transaction **PU03**.	If an employee has left or has been terminated, the payroll should be able to process this employee. Typically, the **Run Payroll Up to Date** needs to be changed.

Table 8.3 Recap of Claims Processing

Claims Processing Step	How to Perform the step in SAP	Explanation
How to clear claims	Create infotype **0267** with wage type **MRP1** so the amount equals the claims amount from the claims report. This step is carried out if the employee has left the company or if you want to clear the claim before the next regular payroll run.	This generates wage type **/563** in the payroll results table **RT** to clear claims. This step has no financial posting impact. This step will be carried out if the employee has left the organization or if you don't want to wait until the next regular payroll (if the employee is still with your organization). If you have a custom schema for regular payroll, you should use the same schema for this run as well.
Clearing claims for taxes and accounts by running off-cycle payroll Type **C**	Create infotype **0221** using the year-end workbench. Use wage types **MRP1** and **/4xx**. The payroll date should be after the earlier off-cycle type **A** run date.	Use the custom payroll schema you normally use for regular payroll. Verify the amounts as well as the sign (positive/negative) for the amounts using the claims report.
Postings	Run FI posting. Run AP posting.	Appropriately use infotype **0221**'s payroll run date and identifiers to post the payroll results.

Table 8.3 Recap of Claims Processing (cont.)

Let's now discuss the next advanced topic, accruals.

> **Note**
>
> It is strongly recommended that you read SAP's standard documentation at *http://help.sap.com* on month-end accruals before starting the next section. It is imperative that you understand SAP's solution on month-end accruals before continuing.

8.2 Accruals

Before starting the discussion on accruals, it might be helpful to explain what defines an *accrual*. Because it is an accounting term, many of the HR/Payroll readers might have difficulty understanding the concept of what an is accrual. To help, accruals are:

▸ Amounts owed by the company that are not yet recorded in the accounting books.

▸ Amounts that are spent in the period, but the cash transactions won't take place within that period.

The accruals method of accounting reports income when earned and expenses when incurred. The other method of accounting—cash-based accounting—reports income when received and expenses when paid. There are rules governing revenue recognition in the accrual method of accounting. (US Securities and Exchange Commission's (SEC) web site has useful resources on this topic. See *http://www.sec.gov*.)

Because accruals sound very accounting-oriented, you may wonder how they impact payroll. To answer the question, let's take an example from US Payroll, as described here:

You have a biweekly payroll and monthly accounting periods. As such, the *From* and *To* dates for the payroll periods and the *From* and *To* dates for the accounting periods will be different. It also means that a payroll period will cut across two different accounting periods. Without the month-end accrual functionality in SAP, payroll expenses would get posted to a period, but they would be split across two periods.

The next section shows you how to configure accruals, and then you'll learn more about the payroll process.

8.2.1 Accruals Configuration

The configuration required for accruals to work in payroll involves wage types and the accruals subschema. The configuration is not very complex for either subschemas or wage types. Let's first discuss the accruals subschema in US Payroll schema **U000**.

Subschema

Chapter 2 listed subschema **UAC0** in the main payroll schema **U000**. This schema, which is small in size, normally requires just a single change. This schema has a simple rule **UAC0** (same name as the schema itself) that controls the switch for calculating accruals. You need to set the switch to either ON or

OFF. Figure 8.5 shows the copy of the rule **UAC0** (it's copy **ZAC0**) in the schema run.

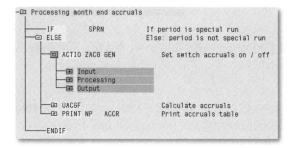

```
─□ Processing month end accruals

     ├───IF        SPRN         If period is special run
     ├─□ ELSE                   Else: period is not special run

         ├─□ ACTIO ZAC0 GEN        Set switch accruals on / off

             ├─□ Input
             ├─□ Processing
             ├─□ Output

         ├─□ UACGF                 Calculate accruals
         └─□ PRINT NP    ACCR      Print accruals table

     └───ENDIF
```

Figure 8.5 Rule UAC0 (ZAC0) to Turn ON the Accrual Switch

Wage Type

Configuration of wage types requires two major tasks: one related to the processing class and another for posting attributes. The processing class **79** value needs to be set up for the wage types that are processed in accruals. You can go through the IMG path (**Payroll USA • Month-end accruals • Basis for computations • Define wage types to be read**), or you can use table **T512W** with transaction **SM31** to maintain this processing class. Next, the finance posting attributes need to be configured, as shown in Figure 8.6. In addition to normal posting attributes, this figure shows that you need two additional entries for the accruals-related posting.

Wage Type	/404	TX ER Social Security Tax
End Date	12/31/9999	

Posting a Wage Type

N.	V	ProcessTyp	Sym...	AATyp	Description of the symbolic account
1	+	Normal processing	1040	C	ER taxes
4	-	Normal processing	10D5	F	Taxes to be paid
9	+	Month end accruals	1040	C	ER taxes
10	-	Month end accruals	10Z1	F	Accrual adjustment account 1

Figure 8.6 Posting Attributes for Wage Type

The example shown in Figure 8.6 shows posting attributes for wage type **/404**. Along with normal posting, this wage type also has an accrual posting, as shown on the third line. Posting attributes are configured using IMG path **Payroll USA • Posting to financial accounting • Activities in the HR-system**.

Dates

For a successful month-end accruals run, there are multiple dates in the configuration you need to understand, as defined here:

▸ **Payroll Period Dates**
The Begin Date for payroll period 13 is 05/30/2004, and the End Date is 06/12/2004.

▸ **Posting Dates**
Figure 8.7 presents the posting dates for the biweekly payroll period 13/2004 as 06/25/2004. Which means that the payroll has ended somewhere after the period end date of 06/12/2004. As a result, the postings need to be carried out by 06/25/2004.

DM...	Period Paramet...	Name per. parameter	Pay.yr.	Py.per	Date
00	04	Bi-weekly	2004	08	04/16/2004
00	04	Bi-weekly	2004	09	04/30/2004
00	04	Bi-weekly	2004	10	05/14/2004
00	04	Bi-weekly	2004	11	05/28/2004
00	04	Bi-weekly	2004	12	06/11/2004
00	04	Bi-weekly	2004	13	06/25/2004
00	04	Bi-weekly	2004	14	07/09/2004
00	04	Bi-weekly	2004	15	07/23/2004
00	04	Bi-weekly	2004	16	08/06/2004

Date Identifier 04 Posting Date

Figure 8.7 Posting Dates for the Payroll Periods

▸ **Closing Date**
Closing dates for the accounting periods are shown in Figure 8.8. Since biweekly period 13/2004 falls in accounting period 5, the closing date is 05/30/2004.

▸ **Latest Document Creation Dates**
In the payroll period example where the biweekly period is 13/2004 with a period end date of 06/12/2004, the pay date (or check date) will normally be after this date. Checks are mailed to employees or bank transfers are made to employee accounts. By then, you're at the *point of no-return* for payroll posting. The latest document creation date will be a later date in the payroll cycle, as shown in Figure 8.9.

After you have configured all of the dates, the accrual process in the payroll subschema creates the accruals table entries, as discussed in the next section.

Figure 8.8 Closing Dates for the Accounting Periods

Figure 8.9 Latest Document Creation Dates

8.2.2 Accruals Process and Posting

In the accruals subschema **UAC0**, the function **UACGF** carries out the accrual calculations and creates **ACCR** table in payroll results. The **ACCR** table holds the entries for accruals posting in finance. Figure 8.10 shows the **UACGF** function in the accruals subschema in payroll.

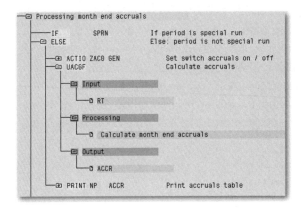

Figure 8.10 Accrual Function UACGF in Payroll

Let's look at the input **RT** table to the function, as shown in Figure 8.11; take note of wage type **2417** for ER dental insurance benefits. This wage type has an amount of $0.10 in the **RT** table. In Figure 8.9, you can see that the posting period 11 has ended on 05/28/2004, which means there are three more days in May that need to be adjusted for in the following period.

A	Wage type	APC1C2C3ABKoReBTAwvTvn	One	amount/one number	Amount
*	/101 Total gross				16.80
*	/102 401(k) Wage				16.80
*	/104 NQP Eligibl				16.80
*	/109 ER benefit				2.86
*	/114 Base wage f				16.80
*	/840 Diff.curr.f01		80.00-		
*	/BD2 EE Dep. GTL				18.60
*	/BE2 EE GTLI Cov				892.80
*	/BX7 BCY EE 402(01				421.90
*	2010 Std Medical01	B 02			0.09-
*	2017 Dental EE p01	B 01			0.07-
*	2041 Dep Care EE01	B 08	0.03		0.03-
*	2310 Std Medical				1.32
*	9C35 Pension Com		80.00		16.80
1	/001 Valuation b01		0.21		
1	/002 Valuation b01		0.21		
1	/BER Benefits ER01				1.35
1	/BT1 EE GTLI Tax01				0.02
1	1001 Hourly rate01		0.21		
1	1200 Regular wor01		0.21	80.00	16.80
1	2317 Dental Empl01	B 01			0.03
1	2410 Std Medical01	B 02			1.41
1	2417 Dental Prov01	B 01			0.10
*	/110 Net payment				0.19-
*	/550 Statutory n				16.80
*	/700 RE plus ER				19.66
*	/559 Payment	01			11.56

Figure 8.11 Input RT Table to UACGF Processing

The output from **UACGF** function processing is the accrual table **ACCR**, as shown in Figure 8.12. For the sample wage type **2417**, you will notice that the biweekly deduction of $0.10 in the **ACCR** table has increased to $0.13. Figures 8.13 and 8.14 explain the rationale behind the $0.13 amount.

```
Table ACCR

GrpRule  WType  Earn.date   Reversal dt  Number              Amount
*        2310   06/01/2004  07/01/2004              0.00                 1.72
1        1200   06/01/2004  07/01/2004            104.00                21.84
1        2317   06/01/2004  07/01/2004              0.00                 0.04
1        2410   06/01/2004  07/01/2004              0.00                 1.83
1        2417   06/01/2004  07/01/2004              0.00                 0.13
```

Figure 8.12 ACCR Table in Payroll Results

```
Analysis of payroll periods (04)14/2004
DateMo. 01
Payroll period from 06/13/2004 to 06/26/2004 with posting date 07/09/2004
Posting period for start date        : 200406
Posting period for end date          : 200406
Posting period for posting date      : 200407
Earliest end date for posting periods      : 06/30/2004
Last payroll period for  calculation 13 / 2004
Last LDCD for this period 06/25/2004
Accruals are calculated in this period
Calculation for future period (estimate)

PP CMod  Factor1       Factor2
01 A     1.00000000    0.00000000
01 K     1.00000000    0.00000000
01 S     1.00000000    0.00000000

Gr WTyp PP C1    BasNumber    BasAmount MD  Fator        EarningDate   Number     Amount
*  2310 00 0000       0.00         1.32 A   1.00000000   06/01/2004      0.00       1.32
*  2310 00 0000       0.00         1.32 A   0.00000000   06/01/2004      0.00       0.00
1  1001 01 0000       0.00         0.00 A   1.00000000   06/01/2004      0.00       0.00
1  1001 01 0000       0.00         0.00 A   0.00000000   06/01/2004      0.00       0.00
1  1200 01 0000      80.00        16.80 A   1.00000000   06/01/2004     80.00      16.80
1  1200 01 0000      80.00        16.80 A   0.00000000   06/01/2004      0.00       0.00
1  2317 01 0000       0.00         0.03 A   1.00000000   06/01/2004      0.00       0.03
1  2317 01 0000       0.00         0.03 A   0.00000000   06/01/2004      0.00       0.00
1  2410 01 0000       0.00         1.41 A   1.00000000   06/01/2004      0.00       1.41
1  2410 01 0000       0.00         1.41 A   0.00000000   06/01/2004      0.00       0.00
1  2417 01 0000       0.00         0.10 A   1.00000000   06/01/2004      0.00       0.10
1  2417 01 0000       0.00         0.10 A   0.00000000   06/01/2004      0.00       0.00
```

Figure 8.13 Analysis of First Period for Sample Wage Type 2417

Note that the posting date for payroll period 14 (see Figure 8.13) is 7/9/2004, and that the payroll period ending date is 6/26/2004. This creates a factor of 0.3 (see Figure 8.14) for the June-July overlap period. Figures 8.15 and 8.16 show the different payroll periods in August so you can see that the factor has changed since the number of days has changed because of the different posting dates. If you closely examine Figures 8.15 and 8.16, you will notice that the factor has changed to 0.7 for the sample wage type **2417**.

By now, you should have a better understanding of month-end accruals. The next section on third-party systems won't be as difficult as accruals!

```
Analysis of payroll periods (04)15/2004
DateMo. 01
Payroll period from 06/27/2004 to 07/10/2004 with posting date 07/23/2004
Posting period for start date          : 200406
Posting period for end date            : 200407
Posting period for posting date        : 200407
Earliest end date for posting periods     : 06/30/2004
Last payroll period for  calculation 13 / 2004
Last LDCD for this period 06/25/2004
Accruals are calculated in this period
Calculation for future period (estimate)

PP CMod  Factor1      Factor2
01 A     0.30000000   0.70000000
01 K     0.28571429   0.71428571
01 S     0.30000000   0.70000000

Gr WTyp PP C1    BasNumber    BasAmount MD Fator       EarningDate   Number      Amount
*  2310 00 0000       0.00         1.32 A  0.30000000  06/01/2004      0.00        0.40
1  1001 01 0000       0.00         0.00 A  0.30000000  06/01/2004      0.00        0.00
1  1200 01 0000      80.00        16.80 A  0.30000000  06/01/2004     24.00        5.04
1  2317 01 0000       0.00         0.03 A  0.30000000  06/01/2004      0.00        0.01
1  2410 01 0000       0.00         1.41 A  0.30000000  06/01/2004      0.00        0.42
1  2417 01 0000       0.00         0.10 A  0.30000000  06/01/2004      0.00        0.03

Analysis of payroll periods (04)16/2004
DateMo. 01
Payroll period from 07/11/2004 to 07/24/2004 with posting date 08/06/2004
Posting period for start date          : 200407
Posting period for end date            : 200407
Posting period for posting date        : 200408
Earliest end date for posting periods     : 07/30/2004
Last payroll period for  calculation 15 / 2004
Last LDCD for this period 07/23/2004
```

Figure 8.14 Analysis of the Second Payroll Period for Sample Wage Type 2417

```
Analysis of payroll periods (04)18/2004
DateMo. 01
Payroll period from 08/08/2004 to 08/21/2004 with posting date 09/03/2004
Posting period for start date          : 200408
Posting period for end date            : 200408
Posting period for posting date        : 200409
Earliest end date for posting periods     : 08/30/2004
Last payroll period for  calculation 17 / 2004
Last LDCD for this period 08/20/2004
Accruals are calculated in this period
Calculation for future period (estimate)

PP CMod  Factor1      Factor2
01 A     1.00000000   0.00000000
01 K     1.00000000   0.00000000
01 S     1.00000000   0.00000000

Gr WTyp PP C1    BasNumber    BasAmount MD Fator       EarningDate   Number      Amount
*  2310 00 0000       0.00         1.32 A  1.00000000  08/01/2004      0.00        1.32
*  2310 00 0000       0.00         1.32 A  0.00000000  08/01/2004      0.00        0.00
1  1001 01 0000       0.00         0.00 A  1.00000000  08/01/2004      0.00        0.00
1  1001 01 0000       0.00         0.00 A  0.00000000  08/01/2004      0.00        0.00
1  1200 01 0000      80.00        16.80 A  1.00000000  08/01/2004     80.00       16.80
1  1200 01 0000      80.00        16.80 A  0.00000000  08/01/2004      0.00        0.00
1  2317 01 0000       0.00         0.03 A  1.00000000  08/01/2004      0.00        0.03
1  2317 01 0000       0.00         0.03 A  0.00000000  08/01/2004      0.00        0.00
1  2410 01 0000       0.00         1.41 A  1.00000000  08/01/2004      0.00        1.41
1  2410 01 0000       0.00         1.41 A  0.00000000  08/01/2004      0.00        0.00
1  2417 01 0000       0.00         0.10 A  1.00000000  08/01/2004      0.00        0.10
1  2417 01 0000       0.00         0.10 A  0.00000000  08/01/2004      0.00        0.00
```

Figure 8.15 Analysis of Another First Period for Sample Wage Type 2417

```
Analysis of payroll periods (04)19/2004
DateMo. 01
Payroll period from 08/22/2004 to 09/04/2004 with posting date 09/17/2004
Posting period for start date      : 200408
Posting period for end date        : 200409
Posting period for posting date    : 200409
Earliest end date for posting periods      : 08/30/2004
Last payroll period for  calculation 17 / 2004
Last LDCD for this period 08/20/2004
Accruals are calculated in this period
Calculation for future period (estimate)

PP CMod Factor1      Factor2
01 A      0.70000000  0.30000000
01 K      0.71428571  0.28571429
01 S      0.70000000  0.30000000

Gr WTyp PP C1    BasNumber    BasAmount MD Fator       EarningDate    Number      Amount
*  2310 00 0000        0.00         1.32 A  0.70000000  08/01/2004      0.00        0.92
1  1001 01 0000        0.00         0.00 A  0.70000000  08/01/2004      0.00        0.00
1  1200 01 0000       80.00        16.80 A  0.70000000  08/01/2004     56.00       11.76
1  2317 01 0000        0.00         0.03 A  0.70000000  08/01/2004      0.00        0.02
1  2410 01 0000        0.00         1.41 A  0.70000000  08/01/2004      0.00        0.99
1  2417 01 0000        0.00         0.10 A  0.70000000  08/01/2004      0.00        0.07
```

Figure 8.16 Analysis of Another Second Period for Sample Wage Type 2417

8.3   Interfacing with Third-Party Payroll Systems— Gross to Net

Before you start learning about the technicalities of interfacing with third-party payroll systems, you might be wondering why there is a need for a third-party payroll system in the first place. There could be many reasons:

▶ Payroll departments want to outsource net processing and check-printing to a third-party. Net processing and check printing involves many logistics, such as maintaining checks, keeping a special printer with secure signature printing, and so on. You then also need to sort, fold, and mail the paychecks. Most payroll departments want to avoid these activities and focus on mainstream payroll activities.

▶ Time clock systems are managed by third-party software.

▶ The economics and cost of running net payroll in-house vs. outsourcing has a significant cost advantage for the company.

▶ Tax processing, tax reports filing, and annual W-2 processing are outsourced; as a result, the net payroll process is outsourced.

▶ In some cases, implementations also use the SAP HR as a system to maintain employee data and run the full payroll in a third-party system.

▶ The implementation team decides to run time evaluation using time clocks in SAP and the results are sent to the third-party payroll system.

235

As a result, gross payroll is run in SAP Payroll and net payroll is run in another system. In some cases, SAP HR is used as the employee master data system and both gross and net payrolls are run in third-party payroll systems. SAP US Payroll has a comprehensive list of features in the *Outsourcing* menu, as shown in Figure 8.17. If you are not familiar with SAP's definitions of gross and net payroll, they are as follows:

▶ **Gross Payroll**

Gross payroll processes the employee master data from the SAP PA module and generates wage types and amounts to be used by the net payroll component. Alternatively, the wage types and amounts are exported to a third-party payroll system for net calculation. Pre-tax deductions and earnings are processed within the gross payroll.

▶ **Net Payroll**

Net payroll processes taxes, post-tax deductions, benefits, and garnishments. The net payroll process uses wage types that were calculated and generated in the gross payroll process. Net payroll creates payroll clusters that are used for all downstream processes, such as account postings, third-party remittance, and statutory tax reporting.

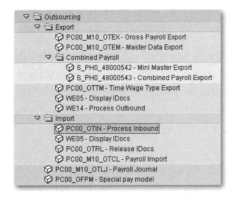

Figure 8.17 Available Outsourcing Functionality in SAP Payroll

Now let's look at an example where we will maintain HR/Employee master data and run gross payroll in SAP, and then outsource net payroll to a third-party system. The steps to follow for this example are:

1. Configure the feature **OTVSN** in Payroll by following the IMG menu path **Payroll USA • Payroll Outsourcing • Configure payroll outsourcing features**. This feature makes a decision that you are going to export gross payroll from SAP to an outside payroll system.

2. Run the payroll using schema **U200** (or an appropriate copy of the schema). Figure 8.18 shows the **U200** schema. Notice that many subschemas are different from what you saw earlier in the standard **U000** payroll schema.

> **Note**
>
> If you will be exporting gross payroll to a third-party for net payroll processing, you are encouraged to learn more about the **U200** subschema.

```
Edit Schema: U200
```

Line	Func.	Par1	Par2	Par3	Par4	D	Text
000010	COPY	UIN0					Initialization of payroll
000020	COPY	U2BD					Basic data
000030	COPY	UPR0					Read previous result of current period
000040	COPY	ULR0					Import previous payroll results
000050	COPY	U2NP					Import previous result of current period
000060	COPY	UMO0					Determine payroll modifiers
000070	COPY	UT00					Gross remuneration
000080	COPY	UREI				*	Travel expense
000090	BLOCK	BEG					Gross cumulation processing
000100	IF		NAMC				else if non-authorized manual check
000110	COPY	U2MC					Process add. payments and deductions
000120	ELSE						Proration and cumulation gross
000130	COPY	U2AP					if non-authorized manual check
000140	COPY	UAL0					Process non-authorized manual check
000150	COPY	UTBS					Save tables for iteration
000160	LPBEG						Begin of iteration
000170	COPY	UTBL					Load saved tables
000180	COPY	UDD0					Process deductions, Benefits
000190	COPY	U2TX					Fill US Tax Tables
000200	COPY	U2NA					Calculate net
000210	LPEND						End of iteration
000220	ENDIF						to: if non-authorized manual check
000230	BLOCK	END					
000240	COPY	XRR0					Retroactive accounting

Figure 8.18 U200 Schema for Exporting Gross Payroll

3. From Figure 8.17, and using the menu path, run the gross payroll export process. Figure 8.19 shows the selection screen for the gross payroll export process.

4. When you run this process, SAP generates the payroll results tables, which are different than the normal **U000** schema. Figure 8.20 shows the payroll results table when you run the **U200** schema payroll. The **GRT** table is used by the export program to send out the payroll results.

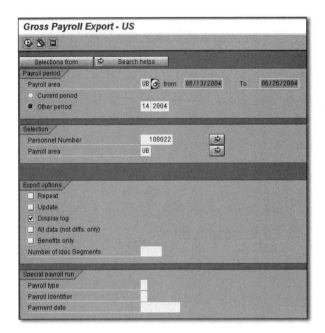

Figure 8.19 Gross Payroll Export Process

Name	Name	Nu...
WPBP	Work Center/Basic Pay	1
CRT	Cumulative Results Table	278
BT	Payment Information	1
V0	Variable Assignment	9
GRT	Output Table from Gross Part	29
BENTAB	Benefits	1
VERSION	Information on Creation	1
PCL2	Update information PCL2	1
VERSC	Payroll Status Information	1
TAX	Employee tax details	2
TAXR	Residence and unemployment tax details	4
TAXPR	Tax proration table	1
TCRT	Cumulated tax results	606
NAME	Name of Employee	1
ADR	Address	1
PERM	Personal Characteristics	1
MODIF	HR-PAY-99: Modifiers	1

Mr. Andrew Robert / Seq.nr. 00043 (08/08/2004 - 08/21/2004)

Figure 8.20 Payroll Results Tables with U200 Schema

5. Figure 8.21 shows the **GRT** table as generated by the export program with wage types and amounts.

6. After the exported files are sent to the third-party payroll provider, the provider will run the required net payroll and return the results. The menu in Figure 8.17 shows the Import menu for taking back the files.

GRT - Export

ESG/PCR	WT	WC	C	C	C	ALP	C1	BT	AB	VBTYP	VOZNR	Unit	Rate	Number of	Amount	Currency	Currency
*	/101	00	00	00	00	00	0000	00	00		00		+000000000000000	+000000000000000	+000000000001680		
*	2010	01	00	00	00	00	0000	00	00	B	02		+000000000000000	+000000000000000	-000000000000009		
*	2017	01	00	00	00	00	0000	00	00	B	01		+000000000000000	+000000000000000	-000000000000007		
*	2041	01	00	00	00	00	0000	00	00	B	08		+000000000000004	+000000000000000	-000000000000004		
*	2310	00	00	00	00	00	0000	00	00		00		+000000000000000	+000000000000000	+000000000000132		
*	9C35	00	00	00	00	00	0000	00	00		00		+000000000000000	+000000000000000	+000000000001680		
1	/BT1	01	00	00	00	00	0000	00	00		00		+000000000000000	+000000000000000	+000000000000002		
1	1001	01	00	00	00	00	0000	00	00		00		+000000000000021	+000000000000000	+000000000000000		
1	1200	01	00	00	00	00	0000	00	00		00		+000000000000021	+000000000000000	+000000000001680		
1	2317	01	00	00	00	00	0000	00	00	B	01		+000000000000000	+000000000000000	+000000000000003		
1	2410	01	00	00	00	00	0000	00	00	B	02		+000000000000000	+000000000000000	+000000000000141		
1	2417	01	00	00	00	00	0000	00	00	B	01		+000000000000000	+000000000000000	+000000000000010		

Figure 8.21 GRT Table in the Payroll Export Process

7. SAP provides schema **U250** (shown in Figure 8.22) for importing the results back from a third-party provider. When you use the menu option **Payroll USA • Outsourcing • Import • Payroll Import**, you will need to use schema **U250** with the payroll driver. Please note that schema **U250** uses tables **T558x**, which you'll learn more about later in this chapter. These tables are used when you want to achieve a mid-year go-live for the US Payroll. You are encouraged to learn more about this schema, especially if you decide to use it for outsourcing your payroll.

Edit Schema: U250

Line	Func.	Par1	Par2	Par3	Par4	D	Text
000050	UPD	YES					Update database (YES/NO)
000060	OPT	INFT					Read used infotypes only
000070	OPT	TIME					Import all time infotypes
000080	IF		ACT				Current Periods Only
000090	COPY	UBD0					Process basic data
000100	IMPRT		0				Import old results for retro's
000110	IMPRT		N				Import current payroll result
000120	RFRSH		RT				Clear RT in case of rerun
000130	RFRSH		CRT				Clear CRT in case of rerun
000140	UFRSH		TCRT				Clear TCRT in case of reun
000150	RFRSH		IT				Delete IT after processing basic data
000160	PITAB	D	AIT				Delete AIT after processing basic data
000170	PITAB	D	CORT				Delete CORT after processing basic data
000180	TRANS	558D					Fill IT from T558B/t558d - Net
000190	PGRT	X25A	GEN	NOAB			Save GRT in AIT
000200	PIT	X252	GEN	NOAB			Move NUM/RTE from GRT to RT
000210	PIT	X250	GEN	NOAB			Generate Import Differences
000220	PITAB	D	AIT				Clear AIT
000230	PRT	X25B	GEN	NOAB			Move RT to AIT
000240	PRINT	NP	AIT				Print alternate IT
000250	PRINT	NP	GRT				Print GRT
000260	PGRT	X260	GEN	NOAB			Save in RT missing GRT's
000270	RFRSH		IT				Delete IT after processing net pay data
000280	TRANS	558B	OUTS				Fill IT from T558B/t558e - Tax

Figure 8.22 Schema U250 for Importing Results Back to SAP

8. For the same employee shown earlier in Figure 8.20, the payroll results will now look normal, as shown in Figure 8.23. The schema **U250** creates the result tables by taking the input from the third-party provider.

Name	Name	Nu...
WPBP	Work Center/Basic Pay	1
RT	Results Table	12
RT_	Results Table (Collapsed Display)	12
CRT	Cumulative Results Table	11
BT	Payment Information	1
V0	Variable Assignment	9
GRT	Output Table from Gross Part	29
BENTAB	Benefits	1
VERSION	Information on Creation	1
PCL2	Update information PCL2	1
VERSC	Payroll Status Information	1
TAX	Employee tax details	2
TAXR	Residence and unemployment tax details	4
TAXPR	Tax proration table	1
TCRT	Cumulated tax results	11
NAME	Name of Employee	1
ADR	Address	1
PERM	Personal Characteristics	1
MODIF	HR-PAY-99: Modifiers	1

Mr. Andrew Robert / Seq.nr. 00043 (08/08/2004 - 08/21/2004)

Figure 8.23 Post Import Payroll Result tables

Subsequently, you will do the accounts posting or any other accounts payable posting as necessary to complete your payroll cycle. Earlier in the book, you learned about the benefits and garnishments integration with US Payroll. However, we didn't cover the remittance of the deductions to vendors, which is the subject of the next section.

8.4 Third-Party Remittance (Accounts Payable Processing)

Third-party processing in SAP US Payroll refers to the payments made to external vendors. Vendors in third-party processing normally fall in one of the three types:

▶ Taxes

▶ Benefits

▶ Garnishments

In some cases, you may have miscellaneous vendors; however, the majority of your third-party processing will be for the three categories explained here.

We have seen in earlier chapters that benefits, taxes, and garnishments are deducted during the payroll and various wage types are generated during the payroll schema run. We have also seen that these wage types reside in employees' payroll result tables such as **RT** and **CRT**. To be able to send the appropriate money and data to vendors, you need to configure and process these wage types with the right attributes. Figure 8.24 shows a simple conceptual representation of the third-party remittance processing using payroll results and vendor details.

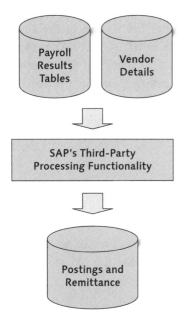

Figure 8.24 Simple Concept of Third-Party Processing

Let's start our discussion with the required configuration.

8.4.1   Required Configuration

The configuration for third-party remittance processing mainly falls into three areas: wage types, vendors, and HR payees. After you configure the wage types correctly and link them to the HR Payee (which are the vendors), you will realize that the process is not that complex.

Wage Types

Wage type configuration for third-party processing falls into two broad areas:

▶ **Processing Classes**

Processing classes **73** and **78** control the third-party remittance and the sign assignment. With deductions, you will typically need to reverse the signs before sending out the money to the vendor. Appendix E lists these processing classes with applicable specifications. You can get to this configuration either from the third-party remittance IMG path **Payroll USA · Third-party Remittance · Wage Type maintenance**, or by using the **T512W** table maintenance dialog box, shown in Chapter 3.

▶ **Posting Attributes**

The GL accounts postings for these wage types need to be in the right order. The IMG menu **Posting to FI · Activities in HR System · Wage type maintenance**, needs to assign the wage type to the right GL account because the corresponding vendor entry will emerge from the third-party remittance posting. To better understand the posting attributes, we'll use a wage type with the associated posting attributes in the next section.

HR Payee Assignment

The wage types to be remitted fall into three broad HR Payee categories: benefits, taxes, and garnishments. Wage type **/403** is used to check the HR payee assignment configuration. The menu path in IMG **Payroll USA · Third-party remittance · HR Payee maintenance · Set up HR Payees for tax remittance** leads us to Figure 8.25. In this figure, you can see that the IRS vendor is linked to wage type **/403** for remittance.

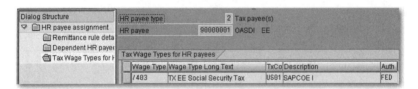

Figure 8.25 Linking Wage Type /403 with the IRS Vendor

To better understand the accounting process, wage type **/403** is discussed further in the next section for clearing an account.

8.4.2 Financial Account Management

For this example, we'll use a sample wage type **/403** to walk through the accounts posting steps:

1. Let's use a wage type from the payroll results, as shown in Figure 8.26.
   Wage type **/403** has an amount of $101.60 that needs to be sent to the IRS
   vendor.

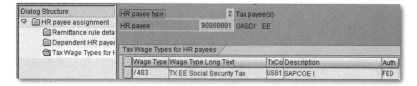

Figure 8.26 Wage Types for Remittance

2. Figure 8.27 shows the symbolic account assignment and the GL account to
   symbolic account assignment. As such, the wage type is posted to the GL
   account 176220.

```
* /401 TX Withhold  01                                    247.12
* /401 TX Withhold  02                                     45.78
* /403 TX EE Socia   01                                    101.60
* /404 TX ER Socia   01                                    101.60
* /405 TX EE Medic   01                                     23.76
* /406 TX ER Medic   01                                     23.76
* /420 TX EE Unemp   02                                      0.33
```

Figure 8.27 GL Account Assignment

3. When the FI posting is run, posting entries are created for wage type **/403**,
   as shown in Figure 8.28.

Wage Type	/403	TX EE Social Security Tax			
End Date	12/31/9999				

Posting a Wage Type						
N.	V	ProcessTyp	SymAc	AATyp	Description of the symbolic account	Ign.CA
1	-	Normal processing	10D3	F	FICA taxes	☐

10D3		176220	
10D3	1	176220	
10D3	2	176220	
10D4		176310	
10D4	1	176310	
10D4	2	176310	
10D5		176210	

Figure 8.28 FI Posting for Remittance Wage Type

4. When the third-party posting run is carried out (you will learn the detailed
   steps in the next section), the vendor posting is also carried out. Figure
   8.29 shows that the IRS HR Payee is linked to vendor **200025** (this configuration is in the same step as in the discussion for Figure 8.25).

HR payee type 2 Tax payee(s)

HR payee assignment

HR payee	Text	Co...	Vendor	Name
70000000	CCRA	4500	71000	Canada Customs & Revenue Ag
70000001	Revenue Quebec	4500	71100	Revenue Quebec
70000200	Ontario Health Tax	4500	71200	Health Tax - Ontario
70000201	Quebec Health Tax	4500	71201	Health Tax - Quebec
70000202	Nfld Hlth/Post Sec Ed Tax	4500	71202	Health Tax - Newfoundland
70000203	Man Hlth/Post Sec Ed Tax	4500	71203	Health Tax - Manitoba
90000000	FIT		200025	Internal revenue service
90000001	OASDI EE		200025	Internal revenue service
90000002	OASDI ER		200025	Internal revenue service

Figure 8.29 HR Payee-Vendor Linkage

5. Vendor 200025 gets an entry for wage types such as **/403**, which are linked to the corresponding HR Payee. Figure 8.30 shows the posting to the vendor account. Note that the amounts $584.60 and $584.62 are a combination of several federal taxes because these taxes need to be remitted to the same IRS vendor. From the payroll results, add wage types **/401, /403, /404, /405**, and **/406** for IRS remittances. The account 176880 will be hit with entries when accounts payable creates payments for these vendors.

		Ven	200025	Internal revenue ser		584.62
		Ven	200025	Internal revenue ser		584.60
		Ven	200016	State of California		369.28
		Ven	200016	State of California		80.99
	S	G/L	176880	HR Clearing Account	2,123.08	
2000	S	G/L	176880	HR Clearing Account	80.99	

Figure 8.30 Vendor Posting from Third-Party Remittance

Now let's get back to the steps to run the third-party remittance process.

8.4.3 Running a Third-Party Process

Unlike the finance posting, which is just a single-step process, third-party remittance requires multiple steps. SAP's standard documentation explains these steps well so the discussion here will be kept short. Figure 8.31 shows the menu path and the various steps that are carried out for the third-party remittance process.

- **Step 1: Evaluation Run Using U500 Schema**
  This schema collects wage types from the payroll results, which have processing classes **73** and **78** configured for third-party remittance. Figure 8.32 shows that the **REMIT** function uses these two processing classes and also generates tables (**C51R6**), which are used for subsequent steps.

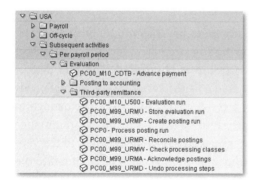

Figure 8.31 Third-Party Remittance Process

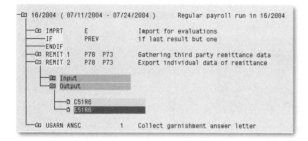

Figure 8.32 Schema U500 Evaluation Run

▶ **Step 2: Storing the Evaluation Run**

This step combines two files (shown in Figure 8.33) and aside from being a prescribed technical step, it has no functional significance. The filenames are generated by SAP in an earlier step and are of a type called **TemSe**. The term *TemSe* comes from Temporary Sequential Data. Spool files (print files) in SAP are also of type TemSe. You can use transactions **SP11** and **SP12** to look at these files.

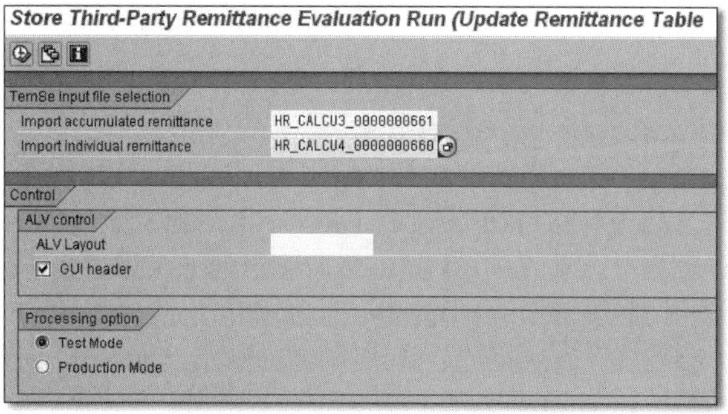

Figure 8.33 Storing an Evaluation Run

▶ **Step 3: Third-party Posting Run**

In this step, you will create the accounts payable/vendor posting documents based on files generated during an earlier step. Refer to Figure 8.34 to see how the due date for processing is controlled. The due date is important because the remittance rule tells the system if the money needs to be sent immediately or within a certain timeframe after the deduction has been made (after running the payroll). Every third-party remittance will have a due date by which the money needs to be remitted to the vendor. For example, with garnishments, the money has to be remitted to the appropriate authorities immediately. In Figure 8.34, all remittances whose due date is less than or equal to 12/27/2006 will be picked up in the run.

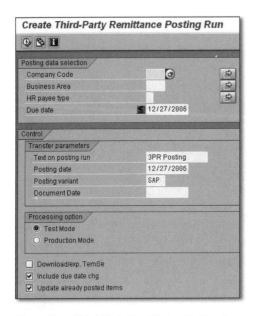

Figure 8.34 Third-Party Remittance Posting Run

▶ **Step 4: Release and Post the Documents to Create Accounting Entries in Vendor Accounts and Appropriate GL Accounts**

The additional menu options from Figure 8.31 (such as the reconciliation and acknowledgment runs) are not mandatory. You can use the reconciliation run if the HR/Payroll users want to know if accounts payable users have actually paid vendors. The acknowledgment program is applicable if your SAP Payroll and Financials systems are in separate environments and perhaps your financials are not running on SAP.

Let's now move on to the last section, where we'll review implementation tips for SAP US Payroll projects. The section is mostly about tips with some exceptions of technical discussion around mid-year go-live of payroll.

8.5 Implementation Tips for US Payroll

The final topic of this book discusses some practical implementation tips. The complexity and the timing of the configuration can be impacted by a variety of factors, as discussed in this section. While you are busy with the configuration and go-live activities, don't lose sight of the post-go-live activities, many of which are discussed in the sections that follow. Many project teams get caught up in a whirlwind of activities soon after the first payroll, and that can cause a backlog in areas like claims processing, financial postings, and third-party postings.

8.5.1 Mid-Year Go-Live

Most US Payroll projects plan to go-live with the first payroll of a new year. The primary reason for this is taxes and year-end financials. After completing W-2s and other tax processing tasks in the legacy system, users typically want to start fresh in SAP, beginning the new year with a new system. This also avoids a mid-year data conversion for payroll cumulated results. However, in some projects, due to other factors, the payroll go-live date can land in the middle of a pay period. The features and data conversion aspects for each scenario are explained in the following sections.

New Year Go-Live

When your SAP US Payroll implementation is going live for the first payroll run of a new year, follow this simple checklist:

▶ Correct data conversion for employee master data as of the go-live date.

▶ Flexible spending account balances for the previous year.

▶ Benefits enrollment data (if the organization has benefits enrollment at year-end in November and December).

▶ Planning and strategy around retroactivity prior to go-live. For example, how will you manage missing overtime for a prior payroll before go-live? You may need to employ manual procedures using infotypes **0015**, **2010**, etc., to manage these cases.

Middle of Year Go-Live

The middle of year go-live has two possibilities: the start of a quarter or the middle of a quarter. Depending on the option you choose, you might have flexibility to load the **MTD** and **QTD** amounts for the wage types. If you follow the IMG menu path **Payroll USA · Transfer Legacy Data**, you will see the options shown in Figure 8.35.

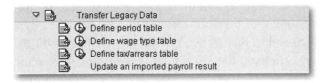

Figure 8.35 Configuration of Tables for Legacy Payroll Data Load

You will need to configure the three tables shown by the three options, as detailed in the following steps:

1. In this step, you prepare the pay period table **T588B** to receive the employee data that is transferred into US Payroll using schema **ULK9**. The schema ignores the period specified in the payroll driver screen and takes the periods from the pay period table **T558B**.

2. However, your pay period table in the SAP system should have all of the periods already configured that you are trying to load.

3. All regular and any bonus or off-cycle runs need to be loaded using this table.

4. Remember that you have to write your own custom data conversion programs to load the tables explained here.

5. In this step, table **T558C** needs to be populated with wage types.

6. Corresponding to each payroll period from table **T558B**, you need to create wage types in table **T558C**. The personnel number will match the two tables together.

7. SAP provides a third table, **T5U8C**, which you use to load the tax and arrears data.

8. In table **T5U8C**, you can use the record type to indicate **T** for tax or **A** for arrears. A field **TaxAu** is provided in the table for tax authority. Once again, the personnel number and payroll period will match the records with other tables.

Once the tables are configured, use schema **ULK9** (by now, I'm sure you have kept track of all of the different schemas used in this book: **U000**, **U200**,

U250, and now **ULK9**) to load these tables into SAP's results tables. Using the standard payroll driver **RPCALCU0** and schema **ULK9** run the payroll.

8.5.2 Volumes and Complexity

If you look at wage types, schemas, and rules, the complexity for payroll is almost the same for a 5,000-employee payroll as it is for a 10,000-employee payroll. However, as the employee population rises, the complexity with unions and payroll schemas and rules goes up as well. If your employee population is spread across multiple states, then the complexity for taxes, garnishments, and benefits will obviously go up. As discussed in Chapter 7, there are certain localities where you will encounter multiple tax authorities which need to be accounted for in the configuration as well as in testing.

8.5.3 Resource Planning and Knowledge Transfers

It is a common complaint that developing, finding, and retaining good SAP US Payroll resources is very difficult. While implementation teams can get help from consultants, it may not be cost-effective in the long run to keep US Payroll consultants on your payroll. In the first year after a go-live, implementations do require lot of help, especially in areas of wage types, schemas, rules, taxes, and year-end processing. You need to plan your budgets and resources so you will have access to the necessary help around key milestones. The typical first-time milestones after go-live are:

- First month-end accrual run
- First accounting period-end
- First quarter-end
- First year-end
- First benefits enrollment
- Union agreements and changes

8.5.4 How to Run a Parallel Payroll

Parallel payroll runs are payrolls that are run in two systems for the same period. For example, you may need to run payroll in SAP as well as in your legacy system at the same time to identify differences. Parallel payroll runs are an integral part of payroll testing cycles, and they also help users ensure that the results are accurate in SAP Payroll. There isn't a single-best method for parallel payroll runs. There are many factors around the parallel runs and whatever works for your implementation team to get to the successful go-live date is good. Here are some questions to get you thinking:

▶ *How many parallel runs are good?* (Hint: You need to test month-end accruals as well as some deductions that only occur in the last payroll of a month.) Two cycles for each pay-frequency is normally good. Run each cycle over and over untildesired degree of discrepancy is achieved.

▶ *Is it possible to compare—dollar-for-dollar—between my legacy system and SAP Payroll?* Since the tax rates and benefit calculations in the new payroll system will have different amounts compared to legacy systems, the differences could be dramatic. For example, you have decided to use two decimal places in SAP US Payroll, while your legacy system used three decimal places.

▶ Are there third-party products for comparing results? There are products available in the market that can be used to compare payroll results. However, they require an additional investment. For large implementations this cost is easily offset by the level of confidence in the payroll results. For employers with 3,000 or more employees, it is nearly impossible to do a full-volume parallel payroll if the comparisons were not automated. The payroll comparison tool of choice should provide allowable thresholds for each wage type (e.g., FICA $.01, regular pay $.03, but certain taxes, such as those for Puerto Rico) with allowable ranges of possibly up to $10. Another driver for the tools selection is the usability of the reports for payroll users—most vendors provide tools with a focus on IT professionals.

▶ *What is the best way to compare results?* (Hint: Take a top-down approach. For example, if wage type **/101** totals match between the legacy and SAP systems, you don't need to drill down into individual earnings.)

▶ *Should I identify unique and difficult test cases to verify in the new SAP Payroll system?* (Hint: Employees with multiple garnishments, employees with complex union rules, etc.)

▶ *When planning to go-live in the first payroll of the new year, how do we manage and compare results while creating W-2s and carrying out year-end adjustments in the legacy system?,* (Hint: Data conversion timing and double data entry for a few days in the legacy as well as SAP systems.)

▶ *Can we choose any two payroll runs to compare results or do we need to select the last two payroll runs?* (Hint: Think of the control record and timing of data conversion cycles.)

8.5.5 Housekeeping Activities

Project teams often ignore the documentation of procedures. In addition, unless you are in a regulated industry such as pharmaceutical, food or financial (FDA or FDIC audits), the procedures are often not documented very well. Because of Sarbanes-Oxley (SOX) compliance requirements, this has been changing across all industries, and there has been more procedural documentation in recent years in other industries as well. US Payroll demands that before, during, and after the payroll, you follow many procedures and housekeeping activities. Some are essential to run the payroll, while others will help you smooth out your run operations. These activities are divided into pre-payroll and post-payroll, as described in the following sections.

Pre-Payroll Checks

When you think of the payroll cycle and control record status, you will realize that after you release the control record and by the time you exit the control record, you don't have a lot of time to solve issues or even review payroll data. As such, it is good practice to run pre-payroll checks to verify the inputs to the payroll process. These checks could be in the form of reports, SAP queries, or even transaction **SE16**-based data analysis. Some examples include:

- Run a report with infotype **0014** or **0015** with certain wage types or amounts greater than a certain threshold. It will help you to catch data entry errors.
- Run a report with overtime hours greater than a certain limit.
- Run a report of new hires and terminations.
- Run a report on promotions and transfers.
- Check on W-4 data changes.
- Check on 401(k) deduction changes.

Some payroll users also compare between the last result and the current result by running a wage type reporter on the total gross or total deductions. Even with that approach, the pre-payroll checks will help you to foresee the changes coming up in payroll results.

Post-Payroll Checks

The post-payroll check procedure is relatively straight-forward compared with pre-payroll checks. The typical post-payroll checklist consists of the following:

- Completing accounts posting.
- Completing third-party remittance posting.
- Running claims report.
- Managing payroll control record status.
- Checking terminations and managing infotype **0003** maintenance.
- Reconciling with finance and accounts payable.

Control Record Management

The more payroll frequencies in your implementation, the more you'll need to manage the control records. You will need someone to manage the status of the control record within the announced time table for the payroll calendar. For example, after you release the control record, users won't be able to maintain the employee master data for the current pay period. If your implementation has multiple payroll areas, control record management will increase exponentially. After users develop confidence with the system, batch programs can be created to release the control record. We have not covered process model functionality in this book, and you can also consider the process models to automate many of the housekeeping activities.

Overpayments and Claims Management

Earlier in this chapter, we discussed overpayments and claims. It is important to manage overpayments immediately after the current payroll run and prior to the next, especially as you get closer to year-end. You will realize that overpayments can create a lot of headaches.

TUBs, Support Packs

Each implementation adopts its own strategy for support packs. Although the time table for support packs depends on other functional teams, Tax Update Bulletins (**TUBs**) are required only by Payroll. Also, the **TUBs** give you the required tax updates, so it is essential that you apply the **TUBs** and test them as soon as you receive the communication from SAP/BSI.

8.5.6 Best Practices to Maintain Wage Types, Schemas, and Rules

Wage types, schemas, and rules are at the heart of your payroll system. Keep in mind the wage type template presented in Appendix B (and also discussed in Chapter 3). Use of this template will help create a paper trail for wage type maintenance. Note the transport number on this template; key data such as the transport number will help you track and figure out changes in the system. In addition, you can always refer to SAP's best practices series documents titled **Best Practices for mySAP HCM** and are available for all SAP HR sub-modules.

When introducing any new rule in payroll, make sure that you test it with real data. There are many third-party products available in the market that allow you to copy employee master data and payroll data from a production system to a test system. It may be a good idea to invest in such a tool so you can get current and real data from the production system for your test environment. You may also want to create your own documentation template for maintaining schemas and rules as we have with the wage type maintenance template in Appendix B. A list of sample best practices for maintaining schemas, rules, and wage types are as follows:

▶ **Schemas:**

　▷ Do not change SAP-delivered schemas. Always copy and create your own custom schemas.

　▷ Use the Documentation option in the schema editor (**PE01**) to document the details of the custom schema.

　▷ Add comments in the schema.

　▷ If you are changing delivered SAP logic in schemas, original lines should be commented and not deleted so you can maintain the trail of changes.

　▷ Follow a standard naming convention for custom schemas. For example, start all names with the letter Z.

　▷ Insert the appropriate heading texts in schemas, so that during a payroll run, the texts can help you to drill down into the schemas.

▶ **Rules:**

　▷ Do not change SAP-delivered rules. Always copy and create your own custom rules.

　▷ Use the Documentation option in the rules editor (**PE02**) to document custom rules.

> ▶ If a rule is intended to be used for a large employee population, make sure that the logic is efficient. The rules logic is almost like programming logic and although it does not affect the processing time a great deal, it has the potential to make it inefficient.

> ▶ Test the rule on the entire employee population (i.e., run a complete payroll) in the test system before launching the rule in the live payroll system. For example, a rule can potentially drop certain wage types if the appropriate logic is missing.

8.6 Summary

You may want to re-read the overpayments and claims processing section in this chapter to better understand the scenarios. It is one of the more complex and deeper topics of this book, and I am sure you will need to practice in your SAP system and create the test cases to check the different scenarios we discussed. I am hopeful that the implementation tips in this chapter will make you think a bit beyond just the configuration and testing.

This chapter also brings us to the conclusion of this book. I hope that it has provided you with the practical knowledge you need to configure and use the SAP US Payroll module. Note that likely the complex topics such as wage types, rules, and overpayments will require further reading and practice on your part. If you like, you can send me feedback at *saphrwriter@yahoo.com*. Best wishes on your SAP US Payroll journey.

Appendix

A   **US Payroll Schema U000** 257

B   **Wage Type Template** 269

C   **Commonly-Used Technical Wage Types** 273

D   **Commonly-Used Model Wage Types** 287

E   **Commonly-Used Processing Classes and Specifications**   299

F   **List of Useful Payroll Operations** 307

G   **About the Author** 317

A   US Payroll Schema U000

The figures shown in this Appendix present the US schema **U000** in a sequentially exploded fashion. If you use transaction **PE01** in the Schema Editor and follow the menu path: **Schema • Display • Print • Expand schema**, you will get an expanded picture of your schema as shown in Figure A.1.

If you take all of the figures shown in this appendix and paste them end-to-end, you will see the entire view of the US schema and its subschemas. Although you can use transaction **PE01** and individually access the subschema, it is important to understand how each subschema is called within the main schema so you can see the logic flow. Each figure has the top heading line from the Schema Editor

▸ Fct (Function)

▸ Par1 (Parameter 1)

▸ Par2 (Parameter 2)

▸ Par3 (Parameter 3)

▸ Par4 (Parameter 4)

The E column with asterisks (*) shows the commented lines in the schema. If you need to, you can return to Chapter 4 to review the discussion on important schema functions.

> **Note**
>
> You should print the schema from your SAP system with the version that you have implemented.

Figure A.1 shows the initial subschemas **UIN0** and **UBD0**, which carry out initial checks as well as process the initial infotypes. You can add your own comments with the function **COM**, as seen in the figure.

Figure A.2 starts at the last line of Figure A.1. Control is passed to subschema **UPR0**, which checks for retroactive accounting and then the schema **XLR0** imports the previous payroll results. (Note: Subschemas starting with **X** are common for all countries; US subschemas start with **U**.)

```
Fct   Par1 Par2 Par3 Par4 L E Text

COPY  UIN0                    * US Payroll:Initialization of payroll
BLOCK BEG                       Initialization of payroll
PGM   ABR                       Program type payroll
UPD   YES                       Database updates performed (YES/NO)
OPT   INFT                      Read only processed infotypes
OPT   TIME                      Read all time infotypes
OPT   DEC                     * Hourly rates with more than 2 decimals
CHECK      ABR                  Check over PA03
OPT   BSI                       Set switch BSI
BLOCK END
                             * END OF COPY UIN0
COPY  UBD0                    * Basic data processing
BLOCK BEG                       Basic data processing
ENAME                           Retrieve employee name
WPBP                            Read org. assignment / basic pay
P0002                           Read personal data
P0006                           Read address
P0207 2                         Read tax data
GON                             Continue with complete data
P0014 UW14 GEN  NOAB            Split WPBP and set APZNR for P0014
PRINT NP   NAM                  Print employee name
PRINT      WPBP                 Print org. assignment / basic pay
PRINT      TAXR                 Print resident authority
PRINT      PERM                 Print personal data
IF         SPRN                 If special run
RFRSH      IT                     Clear internal table IT
ENDIF                           Endif
BLOCK END
                             * END OF COPY UBD0
```

Figure A.1 Subschemas UIN0 and UBD0

```
Fct   Par1 Par2 Par3 Par4 L E Text

                             * END OF COPY UBD0
COPY  UPR0                    * Read previous result of current period
BLOCK BEG                       Get previous result of period for V0
IF         R                    Retro Calculation?
LPBEG      RC                     Loop at prev. results ( still valid
IMPRT      0                        Import old result
PITAB M    OV0                      Merge OV0, V0znr with V0, V0ZNR
PITAB A    PCT
LPEND                              End Loop at ...
ENDIF                            To: Retro Calculation?
BLOCK END                        Get previous result of period for V0
                             * END OF COPY UPR0
COPY  XLR0                    * Import previous payroll results
BLOCK BEG                       Import last payroll result
COM                             Import last payroll result
IMPRT      L                    Import last result
PORT  X006 P06  NOAB            Transfer relevant data to LRT
SETCU                           Prepare CRT (old results)
BLOCK END                       Import last payroll result
                             * END OF COPY XLR0
COPY  UMO0                    * Determine payroll modifiers
COM                             Rule for USA modifiers (UMO1) must be
COM                               called prior to UMOD!!!!
BLOCK BEG                       Determination of payroll modifier
MOD   UMO1 GEN                  Determine US payroll modifiers
MOD   UMOD GEN                  Determine payroll modifiers
BLOCK END
                             * END OF COPY UMO0
```

Figure A.2 Subschemas UPR0, XLR0 and UMO0

Time-related processing is handled in subschema **UT00**, as seen in Figure
A.3. The checks are carried out for positive or negative time tracking.

```
Fct   Par1 Par2 Par3 Par4 L E Text
                              * END OF COPY UM00
COPY  UT00                    * Gross compensation and time evaluation
BLOCK BEG                       General processing of time data USA
IF         SPRN
ELSE
CHKPC                         * Has personal calendar been generated?
PRINT NP   PCI                  Personal calendar: annual view
PRINT NP   PCIP                 Personal calendar: period view
GENPS                           Generate personal work schedule PWS
PRINT NP   PSP                  Print PWS
PARTT                           Partial month parameter
P2003      S**                  Import shift substitutions into PWS
PIT   U010 P01                  Create valuation bases (addition) (tips)
PIT   X013 P01                  Create valuation bases (division)
RAB                             Import absences
IMPRT      L
UNAB
PRINT NP   AB                   Print absences
IF         PDC                  Is PDC active in period?
IMPRT      B2                     Import cluster B2
PRINT NP   ZL                    Print table of time wage types
DAYPR TC00 PDC          *        Day processing of time data
ELSE                             PDC not active in period
DAYPR TC00              * *      Day processing of time data
ENDIF                            Endif PDC
```

Figure A.3 Subschema UT00 for Time Processing

Figure A.4 continues with schema **UT00** and further processing of tables **ZL** and **IT** is carried out in function **ZLIT**, as discussed in Chapter 4. This part of schema **UT00** also prints the part pay period tables. Function **PARTT** from Figure A.3 creates the part period-related tables that will be visible in the portion of the schema shown in Figure A.4. If you need to do any investigation related to time-based payments such as overtime, call-in time, etc., then this subschema provides you with potential clues and answers.

```
ENDIF                           Endif PDC
COPY  XT01              * *  Weekly overtime analysis
PAB                             Edit absence data
PRINT NP   PART                 Print partial month parameter
PRINT NP   PARX                 Print cumulated absences
PRINT NP   ZL                   Print table of time wage types
PRINT NP   IT                   Print IT
P2010 X930 GEN  NOAB            Process employee remuneration info
UTIPS                         * Tip processing
PIT   UTAL P84  NOAB          * Total tip allocation amounts
PRINT NP   ALP                  Table of different payments
PALP  X012 GEN                  Val. bases for different payments
PIT   XALP      NOAB            Increased val.basis+extra pay+premium
IF    UTRR                     * If workweek and hourly paid
COPY  UTR0                     *   FLSA: overtime valuation with reg.date
ELSE                          * Else usual valuation of time wage types
ZLIT            AMS              Time wage types in IT
P0003                           Valuation of time wage types
PIT   X015 GEN  NOAB            Endif
ENDIF                         * Remove val. bases with ALP split
PIT   X009 GEN  NOAB            Incentive wages
COPY  XIW0                      Gross and RT storage for time wage types
PIT   X020 P03                  Gross and RT storage for time wage types
ENDIF
BLOCK END
                              * END OF COPY UT00
```

Figure A.4 Continuation of subschema UT00

After subschema **UT00**, the payroll schema detours slightly and processes non-authorized manual checks. As seen in Chapter 7, if there are any info-type **0221**-related adjustments, processing is carried out by subschema **UMC0**. Figure A.5 shows subschema **UMC0**.

```
Fct    Par1 Par2 Par3 Par4 L E Text

                              * END OF COPY UT00
COPY   UREI                   * Travel expense
BLOCK  BEG                       Gross cumulation and tax processing
IF              NAMC             if non-authorized manual check        (*)
COPY   UMC8                   *   Process Non authorized check         (*)
COM                              US Payroll
COM                              Standard subschema for manual check
BLOCK  BEG                       Processing non authorized manual check
RFRSH        IT                  Delete Wage types from Basic Pay
P0221  UNAM GEN  NOAB            read inf. non authorized manual check
PRINT  NP   IT                   Print IT
PIT    X023 P20  NOAB            Calculate gross amounts
PIT    X024 P41  NOAB            Cumulate gross wages and store in RT
PIT    X025 P04  NOAB            Calculate gross amounts
IMPRT        L                   Import last period results
COPY   UMCE                   * Move old arrrs, ddntk & accr tbls to new
COM                              Non auth manual check final processing
CPYOT       ARRS                 Copy old table arrears    into original
CPYOT       ACCR              * deleted with note 193349
CPYOT       DDNT                 Copy old table deductions into original
UGARN  TBRS                      Take over tables from last result
BENPR                            Benefits: carry forward BENTAB
                              * END OF COPY UMCE
```

Figure A.5 Sub-schema UMC0 for Non-Authorized-Manual-Check

Figure A.6's logic resides in subschema **UMC0**. As a rule of thumb: Unless you see a comment line **END OF COPY**, the subschema has not yet ended. Figure A.6 shows that using processing class **50** (**66** in earlier versions), the subschema processes any goal- and deduction-related wage types for non-authorized manual check. If you need to revisit the goals and deductions wage types, refer back to Chapter 3.

```
                              * END OF COPY UMCE
PITAB  S    AIT                  Save IT on AIT
PLRT   XPPD GEN  NOAB            Forward balances for prepaid deductions
PLRT   XDPM P50  NOAB            Forward balances and deduction totals
PIT    XDPI P50  NOAB            Save balances for processing
PIT    XDPR P50  NOAB            Calculate deduction balance
PIT    UDPT P50  NOAB            Process deduction totals
PIT    UDPC P50  NOAB            Check deducted amount
PLRT   UD11 GEN  NOAB            Create inflow wage type (/Zxx) from LRT
PIT    UD21 GEN  NOAB            Process inflow wage types
PIT    UD32 GEN  NOAB            Store /Xnn in RT
```

Figure A.6 Goals and Deductions Handling in subschema UMC0

Subschema **UTX0** (see Figure A.7) is the US tax subschema that is called from subschema **UMC0** to process taxes for manual check processing. For regular payroll, taxes are processed with the same subschema, but at different places, as you will see later. Note that this schema is using BSI version 6.0

(shown by the line **UPAR1 BSI 60**). At the time of this writing, SAP customers are using BSI versions 6.0 and 7.0.

> **Tip**
>
> SAP includes a program **RPUBTCU0** to test your BSI installation. **OSS** notes 308846 (Version 6.0) and 781272 (Version 7.0) provide additional information.

```
Fct    Par1 Par2 Par3 Par4 L E  Text

PIT    UD32 GEN  NOAB            Store /Xnn in RT
COPY   UTX0                    * Calculate taxes
BLOCK  BEG                       Calculate taxes
UMOD   UMOT GEN  NOAB            Determine modifiers for US tax
ACTIO  UUIM                      Is unemployment insurance mandatory?
IF          SPRN                 If special run, don't accum basic hours
ELSE                             Else, not special run
ACTIO  UWH1 A                    Determine basic work hours
ENDIF                            Endif, special run
PRT    UWH2 P86                  Determine actual work hours
UPAR1  BSI  60                   BSI version flag
UPAR1  CUR  NA                   Override parameters for current payment
UPAR1  DIF  1    22   B          Override parameters for retro difference
UTXOR  1                         Tax authority override before USTAX
USTAX  1    3         1          Call tax calculation routine
UTXOR  2                         Tax authority override after USTAX
UTPRI                            Process tax priority
UOTX0                            Freeze the taxes for retro across year
PRT    UPTX P72  NOAB          * Post tax amount to various Tax Levels.
PIT    UBWG      NOAB            Accumulate unemployment bonus wages
IF          SPRN                 If special run don't calc. time units
ELSE                             ELSE, not special run
PRT    USUI                      SUI: hours & weeks worked; # employees
ENDIF                            ENDIF special run
BLOCK  END

                               * END OF COPY UTX0
```

Figure A.7 Tax Subschema UTX0 for Manual Check Processing

Figure A.8 shows that the manual check subschema **UMC0** has ended, and logic is now passed to another subschema, **UAP0**. Subschema **UAP0** processes infotypes **0014** and **0015**, and it also calls a benefits subschema **UBE1**. **UBE1** processes benefits infotypes **0167**, **0168**, and **0377**. This subschema provides you with details for many earnings and deductions. If you are looking for a place to write custom rules for wage types processed in these infotypes, you should try this subschema.

After subschema **UAP0**, **UAL0** takes control of proration and cumulation. Subschema **UAL0** handles any wage types that need to be processed for middle-of-pay-period proration calculations, as shown in Figure A.9. Rules **XVAL** and **XPPF** were discussed in Chapter 4.

Figure A.9 shows subschema **UTBS** and Figure A.10 shows subschema **UTBL**. Between these two subschemas, various payroll tables (**IT**, **RT**, **TAXR**, etc.) are saved and reloaded for iterative processes.

```
Fct    Par1 Par2 Par3 Par4 L E Text
                              * END OF COPY UTX0
COPY  UXD1                    * Fill currency fields
XDECI FILL RT                 * Fill amount currency field in RT
XDECI FILL IT                 * Fill amount currency field in IT
                              * END OF COPY UXD1
PIT   X030 P05   NOAB         Calculate net
PLRT  UADV GEN   NOAB         Get advance wage types from LRT
PIT   UM40       NOAB         Calculate payable amount
ACTIO UM4A                    Adjust payable amount
BLOCK END
                              * END OF COPY UMC0
ELSE                          else if non authorized manual check (*)
COPY  UAP0                    *  Process add. payments and deductions
BLOCK BEG
P0014 U011 GEN   NOAB
P0015 U015 GEN   NOAB
P0579 U011 GEN   NOAB
P0267 U012 GEN   NOAB
P0165
COPY  UBE1                    *
BLOCK BEG                     Process Benefits
BENPR                         Prepare Benefits Processing
BENUS                         prepare US  Benefits Processing
P0167 BEG                     Process Health Plans
P0168 BEG                     Process Insurance Plans
UGTLI                         Process Group Term Life Insurance
P0377 BEG  1                  Process Miscellan. Pl. (1st call)
P0236 BEG  1                  Process Credit Plans (1st call)
BLOCK END                     Process Benefits
                              * END OF COPY UBE1
```

Figure A.8 Subschema UAP0 and Benefits subschema UBE1

```
Fct    Par1 Par2 Par3 Par4 L E Text
                              * END OF COPY UBE1
BLOCK END
                              * END OF COPY UAP0
COPY  UAL0                    *  Proration and cumulation gross
BLOCK BEG                     Calculate part time factors + gross
IF         SPRN               If period is special run
ELSE                          Else: period is not special run
GEN/8 16                         Create wage types /801 to /816 in IT
PIT   XPPF       NOAB         Determine proration factors
PIT   XCM0 P31                Period lump sums for cost accounting
PIT   XVAL P10                Prorate period gross wages
ACTIO XCH0 A                  Calculate hours for cost accounting
ENDIF                         Endif period is special run
XDECI CONV RT    2            * Convert RT amounts down to 2 decimals
XDECI CONV IT    2            * Convert IT amounts down to 2 decimals
PIT   X023 P20   NOAB         Cumulate gross wages and store in RT
BLOCK END
                              * END OF COPY UAL0
COPY  UTBS                    *  Save tables for iteration
BLOCK BEG                     Saving tables for iteration
IMPRT      L                  Import result from last period
PITAB S    UIT                Save IT —> UIT before iteration
PITAB S    URT                Save RT —> URT before iteration
PITAB S    ATR                Save TAXR —> ATR before iteration
PITAB S    AOA                Save OARRRS —> AOA before iteration
PITAB S    ARR                Save ADTXRT, ARETRO_PERIODS, AOFFSET
PITAB S    AV0                Save OV0 —> AV0 before iteration
PITAB S    BEN                Save BENTAB —> ABENTAB before iteration
BLOCK END                     Save tables for iteration
                              * END OF COPY UTBS
```

Figure A.9 Subschema UAL0 for Proration

```
Fct    Par1 Par2 Par3 Par4 L E Text

                              * END OF COPY UTBS
LPBEG                               Begin of iteration
COPY   UTBL                   *     Load saved tables
BLOCK BEG                           Reloading saved tables
PITAB L      UIT                    Load UIT ——> IT
PITAB L      URT                    Load URT ——> RT
PITAB L      ATR                    Load ATR ——> TAXR
PITAB L      AOA                    Load AOA ——> OARRRS
PITAB L      ARR                    Load retr.tab. (RETRO_PERIODS, offset_o)
PITAB L      AV0                    Load AV0 ——> OV0
PITAB L      BEN                    Load ABENTAB ——> BENTAB
BLOCK END                           Reload saved tables
                              * END OF COPY UTBL
```

Figure A.10 Subschema UTBL to reload Saved Tables

Figure A.11 shows subschema **UDD0** and **UDBS**, which process base amounts for deduction calculation. If you run payroll retroactively, inflow and outflow wage types (**/Z02** and **/X02**, listed in Appendix C) are processed in this subschema.

```
Fct    Par1 Par2 Par3 Par4 L E Text         .

                              * END OF COPY UTBL
COPY   UDD0                   *     Process deductions, Benefits
BLOCK BEG                           Process deductions, Benefits and storage
PRART  U013 GEN   NOAB              Process previous ARRRS table (->in IT)
COPY   UDBS                   * Calculate deduction base
COM                                 US Deduction base calculation
PIT    UD01 P83   NOAB              Eliminate split for deduction base
PRINT NP    LRT                     Print LRT for deduction base
PLRT   UD11 GEN   NOAB              Create inflow wagetype(/Zxx) from LRT
PIT    UD21 GEN   NOAB              Process inflow wagetypes
IF          0                       If: original period
ELSE                                Else: if original period
RFRSH       OLD                       Refresh ORT/VORT (case of no original)
PITAB D     CORT                      Refresh CORT
LPBEG       RC                        Loop over old results
IMPRT       0                           Import previous result
PITAB A     CORT                        Add ORT to CORT
LPEND                               To: loop over old results
PITAB L     CORT                    Load CORT to ORT
PORT   UD30 P83   NOAB              Add AMT=0 entries from ORT (NUM=1)
PIT    UD31 P83   NOAB              Handling in Retrocalc (Clear NUM)
PIT    UD32 GEN   NOAB                Store /Xnn in RT
ENDIF                               Endif: If original period
PRINT NP    RT                      Print RT after Deduction base calc
                              * END OF COPY UDBS
```

Figure A.11 Subschema UDD0 and UDBS for Deduction Base

As seen earlier, the benefits subschema **UBE1** processes some of the benefits infotypes. Figure A.12 shows the second benefits of subschema **UBE2**, which mainly processes infotype **0169** and savings plans. You will also notice that processing class **50** (goals and deductions wage types) logic is used again to process the regular payroll; this class was shown earlier in the context of a non-authorized manual check.

```
Fct    Par1 Par2 Par3 Par4 L E Text

                              * END OF COPY UDBS
COPY   UBE2                   * Process Benefits (2nd time)
BLOCK  BEG                      Process Benefits (2nd part)
BENCM                          Process compensations
P0170  CHK                     Process Spending Accounts
P0169  BEG                     Process Savings Plans
P0377  BEG  2                  Process Miscellaneous Plans(2nd call)
P0379  BEG                     Process Stock Purchase Plans
P0236  BEG  2                  Process Credit Plans (2nd call)
BLOCK  END                     Process Benefits (2nd part)
                              * END OF COPY UBE2
COPY   UDP0                   * Process deduction balances + totals
COM                            Calculate deductions/donations
COM                            Program type.....: Payroll
PIT    URRS GEN  NOAB          Recover arrears for deduction processing
PLRT   XDPM P50  NOAB          Forward balances and deduction totals
PIT    XDPI P50  NOAB          Save balances for processing
PIT    XDPR P50  NOAB          Calculate deduction balance
PIT    UDPT P50  NOAB          Process deduction totals
                              * END OF COPY UDP0
LIMIT                          Process limits on deductions
BENMA  R                       Adj. Employer contr. in retrocalculation
```

Figure A.12 Second Benefits Subschema UBE2

Chapters 3 and 4 discussed the deductions not taken table (table **DDNTK**), which are used when there is not enough money available for an employee's deductions. Figure A.13 shows subschema **XPDD**, which processes the **DDNTK** table.

```
Fct    Par1 Par2 Par3 Par4 L E Text

LIMIT                          Process limits on deductions
BENMA  R                       Adj. Employer contr. in retrocalculation
COPY   XPDD                   * Adjust deductions corr. table DDNTK
BLOCK  BEG                      Process table DDNTK (ded.not taken)
IF          R                   Retroactive accounting ?
PITAB  D    CORT                Refresh table CORT (cumulated ORT)
LPBEG       RC                  Loop using original results
IMPRT       O                    Import original result for period
PITAB  A    CORT                 Cumulate ORT in CORT
LPEND                           End of loop
IF          LPRC               Has loop been processed?
PITAB  L    CORT                Rewrite CORT to ORT
ELSE                           No original result in cluster
RFRSH       ORT                 Initialize ORT
PITAB  D    OV0                Initialize OV0 and OV0ZNR
ENDIF                           to: Has loop been processed ?
ENDIF                          to: Retroactive accounting ?
PRDNT                          Modify deductions with values from DDNTK
BLOCK  END

                              * END OF COPY XPDD
BENMA  O                       Adj. Employer contrib. in original
BENWT                          Process benefits 403(b) tech. WT
PIT    X024 P41  NOAB          Cumulate gross wages and store in RT
PIT    X025 P04  NOAB          Prorate and cumulate gross USA
BLOCK  END

                              * END OF COPY UDD0
```

Figure A.13 Subschema XPDD for DDNTK Table

Figure A.14 shows the same tax subschema (**UTX0**, shown in Figure A.7), except this time, it is used to process taxes for regular payroll.

```
Fct    Par1 Par2 Par3 Par4 L E Text

                         * END OF COPY UDD0
COPY   UTX0                  *    Calculate taxes
BLOCK  BEG                   Calculate taxes
UMOD   UMOT GEN  NOAB        Determine modifiers for US tax
ACTIO  UUIM                  Is unemployment insurance mandatory?
IF          SPRN            If special run, don't accum basic hours
ELSE                        Else, not special run
ACTIO  UWH1 A               Determine basic work hours
ENDIF                       Endif, special run
PRT    UWH2 P86             Determine actual work hours
UPAR1  BSI  60              BSI version flag
UPAR1  CUR  NA              Override parameters for current payment
UPAR1  DIF  1     22   B    Override parameters for retro difference
UTXOR  1                    Tax authority override before USTAX
USTAX  1    3          1    Call tax calculation routine
UTXOR  2                    Tax authority override after USTAX
UTPRI                       Process tax priority
UOTX0                       Freeze the taxes for retro across year
PRT    UPTX P72  NOAB     * Post tax amount to various Tax Levels.
PIT    UBWG      NOAB       Accumulate unemployment bonus wages
IF          SPRN           If special run don't calc. time units
ELSE                       ELSE, not special run
PRT    USUI                SUI: hours & weeks worked; # employees
ENDIF                      ENDIF special run
BLOCK  END

                         * END OF COPY UTX0
```

Figure A.14 Tax Subschema UTX0

Figure A.15 processes garnishments. The garnishment subschema, **UGRN**, starts garnishment processing and handles the disposable net income calculations discussed in Chapter 6. Note that the garnishment subschema runs after taxes are calculated, because taxes must first be taken from an employee's gross income.

```
Fct    Par1 Par2 Par3 Par4 L E Text

                         * END OF COPY UTX0
COPY   UGRN                  *    Calculate garnishments
BLOCK  BEG                   Garnishment calculation: Current period
COM                       * ****************************************
IF          0               Actual period
IMPRT       L             * Import results from last payroll period
UGARN  READ       3         Read garnishments (in IN-period)
UGARN  SETC B     3         Set for check: Active garn., adjustments
IF          GREX           Active garn., adjustm.in current period?
COM                       * There are garnishmnts in current per.
PITAB  S    AIT             Save IT in AIT
PIT    UGIT P59  NOAB       Delete special wage types in IT
UGARN  RFND       3         Refund, wage types in IT
UGARN  SETC A     3         Set for check: Active garnishments
IF          GREX           Active garnishments?
COM                       *    There are active garnishments
PRT    UGRT P59  NOAB        Get necessary WT from RT in IT
UGARN  GETD       3          Get differences from recalculation
PRINT  NP   IT               IT after get differences
XDECI  CONV IT    2        * Convert to 2 decimal digits
PIT    UGDN P59  NOAB        Disposable net
ACTIO  UGGR                  Gross
PORT   UGCL      NOAB      *    Net Garnishments from claims
PIT    UGNG               *    Zero negative gross/net
UGARN  CALC       3            Calculate garnishments
ENDIF                       End: Active garnishments
COM                       * Active garnishments, adjustments
PRINT  NP   IT              IT before save wage types
PIT    UGSV P60  NOAB       Save garnishment wage types
PITAB  L    AIT             Load IT from AIT
ENDIF                       End: Active garnishments, adjustmein IT
COM                       * Independent from active garnishments
```

Figure A.15 The Garnishment Subschema, UGRN

After garnishments have been processed, subschema **UNA0** performs the net calculations, because by now, all earnings and deductions have been processed. Additionally, subschema **UDNT** looks at the **DDNTK** table and uses the priority and arrears configuration (see the discussion in Chapter 3) to decide the final processing of arrears and deductions not taken. Figure A.16 processes the net calculations using subschema **UNA0**. Rule **X040** calculates the payable amount to the employee.

```
Fct   Par1 Par2 Par3 Par4 L E Text

COM                         * Independent from active garnishments
UGARN TBAP         3          Take over unused garnishment orders
ENDIF                         End; Actual period
BLOCK END
                            * END OF COPY UGRN
COPY  UNA0                  *     Calculate net
BLOCK BEG                     Net calculation
XDECI FILL RT               * Fill amount currency field in RT
XDECI FILL IT               * Fill amount currency field in IT
PIT   X030 P05  NOAB          Calculate net
IF         0                  if original period
PLRT  UADV GEN  NOAB          get advance wage types from LRT
PRPRI 0                         Process priority table, Original period
ENDIF                         to: if original period
PIT   X040      NOAB          Calculate payable amount
ACTIO X04A                    Adjust payable amount
BLOCK END
                            * END OF COPY UNA0
COPY  UDNT                  *    Deductions not taken during loop ?
BLOCK BEG                     Processing of deduct. not taken in loop
IF         DDNT               if deductions not taken
ACTIO ULPC                      PCR for loop condition (1 more pass)
ELSE                          no more loop
PREND                           Priority end processing (adjust DDNTK)
ENDIF                         to: if deductions not taken
BLOCK END
                            * END OF COPY UDNT
LPEND                         End of iteration
```

Figure A.16 Subschema UNA0 for Net Calculations

Figure A.17 shows that the schema processes garnishments separately for retroactive payrolls. Figure A.18 continues the retroactive process using subschema **URR0**.

Subschema **UNN0** (see Figure A.19) shows that net processing is further extended using infotype **0009** to create the **BT** table for bank transfers or check processing. If you are using infotype **0011** in the employee master data, the **UNN0** subschema also processes infotype **0011** (see Chapter 2). Subschema **UAC0** (see Figure A.19) is used for month-end accruals, as discussed in Chapter 8.

The last subschema, **UEND** (shown in Figure A.20), concludes payroll processing and exports the results table to payroll clusters. The **RT** tables are written to the employee's payroll record.

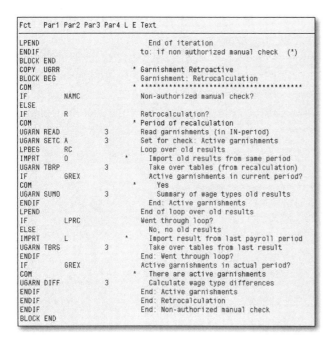

```
Fct    Par1 Par2 Par3 Par4 L E  Text

LPEND                              End of iteration
ENDIF                             to: if non authorized manual check   (*)
BLOCK END
COPY  UGRR                       * Garnishment Retroactive
BLOCK BEG                          Garnishment: Retrocalculation
COM                              * *****************************************
IF         NAMC                    Non-authorized manual check?
ELSE
IF         R                       Retrocalculation?
COM                              * Period of recalculation
UGARN READ            3            Read garnishments (in IN-period)
UGARN SETC A          3            Set for check: Active garnishments
LPBEG      RC                      Loop over old results
IMPRT      0              *         Import old results from same period
UGARN TBRP            3            Take over tables (from recalculation)
IF         GREX                    Active garnishments in current period?
COM                      *          Yes
UGARN SUMO            3             Summary of wage types old results
ENDIF                             End: Active garnishments
LPEND                             End of loop over old results
IF         LPRC                    Went through loop?
ELSE                               No, no old results
IMPRT      L             *         Import result from last payroll period
UGARN TBRS            3            Take over tables from last result
ENDIF                             End: Went through loop?
IF         GREX                    Active garnishments in actual period?
COM                      *          There are active garnishments
UGARN DIFF            3             Calculate wage type differences
ENDIF                             End: Active garnishments
ENDIF                             End: Retrocalculation
ENDIF                             End: Non-authorized manual check
BLOCK END
```

Figure A.17 Garnishments Processing for Retroactive Payroll

```
Fct    Par1 Par2 Par3 Par4 L E  Text

BLOCK END
                                 * END OF COPY UGRR
COPY  URR0                       * Retroactive accounting
BLOCK BEG                          Retroactive accounting
IF         NAMC                    Non-authorized manual check?
ELSE                               Else: Non-authorized manual check?
IF         0                       Original payroll?
PDT   X041 GEN  NOAB                 Provide differences received
ELSE                               Else: Original payroll?
ACTIO X048                          Reset BTEX
LPBEG      RC                       Loop
IMPRT      0                         Import last payroll
PRINT NP   ORT                       Print ORT
ACTIO X048               *           Reset BTEX
PORT  X042 GEN  NOAB                 Form differenes and transfer
PORT  U042 GEN  NOAB                 Form differenes and transfer US
COM                                  wage types that cannot be revised
PIT   X047                           Cumulation of new net pay
PIT   X043               *           Write new amount to data medium
BTFIL                                Transfer BT from last payroll
LPEND                               Endloop
IF         LPRC                     Run through the loop?
PIT   X043                           new amount to data medium
ELSE                               If not
PIT   X047                           Calculate new net pay
PIT   X043                           Transfer new amount to DT
ENDIF                              End if: Run through the loop?
ENDIF                             End if: Original payroll?
ENDIF                            End if: Non-authorized manual check?
BLOCK END
                                 * END OF COPY URR0
```

Figure A.18 Subschema URR0 for Retroactive Payroll

```
Fct    Par1 Par2 Par3 Par4 L E  Text

                               * END OF COPY URR0
COPY  UNN0                      * Net processing
BLOCK BEG                         Net processing
IF            NAMC                If non authorised manual check
PIT   UM60         NOAB             Store net pay for NAMC
ELSE                               Else: non authorised manual check
IF            0                    If in original period...
P0011 X055 GEN NOAB                  Read external bank transfers
PIT   X045 P25                       Process loans
ACTIO X046                           Check bank transfer
PIT   X047                           Cumulation of net pay
P0009 X050 GEN NOAB                  Bank information
ENDIF                                Endif: In original period...
PIT   X060                         Store net pay
P9ZNC W    C                       Check on IT9; Print Zero-Net-Checks
ENDIF                              Endif: non authorized NAMC
BLOCK END

                               * END OF COPY UNN0
COPY  UAC0                      * Month end accruals
BLOCK BEG                         Processing month end accruals
IF            SPRN                If period is special run
ELSE                               Else: period is not special run
ACTIO UAC0 GEN                       Set switch accruals on / off
UACGF                                Calculate accruals
PRINT NP   ACCR                      Print accruals table
ENDIF                              Endif period is special run
BLOCK END
                               * END OF COPY UAC0
```

Figure A.19 Subschema UNN0 and UAC0

```
                               * END OF COPY UAC0
COPY  UEND                      * Final processing
BLOCK BEG                         Final processing USA
PIT   X070 GEN NOAB               Error for whatever w/type is still in IT
BENTB                             Update BENTAB (benefits processing)
ADDCU      P30                    Update cumulative results (table CRT)
IF         0                      Original payroll?
PTCRT UNEG GEN  Y                 Check ytd amounts in TCRT
ENDIF
BENWT                           * Process benefits 403(b) tech. WT
IF         R                      IF retro
UCQRC 1                           Populate T5UQR is cross quarter
ELSE
IF            SPRN                If special run (Not retro)
UCQRC 2                           Populate T5UQR if TR has been run
ENDIF
ENDIF
UTRST                             Build tax reporter index table T5UX1
EXPRT      RU                     Export results to database cluster RU
BLOCK END                         At end of selection
                               * END OF COPY UEND
```

Figure A.20 End of the Schema, with Subschema UEND

B Wage Type Template

Part 1: To Be Completed by Requestor

Basic Details

Type: Earning/Deduction/Benefits   Date: __/__/____

Wage Type Number: ____   Wage Type Short Text: _____

Wage Type Long Text: _____

Data Entry

Permissibility in Infotypes: (0008, 0014, 0015, 0221,2010):_____

Elements: AMT/RTE/NUM: _____

Output

Taxability: Normal / Supplemental   Taxability- Pre-Tax / Post-Tax

Printed on Pay Stub: Y / N

Posting & Reporting

GL Account Number for posting: _____

Vendor Number: _____

Benefits Interface Affected: _____

Wage Type Reporter Variants Affected: _____

Requestor and Signatures

Person Requesting: _____   Signature: _____

Person Testing: _____   Signature: _____

—

Part 2: To Be Completed by Person Configuring

Applicable Processing Classes

Processing Class	Specs	Remark
3 – Cumulation and storage		
6 – Previous pay period process		
10 – Monthly factoring		
20 – Cumulation and storage at end		
24 – Transfer control		
25 – Behaviors after end of payment		
30 – Cumulation update		
41 – Splits		
50 – Deduction goal/Deduction		
59 – Disposable net for garnishment		
60 – Save garnishment WT		
65 – Pre-tax or post-tax		
68 – Payment type for tax calc		
69 – Taxable or non-taxable		
71 – Tax classification		
73 – Third Party sign assignment		
78 – 3PR remittance		
72 – Employee/Employer tax		
76 – Regular or bonus runs		
82 – Set this for ITY 0221 runs		

Cumulation Decisions

Technical Wage Type for Cumulation	Explanation
/101 – Total gross	
/102 – Retirement wages	
/109 – Employer benefits	
/110 – Employee deductions	

Technical Wage Type for Cumulation	Explanation
/114 – Base wages for BSI	
/115 – Bonus wages	

Accumulators

Month To Date (MTD):   Y/N

Quarter To Date (QTD): Y/N

Year To Date (YTD):   Y/N

Handling of Wage Types

Entered by User: Y/N   Infotype for Entry: ____

Generated by System: Y/N

Deduction Treatment

Arrears Processing: Y/N   Type of Arrears Processing: _____

Arrears during Retro: Y/N   Type of Arrears Processing: _____

Payment Model: _____

Payroll Process

Rules that will use the wage type: _____, _____, _____, _____, _____

Subschemas that use the rules: _____, _____, _____, _____, _____

Accounts Interface

Type of Account: Expense / Liability   GL Account: _____

PPMOD Grouping: _____   Vendor Account: _____

Accrual: Y/N   Accrual Account: _____

Approvals and Testing

Payroll Approval: _____

HR Approval: _____

Person Configuring: _____   Signature: _____

Person Testing: _____

Final Release Date for Production: __/__/____

Transport Number: _____

C Commonly-Used Technical Wage Types

Chapter 3 introduced wage types and talked about the technical wage types generated by SAP when the payroll schema is processed. The chapter also covered technical wage types such as **/101** (Total Gross) and **/559** (Net Pay). A complete list of the SAP-delivered technical wage types is presented in this Appendix. You will notice that there are many technical wage types related to taxes while there are others for valuations, totals, and overpayments. Although technical wage types are generated by the system and not user-entered, you may recall from the discussion in Chapter 7 about the Year-End Workbench that some of the tax-related technical wage types are used in infotype **0221** for data entry. We also have referred to some of the other wage types, such as **/G00, /G01** in Chapter 6 on garnishments. The wage types and their descriptions are as given by SAP from table **T512W**.

> **Note**
>
> You should verify the list of wage types in Table C.1 against your current version.

Technical Wage Type	Description
/001	Valuation basis 1
/002	Valuation basis 2
/003	Valuation basis 3
/004	Valuation basis 4
/101	Total gross
/102	401(k) wages
/109	ER benefit contributions
/110	EE deductions
/114	Base wage for BSI
/115	Bonus wages

Table C.1 Commonly-Used Technical Wage Types

Technical Wage Type	Description
/167	Payments/deds./unreduced
/3**	TG Taxable Gross
/3--	TG
/301	TG Withholding Tax
/302	TG Earned Income Credit
/303	TG EE Social Security Tax
/304	TG ER Social Security Tax
/305	TG EE Medicare Tax
/306	TG ER Medicare Tax
/307	TG State Unemployment Ins
/308	TG Social Charge Tax
/309	TG ER Special Payroll Tax
/310	TG ER Unemployment Tax
/311	TG ER Debt Repayment Tax
/312	TG ER Old Fund Liability
/313	TG ER Emplmt Security Enh
/314	TG ER Re-emplmt Placemt Tax
/315	TG ER Job Devmt Assessmt
/316	TG Employment Training Tax
/317	TG ER Health Insurance Tax
/318	TG ER Workforce Devlmt Tax
/319	TG Payroll Expense Tax
/320	TG EE Unemployment Tax
/321	TG EE Debt Repayment Tax
/322	TG EE Old Fund Liability
/323	TG EE Health Insurance Tax
/324	TG EE Workforce Devlpmt Tax
/325	TG EE Hlth, Disbility
/326	TG EE Chauffer's License

Table C.1 Commonly-Used Technical Wage Types (cont.)

Technical Wage Type	Description
/327	TG ER Chauffer's License
/328	TG ER Hlth, Disbility
/329	TG Special Admin Reserve
/330	TG ER Worker Compesatn Tax
/331	TG ER Disability Tax
/332	TG ER Accident Fund Tax
/333	TG ER Medical Aid Fund Tax
/334	TG ER Suplmtal Pension Tx
/335	TG Transit District
/336	TG Dislocated Worker
/337	TG Administrative Conting
/338	TG Employer Investment
/340	TG EE Worker Compensation
/341	TG EE Disability Tax
/342	TG EE Suplmtal Pension Tax
/343	TG EE Medical Aid Fund Tax
/344	TG EE Sen Cit/mntal Hlth
/345	TG EE Senior Citizen Tax
/346	TG EE Mental Health Tax
/347	TG Joint Economic Dev.
/348	TG EE Voluntary Disabilit
/349	TG EE Sen Cit/Mntal Hlt/Tax
/350	TG EE Transportation Tax
/351	TG EE Occupation Tax
/352	TG ER Head Tax
/353	TG EE School Tax
/354	TG ER Occupation Tax
/355	TG EE Railroad Rtmt Tier1
/356	TG EE Railroad Rtmt Tier2

Table C.1 Commonly-Used Technical Wage Types (cont.)

Technical Wage Type	Description
/357	TG ER Railroad Rtmt Tier1
/358	TG ER Railroad Rtmt Tier2
/359	TG EE Railroad Rtmt Tier1
/360	TG ER Railroad Rtmt Tier2
/361	TG Ss. EE Retirement Plan
/362	TG Ss. EE Retirement Plan
/363	TG Mass. ER Retirement Plan
/364	TG Mass. ER Retirement Plan
/365	TG Employer Supplemental
/4**	TX Tax
/4--	TX
/401	TX Withholding Tax
/402	TX Earned Income Credit
/403	TX EE Social Security Tax
/404	TX ER Social Security Tax
/405	TX EE Medicare Tax
/406	TX ER Medicare Tax
/407	TX State Unemployment Ins
/408	TX Social Charge Tax
/409	TX ER Special Payroll Tax
/410	TX ER Unemployment Tax
/411	TX ER Debt Repayment Tax
/412	TX ER Old Fund Liability
/413	TX Er Emplmt Security Enh
/414	TX Er Re-emplmt Placemt Tax
/415	TX Er Job Devmt Assessmt
/416	TX Employment Training Tax
/417	TX ER Health Insurance Tax
/418	TX ER Workforce Devlmt Tax

Table C.1 Commonly-Used Technical Wage Types (cont.)

Technical Wage Type	Description
/419	TX Payroll Expense Tax
/420	TX EE Unemployment Tax
/421	TX EE Debt Repayment Tax
/422	TX EE Old Fund Liability
/423	TX EE Health Insurance Tax
/424	TX EE Workforce Devlpmt Tax
/425	TX EE Hlth, Disbility
/426	TX ER Chauffers License
/427	TX ER Chauffers License
/428	TX ER Hlth, Disbility
/429	TX Special Admin Reserve
/430	TX ER Worker Compesatn Tax
/431	TX ER Disability Tax
/432	TX ER Accident Fund Tax
/433	TX ER Medical Aid Fund Tax
/434	TX ER Suplmtal Pension Tax
/435	TX Transit District
/436	TX Dislocated Worker
/437	TX Administrative Conting
/438	TX Employer Investment
/439	TX Employment Administrat
/440	TX EE Worker Compensation
/441	TX EE Disability Tax
/442	TX EE Suplmtal Pension Tax
/443	TX EE Medical Aid Fund Tax
/444	TX EE Sen Cit/mntal Hlt
/445	TX EE Senior Citizen Tax
/446	TX EE Mental Health Tax
/447	TX Joint Economic Dev.

Table C.1 Commonly-Used Technical Wage Types (cont.)

Technical Wage Type	Description
/448	TX EE Voluntary Disability
/449	TX EE Sen Cit/Mntal Hlt/Tax
/450	TX EE Transportation Tax
/451	TX EE Occupation Tax
/452	TX ER Head Tax
/453	TX EE School Tax
/454	TX ER Occupation Tax
/455	TX EE Railroad Rtmt Tier1
/456	TX EE Railroad Rtmt Tier2
/457	TX ER Railroad Rtmt Tier1
/458	TX ER Railroad Rtmt Tier2
/459	TX EE Railroad Rtmt Tier1
/460	TX ER Railroad Rtmt Tier2
/461	TX Ss. EE Retirement Plan
/462	TX Ss. EE Retirement Plan
/463	TX Mass. ER Retirement Plan
/464	TX Mass. ER Retirement Plan
/465	TX EMPLOYER SUPPLEMENTAL
/550	Statutory net pay
/551	Retrocalc. difference
/552	Differences from prev. per
/553	Recalc. diff. to last payr.
/557	Cash payment
/558	Payment of balance
/559	Bank transfer
/560	Amount paid
/561	Claim
/562	Amount of balance paid
/563	Claim from previous month

Table C.1 Commonly-Used Technical Wage Types (cont.)

Technical Wage Type	Description
/564	Advance payment
/565	Carry-over for subs. month
/566	Carry-over for prev. month
/568	Total reversal amount
/569	Reversal of /557
/570	Reversal of /558
/571	Reversal of /559
/590	Outsourcers' Difference
/5PY	Good Money
/5TC	Net tax claim
/5U0	Tot EE tax
/5U1	Tot ER tax
/5U2	Tot gross-up result
/5U3	Number of paid period
/5U5	Time Mgmt Worked Hours
/5U9	Non-auth. manual check amt
/5UA	Gen Taxable Amount
/5UB	Tax base wage
/5UG	Tax gross wage
/5UH	Worked Hours for SUI
/5US	Standard Worked Hours
/5UT	Actual Worked Hours
/5UU	Taxable Hours
/5UW	Number of weeks for SUI
/5UY	ODR Flag
/5UZ	ODR Eval Flag
/6**	TB Taxable earnings
/6--	TB
/601	TB Withholding Tax

Table C.1 Commonly-Used Technical Wage Types (cont.)

Technical Wage Type	Description
/602	TB Earned Income Credit
/603	TB EE Social Security Tax
/604	TB ER Social Security Tax
/605	TB EE Medicare Tax
/606	TB ER Medicare Tax
/607	TB State Unemployment Ins
/608	TB Social Charge Tax
/609	TB ER Special Payroll Tax
/610	TB ER Unemployment Tax
/611	TB ER Debt Repayment Tax
/612	TB ER Old Fund Liability
/613	TB ER Emplmt Security Enh
/614	TB ER Re-emplmt Placemt Tax
/615	TB ER Job Devmt Assessmt
/616	TB Employment Training Tax
/617	TB ER Health Insurance Tax
/618	TB ER Workforce Devlmt Tax
/619	TB Payroll Expense Tax
/620	TB EE Unemployment Tax
/621	TB EE Debt Repayment Tax
/622	TB EE Old Fund Liability
/623	TB EE Health Insurance Tax
/624	TB EE Workforce Devlpmt Tax
/625	TB EE Hlth, Disbility & W
/626	TB EE Chauffers License F
/627	TB ER Chauffers License F
/628	TB ER Hlth, Disbility & W
/629	TB Special Admin Reserve
/630	TB ER Worker Compesatn Tax

Table C.1 Commonly-Used Technical Wage Types (cont.)

Technical Wage Type	Description
/631	TB ER Disability Tax
/632	TB ER Accident Fund Tax
/633	TB ER Medical Aid Fund Tax
/634	TB ER Suplmtal Pension Tax
/635	TB Transit District Exci
/636	TB Dislocated Worker Asse
/637	TB Administrative Conting
/638	TB Employer Investment Fee
/640	TB EE Workers Compensation
/641	TB EE Disability Tax
/642	TB EE Suplmtal Pension Tax
/643	TB EE Medical Aid Fund Tax
/644	TB Ee Sen Cit/mntal Hlt
/645	TB EE Senior Citizen Tax
/646	TB EE Mental Health Tax
/647	TB Joint Economic Dev. Di
/648	TB EE Voluntary Disability
/649	TB EE Sen Cit/Mntal Hlt/Tax
/650	TB EE Transportation Tax
/651	TB EE Occupation Tax
/652	TB ER Head Tax
/653	TB EE School Tax
/654	TB ER Occupation Tax
/655	TB EE Railroad Rtmt Tier1
/656	TB EE Railroad Rtmt Tier2
/657	TB ER Railroad Rtmt Tier1
/658	TB ER Railroad Rtmt Tier2
/659	TB EE Railroad Rtmt Tier1
/660	TB ER Railroad Rtmt Tier2

Table C.1 Commonly-Used Technical Wage Types (cont.)

Technical Wage Type	Description
/661	TB Ss. EE Retirement Plan
/662	TB Ss. EE Retirement Plan
/663	TB Mass. ER Retirement Plan
/664	TB Mass. ER Retirement Plan
/665	TB Employer Supplemental
/7**	RE Reportable earnings
/7--	RE
/700	RE plus ER shares
/701	RE Withholding Tax
/702	RE Earned Income Credit P
/703	RE EE Social Security Tax
/704	RE ER Social Security Tax
/705	RE EE Medicare Tax
/706	RE ER Medicare Tax
/707	RE State Unemployment Ins
/708	RE Social Charge Tax
/709	RE ER Special Payroll Tax
/710	RE ER Unemployment Tax
/711	RE ER Debt Repayment Tax
/712	RE ER Old Fund Liability
/713	RE Er Emplmt Security Enh
/714	RE Er Re-emplmt Placemt Tax
/715	RE Er Job Devmt Assessmt
/716	RE Employment Training Tax
/717	RE ER Health Insurance Tax
/718	RE ER Workforce Devlmt Tax
/719	RE Payroll Expense Tax
/720	RE EE Unemployment Tax
/721	RE EE Debt Repayment Tax

Table C.1 Commonly-Used Technical Wage Types (cont.)

Technical Wage Type	Description
/722	RE EE Old Fund Liability
/723	RE EE Health Insurance Tax
/724	RE EE Workforce Devlpmt Tax
/725	RE EE Hlth, Disbility & W
/726	RE EE Chauffers License F
/727	RE ER Chauffers License F
/728	RE ER Hlth, Disbility & W
/729	RE Special Admin Reserve
/730	RE ER Worker Compesatn Tax
/731	RE ER Disability Tax
/732	RE ER Accident Fund Tax
/733	RE ER Medical Aid Fund Tax
/734	RE ER Suplmtal Pension Tax
/735	RE Transit District Exci
/736	RE Dislocated Worker Asse
/737	RE Administrative Conting
/738	RE Employer Investment Fee
/740	RE EE Worker Compensation
/741	RE EE Disability Tax
/742	RE EE Suplmtal Pension Tax
/743	RE EE Medical Aid Fund Tax
/744	RE Ee Sen Cit/mntal Hlt
/745	RE EE Senior Citizen Tax
/746	RE EE Mental Health Tax
/747	RE Joint Economic Dev. Di
/748	RE EE Voluntary Disability
/749	RE EE Sen Cit/Mntl Hlth/Tax
/750	RE EE Transportation Tax
/751	RE EE Occupation Tax

Table C.1 Commonly-Used Technical Wage Types (cont.)

Technical Wage Type	Description
/752	RE ER Head Tax
/753	RE EE School Tax
/754	RE ER Occupation Tax
/755	RE EE Railroad Rtmt Tier1
/756	RE EE Railroad Rtmt Tier2
/757	RE ER Railroad Rtmt Tier1
/758	RE ER Railroad Rtmt Tier2
/759	RE EE Railroad Rtmt Tier1
/760	RE ER Railroad Rtmt Tier2
/761	RE Ss. EE Retirement Plan
/762	RE Ss. EE Retirement Plan
/763	RE Mass. ER Retirement Plan
/764	RE Mass. ER Retirement Plan
/765	RE Employer Supplemental
/8++	Valuation wage types ----
/801	Part month factor 1
/802	Part month factor 2
/803	Part month factor 3
/804	Part month factor 4
/805	Part month factor 5
/806	Part month factor 6
/807	Part month factor 7
/808	Part month factor 8
/809	Part month factor 9
/810	Part month factor 10
/811	Part month factor 11
/812	Part month factor 12
/813	Part month factor 13
/814	Part month factor 14

Table C.1 Commonly-Used Technical Wage Types (cont.)

Technical Wage Type	Description
/815	Part month factor 15
/816	Part month factor 16
/817	Part month factor 17
/818	Part month factor 18
/819	Part month factor 19
/840	Diff. curr. from aver. month
/841	Paid leave
/842	Paid sickness
/843	Other paid time off
/844	Paid holidays
/845	Total paid non-work
/846	Total unpaid absences
/852	Overtime hours
/BC1	Reimbursed credits
/BC2	Paid excess credits
/BC3	Forfeit excess credits
/BD1	EE Dep. GTLI Cost
/BD2	EE Dep. GTLI Coverage
/BE1	EE GTLI Cost
/BE2	EE GTLI Coverage
/BER	Benefits ER contributions
/BI1	EE GTL Insurance Ded
/BI2	EE Dep. GTL Insurance Ded
/BO1	EE Child GTL Insur. Ded
/BO2	EE Child GTL Insur. Cov
/BP1	Used credit (FLEX)
/BP2	Avail. credit (FLEX)
/BP3	Overused credit (FLEX)
/BP4	Excess credit (FLEX)

Table C.1 Commonly-Used Technical Wage Types (cont.)

Technical Wage Type	Description
/BP5	Credit plan credit (FLEX)
/BP6	EE Pretax ded. (FLEX)
/BP7	EE credit cash in (FLEX)
/BS1	Spending Acct. Annual Wt
/BT1	EE GTLI Taxable
/BT2	EE Dep. GTLI Taxable
/BT3	EE Child GTL Insur. Imp
/BU1	EE GTL Imp. uncollected
/BU2	EE Dep GTL Imp. uncollect
/BU3	Child uncollected GTL Imp
/BX1	EE pretax (payr)
/BX3	YTD EE pretax
/BX4	YTD ER contr.
/BX5	EE posttax (payr)
/BX6	BCY vested ER (payr)
/BX7	EE 402(g) excpt(payr)
/G00	Disposable net
/G01	Gross for garnishments
/G02	Completely nonexempt
/G03	Garnishment sum
/X02	Outflow(/102)
/Z02	Inflow(/102)

Table C.1 Commonly-Used Technical Wage Types (cont.)

D   Commonly-Used Model Wage Types

During the discussion on wage types in Chapter 2, as well as when we discussed benefits and garnishments in Chapters 5 and 6, we talked about model wage types. SAP provides a model wage type catalog that can be used to copy the model wage types to create your own custom wage types.

This Appendix lists the model wage types delivered by SAP. In the IMG, when you use the **COPY** node at various places, SAP prompts for the appropriate list of model wage types. It is always a good idea to verify the processing classes, cumulations, and other wage type characteristics before deciding to use a particular model wage type. In Table D-1, the model wage types starting with the letter **B** are applicable to benefits-related wage types. As such, when you want to use model wage types for benefits deductions, as we discussed in Chapter 5, you will look for these wage types. All of the other wage types starting with the letter **M** are towards earnings and other deductions, including garnishments as discussed in Chapter 6. The wage types and their descriptions presented in table below are from SAP table **T512W**.

Note
Please verify that the model wage types listed in Table D.1 are available in the wage type catalog in your system, with the SAP version you are running.

Wage Type	Wage Type Text
M001	Hourly rate
M002	Hourly rate, part time
M003	Salary
M004	Supplemental payment
M005	Lead premium
M006	Shift premium
M011	Vacation pay
M021	Tip income

Table D.1 Commonly-Used Model Wage Types

Wage Type	Wage Type Text
M031	Gross up regular method
M032	Gross up result-reg meth
M033	Gross up suppl method
M034	Gross up result-supp meth
M041	Non-tax income
M098	Test wage type
M101	Bonus
M102	Bonus – special pay run
M112	Commission
M113	Severance pay
M114	Uniform allowance
M115	Equipment allowance
M116	Car allowance
M117	Premium pay (% of gross)
M200	United Way donation amt
M201	United Way donation pct
M202	United Way balance
M203	United Way total taken
M204	United Way arrears ded
M205	United Way arrears bal
M206	United Way arrears total
M207	United Way arrears recov
M208	United Way arrs $ purge
M209	United Way arrs % purge
M220	Union dues – amount
M221	Union dues – percent
M222	Union dues – default
M223	Union dues – amt w/arrs
M224	Union Dues arrs $ purge

Table D.1 Commonly-Used Model Wage Types (cont.)

Wage Type	Wage Type Text
M225	Union Dues w/advance
M226	Union Dues advanced
M227	Union Dues prev per adv
M228	Union Dues adv paid back
M300	Tuition reimb-taxable
M301	Tuition reimb-non-tax
M302	Relocation expenses
M303	Health Care FSA Claim
M304	Dependent Care FSA Claim
M720	Donation – United Way
M721	Dntn.balance – United Way
M722	Dntn.total – United Way
M730	401K contribution
M740	Union dues
M741	Union dues
M742	Union dues (no limit)
M750	Tuition reimbursement
M760	Severance pay
M800	Regular working time
M801	Lump sum period hours
M802	On Call
M803	Training (internal)
M804	Training (external)
M805	Regular working time
M806	Lump sum period hours
M807	On call
M810	Sunday premium
M811	Holiday premium
M812	Shift premium

Table D.1 Commonly-Used Model Wage Types (cont.)

Wage Type	Wage Type Text
M850	Training (internal)
M851	Training (external)
M852	Sunday premium
M853	Holiday premium
M854	Shift premium
M855	Bereavement leave
M856	Military leave
M857	Unpaid leave
M858	Family medical leave
M859	Maternity leave
M860	Short term disability
M861	Long term disability
M862	Workers comp injury
M863	Strike/lockout
M890	Comp time balance 1.5
M891	Comp time balance 0.5
M901	Vacation payout
M902	Vacation payout
M903	Sick leave payout
M904	Floating holiday payout
M906	OT comp time payout
M910	Vacation liquidation
M9RN	1099R non-taxable wages
M9RT	1099R taxable wages
MC00	MC payment
MC01	MC withholding tax
MC03	MC OASDI
MC04	MC OASDI (employer)
MC05	MC Medicare

Table D.1 Commonly-Used Model Wage Types (cont.)

Wage Type	Wage Type Text
MC06	MC Medicare (employer)
MC10	Stock
MC41	MC disability
MCOR	Claim of right
MD00	Deduction, C with advance
MD02	Deduction, D, absolute
MD04	Deduction, C without arrears
MD06	Deduction, D with arrears
MD10	Advance for MD00
MD20	Prev. per. advance for MD00
MD30	Advance MD20 paid back
MD50	Arrears with balance recovery
MD60	Recovery for MD50
MD70	Balance for MD60 recovery
MD80	Deduction for MD70 balance
MD90	Total for MD80 deduction
MDRC	Deduction recovery
MG10	Garnish: Creditor
MG11	Pieces
MG20	Garnish: Alimony/Support
MG30	Garnish: Levy
MG40	Garnish: Service charge
MG50	Garnish: Voluntary
MG60	Refund/Stop Payment Alimony
MG70	Refund/Stop Payment Levy
MM00	Overtime base
MM01	Overtime basic remun.
MM02	Overtime (base)
MM10	Overtime 100 % + 25 %

Table D.1 Commonly-Used Model Wage Types (cont.)

Wage Type	Wage Type Text
MM20	Overtime 100 % + 50 %
MM30	Overtime 100 % + 100 %
MMRR	Counter regular rate
MNOC	Noncash taxable
MP10	Claim clearing deduction
MP11	Dntn. balance – ClmClr
MP12	Dntn. total – ClmClr
MQ10	Overtime bonus 25 %
MQ20	Overtime bonus 50 %
MQ30	Overtime bonus 100 %
MQ40	Sunday bonus 50 %
MQ50	PHoliday bonus 100 %
MQ70	Nightshift bonus 20 %
MRP1	Clear claim (Txblty 1)
BA10	Cancer policy after-tax
BA11	Medical 2 EE after-tax
BA12	Retiree Med EE after-tax
BA13	Group Ins EE after-tax
BA14	Medical HMO EE after-tax
BA15	Indemn 90/10 EE after-tax
BA16	Indemn 80/20 EE after-tax
BA17	Medical PPO EE after-tax
BA18	Retiree Med EE after-tax
BA20	Basic Life EE after-tax
BA21	LTD EE after-tax
BA22	Dep Life EE after-tax
BA23	Opt Life EE after-tax
BA24	AD&D EE after-tax
BA25	Life 5 EE after-tax

Table D.1 Commonly-Used Model Wage Types (cont.)

Wage Type	Wage Type Text
BA26	STD EE after-tax
BA27	Travel EE after-tax
BA30	Savings EE After-tax
BA31	401(k) EE after-tax
BA32	Cash Bal EE after-tax
BA33	Thrift EE after-tax
BA34	Savings 3 EE after-tax
BA35	Savings 4 EE after-tax
BA36	Pension EE post-tax
BA50	Car EE after-Tax
BA51	Fitness EE after-Tax
BA52	Legal Ins EE after-tax
BA53	Charity EE after-tax
BA54	Vacation Buy EE after-tax
BA60	EAP EE after-tax
BA61	Health Club EE after-tax
BA62	Pension EE after-tax
BA63	Defer Comp-S EE after-tax
BA64	Defer Comp-B EE after-tax
BA65	Vac Buy EE after-tax
BA70	Stock Purch EE after-Tax
BA71	Alt Stock EE after-tax
BC31	EE age catch-up contrib
BC35	Pension1 compensation
BC36	Pension2 compensation
BC37	Grandf. Pens. compensation
BC40	(CL) Spending Acct. clm.
BE10	Std Medical EE pre-tax
BE11	Dental EE pre-tax

Table D.1 Commonly-Used Model Wage Types (cont.)

Wage Type	Wage Type Text
BE12	Vision EE pre-tax
BE13	Group Ins EE pre-tax
BE14	Medical HMO EE pre-tax
BE15	Indemnity 90/10 EE pre-tax
BE16	Indemnity 80/20 EE pre-tax
BE17	Medical PPO EE pre-tax
BE18	Retiree Med EE pre-tax
BE20	Basic Life EE pre-tax
BE21	LTD EE pre-tax
BE22	Dep Life EE pre-tax
BE23	Opt Life EE pre-tax
BE24	AD&D EE pre-tax
BE25	Life 5 EE pre-tax
BE26	STD EE pre-tax
BE27	Travel EE pre-tax
BE30	Savings EE Pre-tax
BE31	401(k) EE pre-tax
BE32	403(b) EE pre-tax
BE33	Thrift EE pre-tax
BE34	457 EE pre-tax
BE35	Savings 4 EE pre-tax
BE36	Pension EE pre-tax
BE40	Health Care EE pre-tax
BE41	Dep Care EE pre-tax
BE50	Car EE pre-tax
BE51	Fitness EE pre-tax
BE52	Legal Ins EE pre-tax
BE53	Charity EE pre-tax
BE54	Vacation Buy EE pre-tax

Table D.1 Commonly-Used Model Wage Types (cont.)

Wage Type	Wage Type Text
BE60	EAP EE pre-tax
BE61	Health Club EE pre-tax
BE62	Pension EE pre-tax
BE63	Defer Comp-S EE pre-tax
BE64	Defer Comp-B EE pre-tax
BE65	Vac Buy EE pre-tax
BE70	Stock Purch EE pre-tax
BE80	403(b) EE age catch-up
BP10	Std Medical Provider
BP11	Dental Provider
BP12	Vision Provider
BP13	Group Ins Provider
BP14	Medical HMO Provider
BP15	Indemnity 90/10 Provider
BP16	Indemnity 80/20 Provider
BP17	Medical PPO Provider
BP18	Retiree Med Provider
BP20	Basic Life Provider
BP21	LTD Provider
BP22	Dep Life Provider
BP23	Opt Life Provider
BP24	AD&D Provider
BP25	Life 5 Provider
BP26	STD Provider
BP27	Travel Provider
BP31	401(k) Provider
BP32	Cash Bal Provider
BP33	Thrift Provider
BP34	Savings 3 Provider

Table D.1 Commonly-Used Model Wage Types (cont.)

Wage Type	Wage Type Text
BP35	Savings 4 Provider
BP50	Car Provider
BP51	Fitness Provider
BP52	Legal Ins Provider
BP60	EAP Provider
BP61	Health Club Provider
BP62	Pension Provider
BP63	Defer Comp-S Provider
BP64	Defer Comp-B Provider
BP65	Vac Buy Provider
BP32	Cash Bal Provider
BP33	Thrift Provider
BP34	Savings 3 Provider
BP35	Savings 4 Provider
BP50	Car Provider
BP51	Fitness Provider
BP52	Legal Ins Provider
BP60	EAP Provider
BP61	Health Club Provider
BP62	Pension Provider
BP63	Defer Comp-S Provider
BP64	Defer Comp-B Provider
BP65	Vac Buy Provider
BR10	Std Medical Employer
BR11	Dental Employer
BR12	Vision Employer
BR13	Group Ins Employer
BR14	Medical HMO Employer
BR15	Indemnity 90/10 Employer

Table D.1 Commonly-Used Model Wage Types (cont.)

Wage Type	Wage Type Text
BR16	Indemnity 80/20 Employer
BR17	Medical PPO Employer
BR18	Retiree Med Employer
BR20	Basic Life Employer
BR21	LTD Employer
BR22	Dep Life Employer
BR23	Opt Life Employer
BR24	AD&D Employer
BR25	Life 5 Employer
BR26	STD Employer
BR27	Travel Employer
BR30	Savings Employer
BR31	401(k) Employer
BR32	403(b) Employer
BR33	Thrift Employer
BR34	457 Employer
BR35	Savings 4 Employer
BR36	Pension Employer contr.
BR40	Health Care Employer
BR41	Dependent care Employer
BR50	Flex Credit 1 Employer
BR51	Flex Credit 2 Employer
BR52	Legal Ins Employer
BR53	Charity Employer
BR54	Vacation Buy Employer
BR60	EAP Employer
BR61	Health Club Employer
BR62	Pension Employer
BR63	Defer Comp-S Employer

Table D.1 Commonly-Used Model Wage Types (cont.)

Wage Type	Wage Type Text
BR64	Defer Comp-B Employer
BR65	Vac Buy Employer
BR70	Stock Purch Employer
BR71	Alt Stock Employer
BSAL	Benefit Salary
BT40	401(k) Roth Catchup Posttax
BU31	ER age catch-up contrib
BX40	Dep. Care Reimbursement
BX41	Health Care Reimbursement

Table D.1 Commonly-Used Model Wage Types (cont.)

E   Commonly-Used Processing Classes and Specifications

We have referred to processing classes throughout this book. When talking about wage types and rules, you have to talk about processing classes as well. Processing classes decide the behavior and processing of wage types in schemas and rules. This Appendix presents a list of processing classes and their specifications. As discussed earlier in the book, you can add new specifications to the existing processing classes and use them to manipulate the wage types as necessary.

> **Note**
>
> The specifications for each processing class are delivered by SAP and are presented in Table E.1. However, you can also add and configure new values for these specifications. Therefore, you should check the exact list of values in your implementation.

Processing Class/ Specification	Description
Processing Class – 1	Assignment to valuation bases
0	Wage type not included in valuation basis
1	Wage type included in valuation basis /001
2	Wage type included in valuation basis /002
3	Wage type included in valuation basis /001 and /002
4	
5	Division of valuation bases /001 and /004
6	
8	Wage type included in valuation basis /008 – tips
9	Wage type included in valuation basis /009 – tips
Processing Class – 3	Cumulation and storage of time wage types

Table E.1 Commonly-Used Processing Classes and Specifications

Processing Class/ Specification	Description
0	Pass on unchanged
1	Storage, cumulation with ESG for PCR
2	Storage with ESG for PCR and A split
3	Storage, cumulation for hourly wage only
4	Storage with ESG for PCR and A split for hourly wage only
5	Storage, cumulation, accumulation of overtime hours
6	Storage with ESG for pers. calc. rule, cumulation
Processing Class – 4	Summarize WT acc. to TX and SI periods
0	Transfer in summarized form
1	Store in summarized form in RT
2	Summarized allocation according to C1 indicator
3	Summarized allocation according to C2 indicator
6	Transfer without modification
Processing Class – 5	Create net renumeration and total expenditure
0	Store in RT without split indicator
1	Addition in statutory net amount and total expenditure
3	Pass on in summarized form
4	Summarized storage in RT and subtraction in net
5	Summarized storage in RT and addition in total
Processing Class – 6	Enter wage type from old payroll account in LRT
0	Wage type will not be transferred
1	Wage type will be taken from previous payroll
2	Wage type will be taken from same year
Processing Class – 8	Mark wage types for monthly factoring
0	No reduction
1	Reduction with factor /801
2	Reduction with factor /802

Table E.1 Commonly-Used Processing Classes and Specifications (cont.)

Processing Class/ Specification	Description
3	Reduction with factor /803
4	Reduction with factor /804
5	Reduction with factor /805
6	Reduction with factor /806
7	Reduction with factor /807
8	Reduction with factor /808
9	Reduction with factor /809
A	Reduction with factor /801, with rounding 005
Processing Class – 15	Basic formula for creating averages
1	Basic formula 1 for averages of last 3 months
2	Basic formula 2 for averages of last 12 months
A	Calculation of averages with frozen values
Processing Class – 20	Cumulation and storage at end of gross part
1	Pass on unchanged
2	Eliminate wage type
3	RT storage and cumulation
4	RT storage without splits
5	RT storage with ESG for PCR and A split
6	RT storage with A split
7	Pass on in summarized form
8	Route as-is and cumulate
9	Summarized RT storage and cumulation
Processing Class – 24	Transfer Control
0	Effect transfer up to net pay only
1	Always effect transfer in full
Processing Class – 25	Behavior after end of payments/deductions
0	Pass on unchanged
1	Summarized RT storage with transfer indicator
Processing Class – 30	Cumulation update

Table E.1 Commonly-Used Processing Classes and Specifications (cont.)

Processing Class/ Specification	Description
0	Wage type must not be cumulated
1	AMT and NUM of wage type must be cumulated in current year
2	BETRG of wage type must be cumulated in current year
3	ANZHL of wage type must be cumulated in current year
T	Cumulation performed according to table T54C3
Processing Class – 31	Allocate monthly lump sums to cost distribution
0	Wage type does not lead to cost center debits/ credits
1	Calculate paid public holidays
2	Calculate total paid non-work
3	Calculate paid non-work and unpaid absence time
Processing Class – 35	Shift change compensation for substitutions
0	Wage type not included in the calculation
1	Wage type included in the calculation with bonuses
2	Only bonuses are included in the calculation
Processing Class – 41	Cumulation and storage of wage types to be limited
1	Unchanged references
2	Eliminating wage types
3	RT storage and cumulation
4	RT storage without splits
5	RT storage with payroll type and A split
6	RT storage with A split
7	Summarized references
8	Unchanged references and cumulation
9	Summarized RT storage and cumulation

Table E.1 Commonly-Used Processing Classes and Specifications (cont.)

Processing Class/ Specification	Description
B	RT storage with V0 split and cumulation
Processing Class – 59	Garnishments: Calculation of the disposable net
0	Not used for garnishments
1	Transfer to disposable net amount (same sign)
2	Transfer to disposable net amount (sign reversed)
3	Completely non-exempt
4	Used for garnishments
Processing Class – 60	Save garnishment wage types
0	No save in results table, no longer used
1	Save in results table
2	Used after garnishments
Processing Class – 65	415 limit deduction category (pre-tax or after-tax).
A	After-tax deduction
P	Pre-tax deduction
Processing Class – 66 (changed to 50 in newer versions)	Deduction/donation processing
1	Wage type is processed as deduction/donation
2	Wage type is processed as balance
Processing Class – 68	Payment type for tax calculation
1	Regular payment
2	Supplemental payment
3	Cumulative payment
4	Vacation payment
5	Perform gross-up using regular method
Processing Class – 69	Taxable earning or non-taxable contribution
1	Taxable earning
2	Non-taxable contribution
3	Taxable but not taxed

Table E.1 Commonly-Used Processing Classes and Specifications (cont.)

Processing Class/ Specification	Description
4	Taxable but not reportable (1042S)
Processing Class – 70	Work tax area override proration for salaried employees
1	Working hours counter wagetype
2	Prorate according to infotypes 207 and 208, and work tax area overrides
Processing Class – 71	Wage type tax classification
0	Regular taxable wages
1	Regular wages
2	Unemployment taxable only
3	Taxable portion of benefit pay
4	Completely tax free
5	Nonresident taxation
A	Adoption assistant
B	Substantiated business expense reimbursement
C	Cafeteria plans
D	Dependent care reimbursement
E	Employee stock purchase plan
F	Wages accrued at death, paid in the same year
G	Group term life
I	403(b)
K	Group term life insurance
L	401(k) pre-tax contribution
M	<to be defined>
N	Non taxable wages
P	Personal use of company car
R	Tuition reimbursement
S	Severance pay
T	Tips

Table E.1 Commonly-Used Processing Classes and Specifications (cont.)

Processing Class/ Specification	Description
U	Unsubstantiated business expense reimbursement
V	Relocation (non excludable)
W	Relocation (excludable)
Processing Class – 72	Employer/Employee tax
1	Employee tax
2	Employer tax
Processing Class – 73	Third-party remittance sign assignment
1	Reverse the sign
Processing Class – 74	1042S processing
0	50: Other income
F	15: Scholarship or fellowship grants
H	17: Compensation for dependent personal service
I	18: Compensation for teaching
J	19: Compensation during studying and training
Processing Class – 76	Special payroll run
1	Wage type is for special run (e.g., bonus)
2	Wage type is for special and regular payroll run
Processing Class – 78	Third-party remittance
1	Deductions to be remitted
2	Taxes to be remitted
3	Benefits to be remitted to payee
4	Garnishments to be remitted
Processing Class – 79	Wage type group for modifier D (month-end accruals)
0	Not relevant to month-end accruals
1	Wage type group 1 for modifier D (month-end accruals)
2	Wage type group 2 for modifier D (month-end accruals)
Processing Class – 81	Regular/overtime hours (tips processing)

Table E.1 Commonly-Used Processing Classes and Specifications (cont.)

Processing Class/ Specification	Description
1	Regular hours (tipped position)
2	Regular hours (non-tipped position)
3	Overtime hours (tipped position)
4	Overtime hours (non-tipped position)
Processing Class – 83	Calculate percentage deductions during retroactive accounting
1	Take old basis, ignore difference
2	Take new basis to calculate deductions
3	Take new basis if greater than old basis
4	Take new basis if smaller than old basis
5	Take old basis, carry difference forward to next period
6	Take old basis, positive difference to next period
7	Take old basis, negative difference to next period
Processing Class – 84	Non-cash income type for tax calculation
1	Tip income
2	Other non-cash income
3	Indirect tip income
4	Sub-minimum payment
5	Allocated tip amount
6	Gross receipts for tip allocation
Processing Class – 86	Cumulate worked hours for tax calculation
1	Cumulate the number as basic hours worked
2	Cumulate the number as overtime hours
3	Cumulate the number as absence hours

Table E.1 Commonly-Used Processing Classes and Specifications (cont.)

F List of Useful Payroll Operations

This appendix discusses the important and commonly-used Payroll operations. A figure is included with many of the operations to demonstrate how they are used in Payroll rules. Each operation should start at the correct indentation in the rules editor. For example, in the Figures throughout this Appendix, you will notice that the operations are positioned along the plus sign (+) from the top line. Chapter 4 includes examples on how to create custom rules and uses some of these operations in those examples.

ADDCU

Add cumulative table entries operation. This operation is used to create CRT table entries and depends on processing class **30**, which controls the cumulation of wage types. You will find this operation in SAP-delivered rules. Refer to Figure F.1.

000010	BLOCK	BEG			Final processing USA
000020	PIT	X070	GEN	NOAB	Error for whatever w/type is still in IT
000030	BENTB				Update BENTAB (benefits processing)
000040	ADDCU		P30		Update cumulative results (table CRT)

Figure F.1 ADDCU Operation

ADDWT

The most commonly used operation in payroll rules is used to write wage types in the **IT** table. It can be used with a specific wage type or with a wildcard character. You will find this operation in most of the payroll rules. Figure F.2 shows usage of this operation.

000010		D	VWTCL	01
000020	*		ERROR	
000030	0		ADDWT	*

Figure F.2 ADDWT Operation

ADDWTE

This operation is similar to **ADDWT**, however, it writes wage types to the **RT** table. SAP recommends that you write the wage types to the **RT** table when you are done processing them. Typically, you will find this operation toward the end of the payroll schema. Figure F.3 shows that the rule is writing a wage type to the **RT** table when processing class **3** has a specification of **1**.

```
                 ----------+---------+---------+---------+---
    000010               D VWTCL 03
    000020  *              ERROR
    000030  0              ADDWT *
    000040  1              ADDWTE*   ELIMI KTX ADDCU
```

Figure F.3 ADDWTE Operation

AMT

Used for calculations in the current field. When used with a wage type, this field will use the wage type amount. Figure F.4 demonstrates that the **AMT** operation is used to set the amount to a value equal to **50**.

```
              --------+--------+--------+--------+--------+-
    000010            AMT=50   NUM=1    MULTI NAA ADDWT 1001
```

Figure F.4 AMT Operation

CMPER

Compare payroll periods. This operation has many variations for **IN-PERIOD** and **FOR-PERIODS** in payroll and therefore has good usage in retroactive situations. Figure F.5 shows usage of this operation with a variation (**CMPERMM**) where the period number of the **FOR-PERIOD** is compared with the period number of the **IN-PERIOD**. Please note that this operation has many variations depending on whether you are checking **FOR-PERIOD** or **IN-PERIOD**. Refer to the documentation for the operation.

```
    Line     Var.Key  CL T Operation Operatio
             ----------------+---------+-------
    000010               D CMPERRMM 6
    000020  <              ADDWT *
    000030  >              ADDWT 1001
```

Figure F.5 CMPER Operation

DIVID

Divide operation. It is used for dividing two numbers or amounts. Figure F.6 shows that the operation **DIVID** is used to divide Amount (A) with Number (N) and places the resulting amount back in Amount (A). Subsequently, the **ADDWT** operation writes the wage type with a new amount in the IT table. As such, the wage type is written with the amount equal to 10 (50 divided by 5).

```
Line   Var.Key  CL T Operation Operation Operation Operation O
       ---------------+---------+---------+---------+---------+
 000010                   AMT=50    NUM=5     DIVID ANA ADDWT *
```

Figure F.6 DIVID Operation

ELIMI

Eliminate split indicators operation. It is used to eliminate different splits such as cost center, bank transfer, and variable assignment splits, which are created because of the Benefits and Time Management modules. A complementary operation, **SETIN,** is used to revert the required splits. SAP uses many different split indicators, as follows:

- ▸ R: Employee subgroup grouping
- ▸ A: Work center period
- ▸ K: Cost accounting
- ▸ U: Bank transfer
- ▸ X: Variable assignment
- ▸ Y: Absence assignment
- ▸ Z: Time unit

Figure F.7 shows the use of the **ELIMI** operation. In the example rule of Figure F.7, all splits are eliminated because the **ELIMI *** operation is used.

```
       ----------------+---------+---------+---
 000010              D VWTCL 59
 000020  *
 000030  1             ELIMI *    ADDWT *
 000040  2             ELIMI *    ADDWT *
 000050  3             ELIMI *    ADDWT *
 000060  4             ELIMI *    ADDWT *
```

Figure F.7 ELIMI Operation

ERROR

When used during the decision making of a rule, this operation terminates the processing. In payroll logs, SAP typically displays the personnel number, wage type, and processing class that caused the error in the rule. Onscreen, such errors are visible with red highlights.

GCY

Continue processing with rule operation. This operation is used to drive one rule from another; however, logic does not come back to the original rule. In Figure F.8, the logic is sent to rule **U111** using **GCY** operation.

Figure F.8 GCY Operation

MULTI

Multiplication operation. This operation uses three elements of wage types, as seen in Chapter 3: Number (N), Amount (A), and Rate (R). For example, **NRA** multiplies Number with Rate and moves the result to the Amount field. **NAA** multiplies Number with Amount and moves the result to the Amount field. Figure F.4 uses the **MULTI** operation; the wage type amount multiplies 50 by 1 to equal 50.

NEXTR

Processes the next line in a rule. When the logic in one line is too long for the line size, you can extend it to the next line number with this operation. Remember that the rules editor only recognizes the operation at a particular indentation, limiting the space on one line. Figure F.9 shows the overflow of logic from lines 30 and 40; the **NEXTR** operation is used in both of those lines to continue the logic to the next lines.

```
         --------------+---------+---------+---------+----
000010           D VWTCL 83
000020  *            ADDWT *
000030  1            AMT-0 *    ZERO= N    NEXTR        1.
000040  1       1    VALBS=1    ADDWT *    NEXTR
000050  1       2    WGTYP=*    AMT=0 *    ADDWT *
000060  2            ZERO= N    ADDWT *                 2.
000070  3       D    AMT-0 *    ZERO= N    AMT?0        3.
000080  3  *         FILLF A    ADDWT *
000090  3  <         VALBS=1    ADDWT *    NEXTR
000100  3  <    1    WGTYP=*    AMT=0 *    ADDWT *
```

Figure F.9 NEXTR Operation

NUM

Calculation in the number field operation. This operation is used with a wage type to manipulate the **NUM** field of wage types. For example, you can move a particular value into a number field or you can move zero into the number field. Figures F.4 and F.6 demonstrate use of **NUM**.

OPIND

Operations indicator operation. This operation is used to change the signs of fields from negative to positive, or vice versa. Figure F.10 uses this operation to reverse the sign of the wage type currently processed by that rule.

```
000040  *** *        D VWTCL 10
000050  *** * *        OPIND    ELIMI A
000060  *** * 0        OPIND    ADDWT *
```

Figure F.10 OPIND Operation

OUTWP

Workplace and basic pay data operation. This operation has many variations to read different fields in enterprise and payroll structures. In the rule editor, use **OUTWP** to do a pull-down in the Operation field and the system displays the variations of the **OUTWP** operation. Depending on the decision logic, you need to use the correct one. For example, if you want to make a decision on an employee group, then look for **OUTWPPERSG**. Figure F.11 uses a decision on an employee group.

F | List of Useful Payroll Operations

000010		D	OUTWPPERSG		
000020	1		ADDWT *		
000030	2		OPIND	NUM=2	| MULTI NAA ADDWT *

Figure F.11 OUTWP Operation

PCY

Run one personnel calculation rule from another. Unlike operation **GCY**, in this case, the logic returns to the original rule. Figure F.12 shows the usage of the **PCY** operation where rule control is passed to a new rule. Please note that these sample rules are created to demonstrate exact operations; the logic is only meant for the sample.

000010		D	OUTWPPERSG		
000020	*		ADDWT *		
000030	1		ADDWT *		
000040	2		OPIND	NUM=2	MULTI NAA ADDWT *
000050	3	P	PCY U111		
000060	4		OPIND	AMT=50	MULTI ANN ADDWT *

Figure F.12 PCY Operation

PRINT

Print the current table entry to display the current table entry in the schema run.

RESET

Resets the split indicators. For example, when you use the **ELIMI *** operation, you eliminate all split indicators. If you need to reset only the **K** indicator, use the **RESET K** operation, as shown in Figure F.13.

000010			ELIMI *	RESET K

Figure F.13 RESET Operation

RETRO

Helps you to verify whether the payroll is in retroactive calculation. Use of this operation is discussed in Chapter 4.

ROUND

Rounding off while reading a wage type. You can use this operation to round off an amount, numbers, or rates. Figure F.14 shows an amount rounded up by 5. The **ROUND** operation has many variations which can be used to either round the **AMT**, **NUM**, or **RTE** fields up or down. As shown in Figure F.14, you can round to the next 5, 10, and so on.

Figure F.14 ROUND Operation

RTE

This operation is used for rate calculations with a wage type. Figure F.15 shows how the **RTE** (Rate) operation is used to set the rate to a particular value, or to use mathematical operations with **RTE**.

Figure F.15 RTE Operation

SUBWT

This operation subtracts wage types from or to a subsequent wage type. This is useful when you need to create a new wage type based on a difference of two other wage types. In Figure F.16, the rule makes a decision on the wage type. In line 20, wage type **2001** is created with negative **AMT**, **RTE**, and **NUM** values as they are in wage type **1000**. Similarly, in line 30, wage type **2002** is created from **1001** with the **SUBWT** operation.

Line	Var.Key	CL	T	Operation	Operation	Ope
000010			D	WGTYP?		
000020	1000			SUBWT 2001		
000030	1001			SUBWT 2002		

Figure F.16 SUBWT Operation

TABLE

This operation prepares access to tables. Used to read infotype-based tables, or **T511K** tables. The operation limits your ability to read every infotype in the rule. In Figure F.17, the rule is reading table **PA0007** (planned work schedule infotype), and based on the value of a certain field from the table, a decision logic is built into the rule.

```
    --------------+----------+----------+----------+
000010              D  TABLEP007 NUM= ZTERFNUM?0
000020  >           D  NUM?9
000030  > >            ADDWT *
```

Figure F.17 TABLE Operation

UMOD

This operation sets up US modifiers. It has three variations to set employee group, tax area, or to set the taxation always on residence tax area.

UTAXR

This operation sets up US resident tax area or tax authority.

VAKEY

Variable key position. This operation is used to make decisions based on values of fields that are read in rules. Similar to the **OUTWP** operation, this operation too has many variations to use different fields to make decisions. Figure F.18 shows rule **U011**, which makes a decision on the payroll type (A or B).

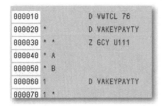

```
000010            D VWTCL 76
000020  *         D VAKEYPAYTY
000030  * *       Z GCY U111
000040  * A
000050  * B
000060  1         D VAKEYPAYTY
000070  1 *
```

Figure F.18 VAKEY Operation

VALEN

Set the length of a variable key. You can use this operation prior to the **VAKEY** operation to read only part of the key based on the length set. Figure F.19 shows the delivered SAP rule (**X009**), which uses this operation to set the length to 2.

```
000010              D VAKEYALZNR
000020 *            D VALEN 2    WGTYP?
000030 * **         D AMT?0.00
000040 * ** *         ADDWT *
000050 * ** =
000060 * /0
000070 N             ADDWT *
```

Figure F.19 VALEN Operation

VWTCL

Reads specifications of the processing class and makes a decision. This is a commonly-used operation. If you create a new specification for the processing class and decide to use it in rules, this operation will help with decision making. You will find plenty of examples in the rules SAP supplies to verify the processing class. Figure F.20 shows a decision being made on processing class **5**. When the specification for processing class is **0**, **1**, **3** or any other value (*****), different lines in the rule will be executed based on decision logic.

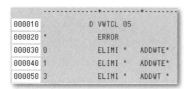

```
000010              D VWTCL 05
000020 *              ERROR
000030 0              ELIMI *   ADDWTE*
000040 1              ELIMI *   ADDWTE*
000050 3              ELIMI *   ADDWT *
```

Figure F.20 VWTCL Operation

WCWP

Get the current calendar month or week. This operation is useful when you need to make a payroll decision based on a particular time of the year.

WGTYP

Set the wage type. This operation is used to verify whether you are reading a certain wage type and following the rule's logic. See Figure F.16 for usage of this operation.

ZERO

Initialize current fields. Nullify the values.

G   About the Author

Satish Badgi has been involved in the US payroll market for over 10 years. His implementations of SAP HR/Payroll cover many industries, such as manufacturing, public sector, utilities, and finance. In addition, he has conducted training courses for customers in the HR and Payroll area, and is a regular presenter at ASUG conferences and events. Satish also writes for HRExpert newsletter and the SAPTips community.

Index

/4xx
  tax wage types 200
1042S
  statutory reporting 127
1042S processing 194
1099
  overpayment adjustments 217
401(k) 21, 52, 73, 77, 153
  catch-up contributions 158
  change in contribution 43, 44
  contribution changes 168
  contributions
    deduction 56, 58
  deduction changes 251
  deductions 58
    infotype for 193
    wage type 197
  wage type 69
  wage type assignment 159
401KL
  constant 157
403(b) 153
457 153

A

Accounts Payable (AP) 22, 147, 172, 246
ACCR table 231, 233
accruals 16, 22, 227, 232
  configuration 228
  defined 227
  process and posting 231
  subschema 228
acknowledgment program 246
ADDCU 110, 307
additional master data infotypes 34
Additional Payments and Deductions 45
ADDWT 307, 309
ADDWTE 308
ad-hoc query
  reporting 49
ADJT sub-type 206, 207
adjustment date 208
adjustments 213
ADP 23

advanced topics 217
after tax deduction
  wage type for 162
allowable disposable net income 176
amount 60
AMT 308
  wage type element 60
annual reports 214
arrears
  net pay 82
  retroactive 93
  table, ARRRS 112
arrears processing 75, 91–93, 98
ARRRS 94, 116
audit report 214
author's email address 254

B

B
  wage types, starting with 56
B2 time clusters 110
balance
  goal amount 75
balance and deduction 75
balance sheet 96
balance sheet accounts 58
bank account
  direct deposit of pay 36
bank transfer 230, 266
  net processing 118
base wage for BSI
  wage type 69
basic pay 35, 56, 124
  infotype for 192
  wage type for 78
benefit 21, 106, 114
  401(k) 21
  enrollment data 247
  flexible spending accounts 21
  health insurance 21
  life insurance 21
  pension 21
  providers 167

benefits
  data 32
  deductions 287
  different cost types 150
  integration 151
benefits constants table
  shortcut to maintain 156
benefits-payroll integration
  diagram of 145
benefits-related wage types 287
best practices 253
  maintaining schemas, rules, and wage
    types 253
Bill of Materials
  schema 102
biweekly payroll 90, 100, 228
bonus
  pay 60
  payments 45, 206
  payroll run 248
Bonus and Off Cycle 45
BSAL
  base salary wage type 160
BSI Tax Factory 23, 26, 69, 78, 80, 113,
  189
BT table 266
Business Solutions Inc.
  web site 23

C

C51R6 244
call-in time 259
car allowance
  permissibility 58
cash advances
  processing 76
cash-based accounting 228
catalog
  US wage types 54
catch-up contributions 148, 153, 158
  401(k) 21
CCPA 176, 178
Ceridian 23
check date 230
CHECK function 108
check processing 266
checks
  replacement 206

child support 173
  multiple payments, division of disposable
    net income 185
  wage type 180
claim generation process 218
claims 212, 218
  clearing 223
  handling 217
  identifying in payroll 220
  strategy 221
claims processing
  diagram of 218
claims report 218, 220, 225
  example of 220
clearing account 97
clearing claims 224
  employee payment plan 226
  payroll forgiven 222
  payroll not forgiven 223
clearing process
  claims report 221
closing date 230
clusters 27
  time 110
CMPER 308
comments
  asterisk 257
compare payroll periods
  CMPER 308
comparing results
  third-party products 250
constants 161
  defined 155
  table 155
Consumer Credit Protection Act (CCPA)
  176
contribution limits
  for HCA and DCA 165
control record 25, 252
  bypassing the check 108
  payroll calendar 23
Controlling (CO) 22
COPY function 104
Cost Center Accounting (CCA) 22
Costs tab
  infotype 0167 149
country code 10 61
coverage amount 161
cross-year tax calculations 32

CRT 89, 147, 307
  payroll table 206
  results table 241
cumulation 52, 57, 59, 68–73, 77, 84,
  88, 89, 114, 261
  year-to-date 27
cumulative results table 89, 118
current calendar
  get month or week 315
custom naming specifications 105
custom schemas
  defined 100
custom tax models
  creating 197
custom wage types 287
customer name space
  for constants 157

D

data errors in payroll
  table of 47
Data Medium Exchange (DME) 83
data processing, basic
  subschema for 108
DCA (Dependent Care Account) 164
DDNTK 93, 116, 266
decision logic 315
deduction
  defined 56, 72
deduction calculation 263
deduction models
  annual maintenance 90
deduction not taken 93
deduction wage types 75
  steps for configuring 74
deduction-related wage types 260
deductions 72
  involuntary 29
  not-taken 91
  post-tax 53
  pre-tax 53
  Priority A 92
  priority and arrears 91
  priority levels 92
  remittance to vendors 240
  taxes 52
  technical wage types for 77
  voluntary 29

deductions and earnings infotype 44
deductions not taken table 264
Department of Health and Human Services
  web site 177
Dependent Care Account (DCA) 164
dialog wage type 56
  creating 65
  deductions 72
dialogue 64
direct deposit 36, 83
disposable income 176
  defined 176
disposable net income 22, 71, 117, 173,
  176, 184, 265
  concept of 178
  rules 173
DIVID
  divide operation 309
DME Workbench 83
documentation 251
drill down 123
  defined 109
due date 246

E

earliest retroactive date 31
earning wage type 57
  processing classes, table of 71
earning wage type M003 79
earnings 36, 64, 236
  defined 53, 56
  entering with infotypes 66
  taxes 53
earnings and deductions 261
  infotype 44
EE pre-tax deductions 220
elements
  wage types, of 59
ELIMI 138, 309, 312
  eliminate split indicators 309
employee cost 150
employee data
  normal 32
  transactions for managing 32
employee events
  changes to health plan coverage 167
employee life events 43

employee master data 266
  infotypes 29, 32
  infotypes in 27
Employee Remuneration 37
Employee Self Service (ESS) 31
employee-dependent deductions 33
employer contribution
  wage type for 162
employer cost 147, 151
employer tax 194
END OF COPY 260
ERROR 310
error conditions 123
error-free report
  test run 66
errors
  detecting 101
  reporting 203
ESS
  Employee Self Service 31
evaluation classes 58
executive employees 58
expense 96
expense accounts 58
export, results table 266
External Bank Transfer 46

F

factoring 70
  wage types 70
Federal Consumer Credit Protection Act
  (CCPA) 176
Federal Insurance Contribution Act
  (FICA) 162
federal tax levy wage type 180
federal taxes
  wage types for 81
FI posting 243
FICA 53, 162
Finance Integration (FI) 22
financial account management 242
flexible spending accounts 21, 146, 164,
  247
  deduction 56
forced retroactive payroll 31
foregiveness
  write off amounts owed 224
Form 941 212

FOR-PERIOD 308
FSA
  flexible spending account 164
  lifecycle, diagram of 164
  outsourcing 165
functions 103, 105
  CHECK 108
  COM 257
  COPY UBE1 114
  COPY UBE2 115
  COPY UDP0 116
  DAYPR 110
  GEN/8 115
  IF 117
  LIMIT 116
  P0002 108
  P0006 108
  P0009 118
  P0011 118
  P0014 108, 114, 124
  P0015 114
  P0103 127
  P0167 114
  P0168 114
  P0169 115
  P0170 115
  P0207 108
  P0221 111
  P0267 114
  P0377 116
  P2003 110
  P2010 110
  P9ZNC 118
  PARTT 110, 259
  PRDNT 116
  PRT 117
  UACGF 231
  UGARN 117
  UPAR1 113
  USTAX 113, 125
  WPBP 108, 137
  ZLIT 110, 259
Funds Management (FM) 22

G

garnishment 21, 107, 117, 240, 265
  calculation of 185
  configuring 172

data 32
document 172
impact on earnings and deductions 180
limit amounts 176
multiple 173, 179
order 172, 186
order type 175
process flow diagram 171
subschema 116, 181
garnishment deductions
calculation of 186
garnishment infotypes
infotype 0194 172
infotype 0195 172
infotype 0216 172
garnishment subschema 181, 265
view during run time 186
garnishment wage types
managing 180
GCY 310, 312
General Ledger (GL) 22, 147, 242
goal amount
balance 75
goal and balance wage type 75
goal-related wage types 260
goals and deductions wage types 263
go-live
mid-year 247
new year 247
good money 82, 221
defined 82
wage type for 82
GRORD
garnishment order table 186
gross
calculation 107
taxable 201
total 56
gross compensation
subschema for 109
gross compensation and time
subschema for 109
gross earnings and deductions
wage types for 81
gross income
for taxes 265
gross pay
earnings 53
pre-tax deductions from 53

wage type 69
gross payroll 236
defined 236
exporting 237
Gross to Net 235
Group Term Life Insurance 160
GRREC
garnishment records table 186
GRT table 237, 238

H

Health Care Account (HCA) 164
health expenses
qualified 165
health insurance
deduction 56
health plan deductions 58
health plans 39, 146, 167
infotype for 193
HIS 49
HR Payee 242, 243
Human Capital Management
HCM 19
human resources
HR 19

I

identify claims 226
IMG 67, 75, 90
implementation tips 247
Import menu
net payroll 238
imputed income 53, 147, 160–163
income
imputed 53
non-cash 194
Industry Solution-Public Sector 126
inflow wage type 112
infotype
0003 31, 223, 252
0006 38
0008 30, 35, 53
0009 36, 266
0011 46, 266
0014 39, 44, 53, 76, 90, 226, 261
0015 45, 53, 76, 226, 261
0041 148

0057 39, 53
0167 39, 146, 149, 261
0168 161, 261
0169 53, 146, 153, 263
0170 146, 165
0172 165
0207 38
0208 38
0209 190
0210 47, 190
0221 224, 260, 273
0234 190
0235 191
0267 45, 222–224, 227
0377 261
2010 35, 37
infotype 0014
  date range in 53
infotype 0167
  for health plans 53
infotype 0168
  for insurance plans 146
infotype 0169
  for savings plans 44
infotype 0170
  for Flexible Spending Account plans 165
infotype 0194
  garnishment document 172
infotype 0195
  garnishment order 172
infotype 0207
  residence tax area 108
infotype 0216
  garnishment adjustment 172
infotype 0221
  creating 203
  off-cycle payroll 202
  year-end adjustments 202
  year-end workbench 225
infotype 0267
  claims processing 45
  overpayments 45
IN-PERIOD 308
input combination field 67
Input Table 124
insurance plans 146, 160, 167
  infotype for 193
integration 96, 145
interfaces 146

Internal Revenue Service (IRS) 41, 53, 57, 192
investments
  capturing 154
IRS remittances 244
  wage types for 244
IS-PS
  (Industry Solution-Public Sector) 126
IT table 182, 307

K

K operation
  RESET 312

L

latest document creation dates 230
legacy code 101
legacy data
  transfer 248
legacy systems 249
loans
  personal, processing 76

M

M
  wage types, starting with 56
mandatory master data infotypes 33
manual check
  non-authorized 260, 263
manual checks
  processing 206
master data 32, 236
  HR/employee, maintaining 236
Medicare taxes 81, 191
Membership Fees 39
middle of pay period 261
mid-year go-live 247, 248
minus sign
  deductions 72
model wage type 56, 61, 65, 66, 72, 151, 158, 162, 180, 222, 226, 287
  collection 56
  commonly used 287
  copying 287
  starting with B 287
  using 61

model wage type catalog   24, 56
model wage type MG20
   garnishments   180
month-end accruals   228, 233, 266
MULTI
   multiplication operation   310
multiplier
   RTE   61

N

naming
   custom   105
negative time tracking   258
net calculation   107
   subschema UNA0   266
net pay   30, 36, 52, 53, 117
   calculating, subschema for   117
   defined   82
   negative amounts   82
   wage type for   78
net payroll   235, 236
   defined   236
   outsourcing   235
new year go-live   247
next line in a rule operation
   NEXTR   310
NEXTR   310
non-authorized check   111, 225, 260,
   263
non-cash income   194
non-resident
   alien   126
   taxes   192
Non-taxable   193
NRA   126
   multiplies   310
   non-resident alien   126
NUM   311
   wage type element   59
number   59
numbering scheme   61

O

off-cycle   45, 100, 209, 210, 248
off-cycle payroll   206
   infotype for   202
   Type A   222

Type C   225
   with infotype 0267   223
one-time deductions   45
one-time payments   45
   infotype for   192
OPERATION   133
operation limits   314
operations   103, 105
   ADDWT   139
   CMPER   139
   commonly-used   307
   ELIMI   138
   MULTI   139
   OUTWP   135
   OUTWPPERSG   135
   RETRO   138
   ROUND   138
   SETIN   138
   VWTCL   136
   XMES   140
OPIND
   operations indicator   311
order type   174
   garnishments   175
Organization Management   13
output of a payroll process   27
Outsourcing menu   236
OUTWP   311, 314
   workplace and basic pay data   311
OUTWPPERSG   311
overpaid taxes   221
overpayment   202, 203, 217
   claim   217
   clearing in payroll   223
   processing   217
override methods   190
overtime   89, 259
overtime pay   37, 61
   posting to payroll expenses   58

P

PA0007
   planned work schedule infotype   314
parallel payroll   249, 250
part pay period tables   259
pay
   basic   56
   net   53

pay frequency   22
pay period   30
  adjustments at middle   108
pay period table   248
paycheck   83
paychecks
  replacement, lost or stolen   206
payment method field   36
payment models   90
payment plan   222
  clearing claims   226
payments
  bonus   206
payroll
  biweekly   90, 100
  clusters   266
  control record   23
  data   32
  equation   29, 52
  indicator   206
  initialization, subschema for   108
  menu   220
  off-cycle   206
  period   139, 230, 233
  process   25
  processing   86
  reconciliation report   213
  results table (RT)   59, 78
  status   41, 203, 226
  tables   206
  weekly   100
Payroll Calculation Rules (PCR)   24, 130
payroll calendar
  sample   40
payroll control record   20, 30, 41, 47, 99,
  100
payroll cycle
  diagram of   47
payroll driver   26, 31, 99, 101, 121, 206,
  209
  RPCALCU0   209
payroll expenses
  posting to a period   228
payroll operations
  list of   307
payroll process   25
payroll reconciliation report   213
payroll results   76, 79, 86
  → payroll clusters

reversing   206
paystub   51
  additional features   54
  example of   51
PC_PAYRESULT
  transaction   86
PCR (Payroll Calculation Rules)   130
PCY   312
PE01   253
PE02   253
pension calculations   69
performance reward payment   45
permissibility   56, 57, 68, 85, 211
Personnel Administration   13, 32, 86
piano boxes
  permissibility   68
plan data tab   149
planned work schedule infotype
  PA0007   314
plus sign
  positioning of operations   307
posting
  AP   97
  GL   96
posting attributes   242
  configuring   229
posting dates   230
post-payroll checks   252
post-payroll process   25, 59
post-tax deductions   53, 73
  examples of   73
  infotypes for   53
pre-payroll
  checks   251
  data verification   47
  process   24
  verification tools and reports   31
pre-tax   57, 72, 77, 155
  deductions   53, 73, 148, 193, 220, 221,
    236
  deductions, infotypes   53
  deductions, Section 128   150
  deductions, wage type for   162
PRINT   312
priority A
  deductions   92
processing class   57, 62, 68, 69, 71, 79,
  136, 193, 229, 242, 299
  5   57

30 307
50 77, 260, 263
  replacement for 75
59 57, 176, 182
65 57
  pre-tax deductions 84
66 75, 112, 260
71 193, 197, 210, 222, 223
73 244
78 244
adjusting 68
earning wage types, table of 71
P66 112
table of 193
table of commonly used 62
processing module
  third-party 145
production mode
  running Tax Reporter in 211
proration 114, 261
provider 146
  cost 151
provider contributions
  wage type for 162
providers 146

Q

quarterly reports 212

R

rate 59
reciprocity
  local tax authority 191
reconciliation run 246
recurring payments
  infotype for 192
referral bonus 45
reimbursements 222, 224
remittance
  processing 241
  rules 173
  third-party 58
  third-party, due date 246
  to benefits providers 167
replacment checks 206
reporting errors 203
reports

annual 214
audit 214
payroll reconciliation 213
quarterly 212
RESET 312
residence tax authority 27, 38
residence-related tax areas 196
resource planning 249
results table 124
  creating 240
  export 266
retirement plan deductions
  annual limits 155
retirement plans 153
retirement savings plans 153
RETRO 138, 312
retroactive accounting 24, 30, 31, 44,
  112, 115, 213, 218, 220
  arrears 93
  calculation, RETRO operation 312
  data change 31
  definition of 30
  payroll 263, 266
  payroll, forced 40
retroactivity 218
ROUND 313
RPCALCU0 99, 249
  US Payroll driver 121
RPCLMSU0 220, 226
RPCPCC00 96
RPDLGA20
  wage type utilization report 181
RPUBTCU0 261
RT table 147, 232, 308
  payroll table 206
  results table 232, 241, 308
RTE 313
  wage type element 59
rule UGARN
  calculation of garnishments 185
rules 98, 103, 105, 114, 128
  maintaining, best practices 253
  running error-free 140
  running, step-by-step process 141
  U011 314
  UAC0 229
  UD** 116
  UD11 112, 116
  UD21 112, 116

UGARN 117
UGDN 117, 184
UNAM 111
UPTX 113
UW14 109, 124
writing in US Payroll 128
X013 110
X020 110
X023 112, 115
X024 112, 116
X025 112, 116
X040 266
XPPF 115, 261
XVAL 261
ZRU1 114, 131
rules editor 129, 253, 307
running balance
 wage type for displaying 75
running payroll 208

S

salary increase
 infotype for 30
sales commission 60
SAP configuration
 golden rule of 106
SAP documentation 29, 83, 96, 101
SAP Service Marketplace 157
Sarbanes-Oxley 251
savings bonds 21, 57, 73, 127
savings plans 44, 128, 146, 153, 168, 263
 infotype for 193
schema 14, 26, 54, 98, 113, 147, 220, 237, 244, 248
 defined 101
 maintaining, best practices 253
 U000 257
 U000, US Payroll schema 228
 U200 237
 U250 239
 UDD0 92
 ULK9 248
 USPS (US Public Sector) 126
 XLR0 257
schema editor 103, 120, 121, 253
Section 128
 pre-tax deductions 150

SETIN 309
sign reversal 77
slash
 technical wage types, starting with 56, 62
social security
 number 54
 tax types 81
 taxes 80, 191
SOX 251
specification
 processing classes 62
split 78, 108, 113, 200
split indicators
 eliminating 309
spool files 245
state taxes
 wage types for 81
State Unemployment Insurance 190, 212
statutory reporting 127
student tax treatment 192
subschema 99, 104, 187, 193, 200, 228
 QPCD 128
 UAC0 231, 266
 UAL0 114, 261
 UAP0 114, 261
 UBD0 257
 UBE1 114, 263
 UBE2 127, 263
 UDBS 263
 UDD0 115, 263
 UDNT 266
 UEND 118, 266
 UGRN 116, 265
 UIN0 257
 UMC0 111, 208, 260
 UNA0 266
 UNAO 117
 UNN0 118, 266
 UPNR 127
 UPPT 127
 UPR0 257
 URR0 266
 UT00 109, 258
 UTBS 261
 UTX0 112, 260, 264
 XPDD 264
subsequent maintenance node 197

SUBWT 313
supplemental rates 64, 191, 192
support packs 61
symbolic account assignment 243

T

T511K tables 314
T588B 248
tables
  558A 107
  5U8A 107
  5U8C 107
  ACCR 231
  ADR 109
  ARRRS 112, 116, 125
  BT (bank table) 118
  C1 111
  CRT 118
  DDNTK 112, 116, 264
  GRDOC 117
  GRORD 117
  GRREC 117
  IT (input table) 109, 111–117, 259
  NAME 109
  PARX 110, 111
  RT 117, 118, 125, 227
  RT (results table) 113
  T511K 128, 156
  T511P 156, 157, 160, 161
  T512W 56, 69, 151, 200, 229, 242
  T558C 248
  T558x 239
  T5U8C 248
  TAXR 109, 113
  TCRT 113, 201
  V0 113, 114
  WPBP 109, 125
  ZL 111, 259
tax 21, 78, 107
  area 195, 199
  class 194, 197, 200
  classification 210
  data 32
  deductions 38, 52
  infotypes 190
  levels 195
  levy 171
  Medicare 191

  non-resident 192
  override 191
  processing 112, 125, 189
  rates 80
  schemas 38
  social security 80, 191
  student 192
  types 81, 196, 199
  unemployment 196
  wage types 38, 52, 80, 81, 189
  withholding 196
  year 73
  year-end adjustments 202
tax adjustments
  year-end 202
tax and arrears data
  table T5U8C 248
tax authority 38, 81, 109, 125, 191, 194,
  195, 207, 248
  attaching a tax model to 198
tax calculations
  post-tax deductions 73
tax combo 84
  withholding taxes 199
tax implications
  overpayments 217
tax model 15, 189, 194, 197, 201
  attaching 198
  creating custom 197
  processing class for 193
Tax Reporter 27, 189, 202, 210, 211
  running in test mode 203
  steps before running 212
Tax Update Bulletins (TUB) 212, 252
tax withholding
  additional 47
taxable
  base 201
  gross 201
  income 202
  salary or earnings 221
  wages 222
taxed-when-earned calculation 206, 207
taxes and accounts posting
  Type C 225
TCRT
  payroll table 206
technical wage types 56, 62, 70, 71, 81
  earnings 71

starting with a slash (/) 180
Temporary Sequential Data 245
TemSe 245
termination
   employee, example of 219
test mode 202
   running Tax Reporter in 211
Test Run button 66
third-party
   payroll systems 235
   posting 246
   processing module 145
third-party process
   running 244
third-party remittance 27, 58, 77, 240
   due date 246
time clusters 110
time evaluations 35, 37, 109
time management 109
time wage types 111
time-based payments 259
time-related processing 258
tips
   processing class for 194
total benefits 77
total deductions 77
total gross 56
transaction data 40
transaction data infotypes
   table of 41
transactions
   PA20 32
   PA30 32
   PAUX 203
   PAUY 203, 204
   PC_PAYRESULT 86
   PE01 103, 257
   PE02 129
   PE04 138
   PU03 226
   SE16 251
   SE38 220
   SM31 68, 229
   *SM31, benefits constant table, mainte-
      nance* 156
   *SM31, used to display wage type table
      T512W* 182
true cumulation
   cumulation 89

TWEG 207
Type C
   off-cycle payroll 209

U

U000 99
   US Payroll schema 99
UACGF function 232
UBD0
   subschema for basic data processing 108
UBE1
   benefits subschema 193
UBE2
   benefits subschema 193
UCLM
   claims schema 220
UINO
   subschema for initializing payroll 108
UMOD 314
UNA0
   subschema for net calculations 104
unemployment tax 196
   infotype 0209 190
union dues 21, 39, 57
   garnishments, priority related to 92
   permissibility 58
unions 20
United Way
   garnishments, priority related to 92
   model wage type 61
US modifiers 314
US Payroll
   components of 26
   equation, diagram of 30
   process, diagram of 25
   schema 99
   uniqueness 20
US public sector
   accruals 22
US resident tax area 314
US schema
   changing 119
US subschemas
   table of 106
US tax subschema 260
US tax year 73
US wage type catalog 54
USTAX function 200

UT00
   subschema, gross compensation and time
      109
UTAXR   314
utilization report
   wage types   84
UTX0
   subschema for tax calculations   104

V

VAKEY   314
VALEN   315
valuation   71
valuation of wage types   110
variable assignment split   309
variable key
   length of   315
variable key position   314
vendor   147, 244
vendor 200025
   IRS, tax posting to   243
vendor posting   246
voluntary deductions   33
voluntary garnishments   176
VWTCL   315

W

W-2   214
   audit report   210
   test run   225
W-4   32, 41
   changes to data   47
   data changes   251
wage type   26, 35
   /101, total gross pay   273
   /110, garnishments, defined   181
   /117, pension plans   70
   /403   242
   /404   229
   /559, net pay   273
   /559, transfer funds to bank account   83
   /560   220
   /561   220
   /561, clearing   224
   /563   224
   /5U0, gross tax deductions   81
   /5U9   209, 225

/BT1   162
/G00, disposable net income   180, 184
/G01, gross wage amount   180
/X02   263
/Z02   263
1001   222
1002   222
1200   60
2417   232
3021, for child support   180
3022, for federal tax levy   180
assigning to an infotype   86
assignment
   for 401(k)   159
BA13, after tax deduction   162
BE13, pre-tax deduction   162
BE14, pre-tax HMO EE costs   151
benefits-related   287
BP13, provider contributions   162
BP14, HMO provider costs   151
BR13, employer contributions   162
BR14, HMO employer costs   151
Catalog   61
categories   58
characteristics   67
configuring   54
cumulation of   307
defined   51, 54
dropped   184
elements of   59
factoring   70
group   65
in groups   80
lifecycle   54
lifecycle, diagram of   55
M720
   United Way   61
maintaining, best practices   253
manipulation   299
MFT1   222
MFT1, copying   222
MG20   180
model, starting with B   287
MRP1   223, 225, 227
MRP1, copying   223
numbering   61
permissibility   68
posting   96
posting to expence accounts   58

printed or non-printed 58
reporter 118
  payroll report 87
technical, table of commonly-used 273
template 269
testing 84
time 111
utilization report 84, 181
valuation 110
WCWP 315
weekly payroll 100
WGTYP 316
withholding overrides 190
withholding tax 196
  wage type for 78
work tax 38, 201
workplace and basic pay data
  OUTWP 311
work-related tax areas 196
WPBP function 108
write-off 222

X

X009 315

Y

YANA 208
  subtype of infotype 0221 206
YAWA 208
  subtype of infotype 0221 206
year-end
  adjustment workbench 224
  adjustments 111, 189
  off-cycle payrolls 107
  tax adjustments 202
year-end workbench 189, 202, 204, 273
  accessing 204
year-to-date cumulations 27
YTD 54, 71, 77, 118

Z

Z
  constants, customer name space 157
ZERO 316
zero net pay 82, 83
Zero-Net-Checks 83

Complete details on customization and application of the New General Ledger

Techniques for flexible reporting and faster execution of period-end closing

Comprehensive information on integration and migration

approx. 300 pp., 69,95 Euro
ISBN 978-1-59229-107-6, Aug 2007

New General Ledger in mySAP ERP Financials

www.sap-press.com

E. Bauer, J. Siebert

New General Ledger in mySAP ERP Financials

Faster, more efficient, and more transparent: This book enables you to implement and use the new General Ledger in mySAP ERP Financials. Readers get an insightful overview of all the most important new functionalities and advantages that the new GL has to offer. You'll quickly learn about the definition of ledgers and document breakdown, with the help of practical examples.

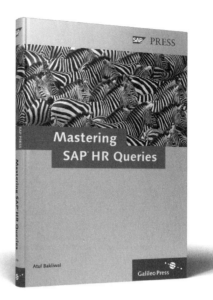

Mastering SAP HR Queries

www.sap-press.com

Atul Bakliwal

Mastering SAP HR Queries

Discover the untapped potential of HR Queries

Learn about SAP's HR Query functionality from the inside out. Readers of this detailed reference get in-depth and practical explanations of vital concepts like logical databases, using query variants, security and local fields, and much more. The comprehensive coverage is tightly focused, specifically on the SAP HR Query functionality, which makes this book an enormous help for readers who need to leverage the valuable, yet under-utilized, potential of queries for a specific project, or in their daily work.

Increase company productivity by learning to use HCM Performance Management efficiently

Prepare for, design, implement, and configure your HCM implementation

Learn to enhance performance management, drawing from business best practices

approx. 350 pp., 69,95 Euro / US$ 69,95
ISBN 978-1-59229-124-3, Sept 2007

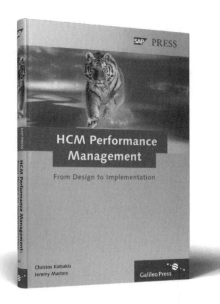

HCM Performance Management

www.sap-press.com

Christos Kotsakis, Jeremy Masters

HCM Performance Management: From Design to Implementation

This comprehensive reference is indispensable for HR professionals learning how to work with HCM Performance Management, which is integral to identifying and retaining key talent within your organization. The authors take you on a guided journey, from design to implementation, and provide volumes of insights to help increase your company's productivity. First, learn about performance management process design, supplemented with practical and insightful case studies. Then, you'll discover, step-by-step, how to implement your own performance management application. Based on the R/3 Enterprise Release (4.7), this book also provides coverage specific to mySAP ERP 2005.

Interested in reading more?

Please visit our Web site for all
new book releases from SAP PRESS.

www.sap-press.com